Praise for Terry Grosz's books:

"Environmentalism meets Indian Jones in these rip-snorting tales of a former wildlife conservation officer. ... A bear of a man— six-foot-four, over 300 pounds—Grosz relates his exploits in adventures full of slam-bang action and bravado tempered by a coolheaded sense of humor."   —*Publishers Weekly*

"Having had the privilege of working with Terry Grosz on wildlife stories, I knew he was a master game warden. What I did not know is that he is also a master raconteur. His adventures in 32 years of enforcing wildlife law astonish even his fellow wardens, and he tells them in a way that keeps you turning the pages till there aren't any more."   —Ted Williams, editor-at-large, *Audubon* magazine; conservation editor, *Fly Rod & Reel*

"His collection of tales needs to be told, for it helps combat an enormous problem concerning our country's natural wildlife. Grosz is obviously a very committed individual—and also a natural storyteller. ... [These stories] relate many close calls with mother nature: wild creatures and savage lawbreakers. ... Those who cherish the outdoors for hunting and fishing as well as those involved in environmental studies will benefit from this work."   —*Booklist*

"From the first chapter till the last, the reader will find no dull moments. This is one of those books that are hard to put down once you start. ... After you finish Terry's book, you will be looking forward to the next in the series."   —*International Game Warden*

"[Terry Grosz] paints a stirring picture of the constant struggle to protect our outdoor resource from a constant assault from lawbreakers. ... [A] brisk, sometimes swashbuckling account of Grosz's running duels with a variety of miscreants from market hunters to garden-variety poachers. A wonderful storyteller, Grosz keeps the reader in an almost constant tingle."   —Charlie Meyers, *The Denver Post*

"Because wildlife is important, wildlife law enforcement officers are important, and Terry 'Tiny' Grosz was one good one. He recounts his lively and dangerous career as a wildlife cop in the same exuberant, unpretentious style it was lived—something like Louis L'Amour meets Mike Hammer."
　　　　—David Petersen, author of *Heartsblood* and *Ghost Grizzlies*

"The book is a page-turner, a remarkable if not heroic glimpse inside the cat-and-mouse competition between wildlife enforcement and wildlife poachers."　　　　　　　　　　—*The Reel News*

"We're the top-dog species on this planet. Even the most wily or fearsomely armed critter stands little or no chance against a thoughtful and well-armed human. And when you add malicious amusement and avarice to the mix, entire species quickly find themselves running for their lives—and into the black void of extinction. Or at least that's how it would be if it weren't for a small group of incredibly dedicated wildlife officers who possess the unrelenting spirit (and occasionally, even the mass) of a protective mother grizzly. In Terry Grosz you will meet such an officer—and find out, in very vivid detail, why it's a terribly bad idea to violate the hunting laws regarding one of his treasured creatures."
　　　　—Ken Goddard, author of *First Evidence* and *The Alchemist*

"Our thin cadre of wildlife agents scattered across the American landscape are some of our finest law enforcement professionals. Often away from family and home, placed in lonely and dangerous situations, they confront devious characters and unpredictable events in their continuing fight to protect our irreplaceable wild resources. Agent Terry Grosz, one of the nation's best, gives us well written, hearty tales packed with high stakes, drama, tears and laughter."
　　　　—John F. Turner, former director, U.S. Fish & Wildlife Service

No Safe Refuge

No Safe Refuge

Man as Predator in the World of Wildlife

Terry Grosz

Johnson Books
BOULDER

Published by Johnson Books, a division of Johnson Publishing Company, 1880 South 57th Court, Boulder, Colorado 80301. Visit our website at www.JohnsonBooks.com. E-mail: books@jpcolorado.com.

9 8 7 6 5 4 3 2 1

Cover design: Debra B. Topping
Cover photo by Jim Klett, special agent for the U.S. Fish & Wildlife Service, Devil's Lake, North Dakota, 1983.

A note on the photo section: These pictures were supplied over the years to the author for teaching purposes. In all cases where the provenance of the photographs are known, we have contacted the photographers and the pictures are used with their permission. In those cases where the source of the photos could not be traced, we are unable to acknowledge the photographers by name, but nevertheless we thank them anonymously for their contribution to conservation law enforcement.

Library of Congress Cataloging-in-Publication Data
Grosz, Terry.
    No safe refuge: man as predator in the world of wildlife / Terry Grosz.
        p. cm.
      ISBN 1-55566-298-6
      1. Poaching—United States. 2. Wildlife crimes—United States. 3. Wildlife conservation—United States. 4. Grosz, Terry. I. Title.
      SK36.7.G76 2003
      333.95'4137'0973—dc21   2003011193

Printed in the United States by
Johnson Printing
1880 South 57th Court
Boulder, Colorado 80301

Printed on ECF paper with soy ink

Contents

Preface

IN THIS FIFTH BOOK, titled *No Safe Refuge: Man as Predator in the World of Wildlife*, the reader is treated to a cross-section of stories encompassing wildlife law enforcement in America. The stories involve the author's activities when serving over the years as a California Fish and Game warden, a U.S. game management agent, and a special agent for the U.S. Fish and Wildlife Service. Woven into these true stories of men who went astray are such unfortunate targets as pheasants, mule deer, black brant, and all manner of ducks and geese in between. There is even a taste of cattle trespassing on a waterfowl production area (like a mini national wildlife refuge) in North Dakota that takes a truly unique turn down the family "trail." In my four previous books, the reader was exposed to the scene of resources routinely being grossly impacted or destroyed because of human stupidity and greed. However, the illegal killing in this book's stories seems to exhibit an unusual life of its own with a distinctly unique intensity of killing—an intensity shown by the huge numbers of arrests and citations issued as a result. My previous books are showcases of such thoughtless destructive activities throughout the world of wildlife, but with none of the savagery and frenzy of killing demonstrated in this book. Every story is replete with twists and turns, but all share the common thread of intentional and intense killing by almost fanatically dedicated shooters. Hence, the title is more than appropriate for the stories contained here.

In "Pheasants Galore and Outlaws Too," you can't help but rejoice in the numbers of birds depicted from days past, densely weed-grown fields, pleasant fall afternoons, and the pleasures they brought to the American hunting public. Then you are brought up short by the greedy and uncontrolled killings at every turn, a scenario of rabid killing for killing's own sake. Today in the Sacramento Valley, where this story unfolded, there are still pheasants, but not like in former days. Loss of habitat plays a pivotal role in any animal population's health and I'm sure does so today for pheasants in the valley. However, uncontrollable killing has long-term consequences. Just think what the genetics of that historical brood stock might have brought to today's pheasant population in the valley had lived, though I realize one can't "stockpile" game. Keep in mind the small amount of ground I covered as an officer trying to rein in the illegal killing. Imagine how many outlaws I missed ... *and imagine the numbers of pheasants they killed!* I wonder what impact the West Nile virus will have on today's diminished pheasant populations? As always, I expect my readers to look down the road beyond the words spilled out on these pages. In so doing, they will discover the ugly long-term reality of those illegal moments.

In *"Crunch,"* you will find upstanding Christian men who slaughtered hundreds of mule deer for distribution throughout the illegal commercial meat markets in the Sacramento Valley. They were *so* dedicated and possessive of their killing way of life that they thought nothing of harming those protecting such wildlife. Again looking down the road, we can only guess what those slaughtered animal populations represent in lost genetics that could have enhanced today's diminished mule deer herds. Such enhancement could have been of inestimable value in light of today's nationwide concerns over chronic wasting disease and its horribly destructive effects on deer populations. In "Marsh Madness," you will find yourself surrounded by hundreds of thousands of migratory waterfowl—and hundreds of out-of-control shooters. The waterfowl were so plentiful that in the dim morning light, one was in constant danger of being struck by their hurtling bodies as they hammered through the air trying to find refuge from the madness and killing lead shot erupting from below. Without a doubt, it was one of the most intense killing fields I ever experienced as a conservation officer in my thirty-two years of service. I wrote more citations in one morning for early shooting and over-limits than many conservation officers will write *in a year!* As I write these words today, the populations of many species of waterfowl represented that morning have declined so drastically that even states such as California, ever greedy for the largest bag limits and longest seasons, have backed away from such destructive management practices. As if that decline isn't bad enough, Tule Lake, historical home to the hordes of waterfowl in the story, is nothing more today than a mudhole because of farmers' greed in taking most of the basin's water for their thirsty crops—crops that for the most part are in great supply and hardly needed for the nation's health. Today the masses of ducks, geese, and swans are gone from Tule Lake. Again, what impact will the West Nile virus have on these diminished waterfowl populations?

In "A Casket Full of Ducks," you will get an up-front look into the souls of a pair of old-fashioned market hunters—killers of such mettle that they went to extremes to circumvent the law in order to appease their raging desire to kill and to enrich themselves through the hungry illicit markets. Both are dead now, but for forty years they practiced their trade, killing everything and anything that carried a financial reward for its flesh. Again, who knows how many creatures they killed before being brought to justice? Thirty thousand, forty thousand ... *more?* Only God will ever know, and I have a feeling that since their passage into the great beyond, he has had a word or two with these chaps regarding their behavior toward the critters He created. Again, the waterfowl they pursued the hardest, especially the graceful pintail, are showing drastic signs of population reduction because of overharvest, drought on the breeding grounds, and loss of habitat on the wintering grounds. Population figures at the time these words were written show reductions of 50 percent or more! And today in the Sacramento Valley of California, the millions of whistling wings that could be heard when this story was lived are heard no more. I doubt they will ever again rule the skies in such unbelievable and magnificent numbers.

In "Aughhhh ... Holy Mary, Mother of God!" you will get a close look at one of the Creator's "kin" ... a man supposedly in tune with the well-being of all of God's creatures, large and small. In this particular instance, *too* tuned in to the critters, it seemed! Before the smell of burned gunpowder drifts away, one is reminded that *every* walk of life includes the good, the bad, and the ugly. Again, the target of that man's intentions is now showing signs of decline, in part because of overharvest, both legal and illegal. It is ironic when what God created for all to enjoy is illegally taken by one of his own ministers.

In "Perils of the Black Brant," the carnage continues as specialized methods of hunting favored on the north coast of California allow for a particularly far-reaching overharvest. This slaughter is rendered even more deadly by the fact that the birds are in mated pairs during hunting season, and to kill them at that moment in time interrupts the breeding cycle. The remaining birds have to begin the courtship process again, using up limited vital reserves needed for brood production. In my opinion, one sees the black brant being overshot because of political lobbying for "hunter opportunity." The reasoning is nothing more than allowing an open season on a declining species in order to sell a few more hunting licenses. Because of this overshooting in Mexico and the United States, with its resulting population decline, a related issue has reared its head. There is serious concern among some of California's waterfowl managers that if they close the season now to protect the brant (a proper wildlife management decision), the environmental and antihunting communities will sue to make the closure permanent.

Wildlife management exercised at the polling places is almost always problematic. In the end, the wildlife the goodhearted but misinformed voters are trying to protect by stockpiling populations end up dying horrible deaths due to overcrowding, starvation, disease, or worse. When I was in college in Arcata, I saw thousands of black brant resting in Humboldt Bay as they interrupted their migration to their breeding grounds in the Arctic. Less than ten years later, when I returned to the area as a U.S. game management agent, they had declined by about tenfold through overshooting and loss of habitat. You will find that when God did not respond to my request for assistance in corralling the brant killers, the law of the Old West quickly prevailed. The black brant is another likely prime candidate to feel the deadly effects of the West Nile virus in light of its arctic nesting grounds, home to seemingly a million mosquitoes per square inch during nesting season. There is no doubt that when the infected mosquitoes reach the high arctic, home to hundreds of thousands of ducks, geese, brant, and swans, the disease will take a terrible toll. To date, there is no known way to protect wild creatures against the virus.

In "It's a Very Small World," you will get a view of those who will kill until hell freezes over, then look for more critters as they wait for hell to thaw! Not because they have to, mind you, but because they truly enjoy the blood sport of killing. You will also get a glimpse into the thought processes of this unique brand of killers as they go to great lengths—and distances—to pursue their "sport." I hope you will begin to understand just how deadly this brand of killer can be, by realizing the odds the hard working conservation officers face in eradicating such behavior. Again, the preferred targets of these predators, especially the scaup, canvasback, and pintail, are on the verge of some pretty low population numbers. When this was written, several species' populations had dropped by almost fifty percent! Habitat and drought have played a big hand with those numbers, but overharvest by those long on shells and short on the trigger pull have not helped. And the beat goes on. ...

In "Uncle John's Cows," you will get a dose of old-fashioned, hardheaded arrogance—"Hurrah for me and to hell with you." Plant populations deserve protection not only for the soil protection they offer but because of the wildlife habitat they provide. In the prairies of the United States, viable plant communities are absolutely key to wildlife survival, especially in winter and spring. If proper habitat is not available, many migratory species just keep flying farther north in that quest. Flying farther uses up precious fat reserves and often means reduced broods, or no broods at all. Then the species spends the short months of summer trying to store up enough fat reserves for the energy-robbing migration south. If they are unable to get the hell out of Dodge when the winter storms come rolling out of the Arctic, they freeze to death or end up as fox food.

Many of the dirt farmers, in order to plant every living foot of space, are wont to turn everything to dirt, or "moonscape." For those living on the northern plains facing the short growing season, that is sometimes the only way to survive. The strategy is rough on the overall environment but is seen as necessary by the tillers of the soil. However, many times the only remaining cover is on lands belonging to the state and federal governments, held in trust for wildlife and recreation. In this story you will enjoy the ride I had to take in order to maintain a small piece of vegetated land for the arrival of spring waterfowl migrants. Hang on to your hat; the story has a "sunfishing" twist that will throw most "riders."

In "The M-1 Abrams Tank," you are in for a different ride, and not the tracked-vehicle kind. The story relates just how far members of the "thin green line" sometimes have to go in order to bag the bad guys and get the job done. It's a story of a close call, but again my pair

of guardian angels worked overtime to allow a clean escape and ultimately a roundup of the miscreants. Again the animal targets, especially the black duck, greater scaup, and canvasback are in trouble
because of man's inhumanity to man in general and the market
hunters' heavy trigger fingers in particular.

In "The Cornfields of Wisconsin," you find not only game hogs in
abundance but many of the landed gentry trying to protect such killing
behavior. This is a story of how we fought the weather, mud, fog, misguided landowners, and those pulling the triggers as if the resource were
inexhaustible. In reality, the only inexhaustible thing was the ethics and
efforts of my officers as we ran those goose-killing bastards to ground.
Some great twists and turns occurred in those cornfields, which I remember today, some twenty-three years later, with each bowl of corn
flakes I eat. ... The grin accompanying my bowl of cereal can be
matched only by the glint of happiness in the collective eyes of a healthy
Canada goose population. For a change, the target in this story is one
of the very few species that somehow is holding its own in population
numbers. However, in light of the extensive and across-the-board
killing that took place, one has to wonder how much more numerous
the populations could have been, or how much stronger the genetics of
those regional species, especially the giant Canada goose (bet you
didn't know such a species existed, did you?), if this level of illegal
killing had not occurred. These birds are another potentially prime candidate for the West Nile virus because of their nesting habits. Only time
will tell if the Canada goose populations maintain their health.

Sitting back and looking at this book's contents, I realize it is probably one of the saddest volumes I have written. Every chapter has
from one to a handful of renegades hell-bent on the destruction of the
critters. And in every story a ton of killing had occurred, or was taking place! Even in the chapter dealing with cattle trespass, the 350-plus
trespassing cattle made a moonscape of the waterfowl production
area, so much so that the migratory species calling that wetland area
home come spring had to move on. Even the events of this chapter
caused a loss of critters through human interference. And that didn't
even cover the winter's loss of endemic critters that depended on that
waterfowl production area's cover against the Arctic's wintry blasts.

No matter how hard I tried or how cleverly I approached problems, the killing was of such magnitude that I couldn't help but real-

ize I was losing the war. And it wasn't mine to lose! This knowledge brought a heavy sense of loss to my heart and soul for all the years I dedicated to the fight of protecting our national heritage. The American people expected more of their resource caretakers, and I was just not getting it done. Going to sixteen-hour days and seven-day weeks only raised the number of miscreants cited or booked in jail until they numbered several thousand. It seemed as if the more I apprehended, the more I discovered rattling around in the leaf litter, itching to go forth and do their destructive thing. I often asked the Creator for help and guidance in despair when the killing got ahead of me, particularly nasty, or just plain out of control. Aside from the whirring wings of my two guardian angels and my body more or less holding together and not getting killed or injured, it seemed pretty silent on the ethereal end. I took that silence as an instruction to "get off your dead hind end and work harder," so I did. I had hoped for more. ... But now that I think back over time, I realize that I got everything I needed, and then some.

So don't despair when I do in this book's stories, but do smile and rejoice with me when I run a particularly nasty killer to ground. Also, enjoy with me my times in the outback when I had a moment to relish God's creations. Look for the stories between the lines, and look down the road at the results of every action—or lack thereof. The purpose of my efforts is not only to inform and educate but, through my eyes, to make you better caretakers of our national heritage. You may begin with the realization that there will come a time when you expect a particular element of the wildlife or plant community to be there, *and it won't!* It won't be because the "thin green line" didn't care or want to do better. It was because there just weren't enough of us to go around. Or we were not in the right place at the right time. Or you, the public, didn't get off your collective hind ends in time to give us and your resources a hand. Whatever the reason, *we all lost!* Give us a hand in this battle, America—but *hurry.*

Acknowledgments

IN THE JOHNSON BOOKS "FAMILY," there has always been an exceptional ethic, literary talent, and friendliness. Those folks were always there for the author, the story to be told, and their reading public. Appreciating the enrichment and values those personalities brought to my books and to me as a writer, I have in a small way individually memorialized their achievements through the Acknowledgments sections of my books.

I saved acknowledging a very special person for this book, not because she was last in line but because it took me time to understand and appreciate her abilities. Stephanie White, accounts coordinator, is one exceptional young lady. Meeting this tall, dark-haired individual for the first time made a lasting impression. Her beautiful smile quickly put me at ease with its genuine projection of being happy to make my acquaintance. Her flashing dark eyes and equally sharp wit telegraphed the fact that I was dealing with a self-sufficient woman. She had the inner toughness of a Winchester rifle, yet also projected a proportional softness. It became apparent to one used to "reading" people that I was dealing with a woman full of some of the Missouri genes that made those folks such hardy pioneers and the strength of the nation. Being deadly efficient professionally was part of her joy in life. Never once in six years of professional association did I ever want for her administrative services. Requests were quickly translated into action, and the product was such that I could "take it to the bank." During my thirty-two-year career before I became a writer, I met many exceptional women administrators. Stephanie would rank at the top with the very best, a fact that should make her parents proud.

She is a unique woman, outstanding professional, and dear friend. To her I acknowledge those professional achievements. You truly are an exceptional young lady!

Dedication

THIS BOOK IS DEDICATED in loving memory to Robert "Bob" Herkert, who returned to his Maker on December 19, 2000, at the young age of 42. Bob was a loving husband and partner to wife Audra; dedicated father to Hannah and Hans, the "Lights of His Life"; a man of the soil and an avid sportsman. Throughout his life, he totally dedicated his heart and soul to that of his family and friends. Being a kindred spirit of the land, he also made time for his beloved rice fields, not only for the simple pleasure they brought and the food they provided his fellow man, but for the thankful migratory waterfowl arriving after an exhausting flight from beyond the north wind. Bob found deep joy in sunrises, decoy sets, flooded rice fields, and a brace of pintail gracefully winging in, all happily shared with his son, Hans. That experience was matched only by salmon fishing on the Sacramento River at sunset with his daughter, Hannah.

It is in Bob's spirit that we celebrate his joy of life, love, easy laughter, warm hugs with arms that always made us feel safe, other special family memories, and his love for the flocks of waterfowl in the rice fields that lifted one's soul. It is also to that spirit we will forever remember the husband, partner, father, and best friend who had such a deep love for us and reverence for all of God's creations. We shall always see his spirit in the sunrises, feel his nearness and touch in the soft breezes, sense his guidance as we travel through life, and quietly comprehend his joys during our successes.

You were our life's joy and eternal love. We miss you dearly. ...
Audra, devoted wife; Hannah (13), daughter and "favorite date"; and Hans (16), son and best friend.

Colusa, California, 2003

one

Pheasants Galore and Outlaws Too

IN THE SUMMER OF 1967, I transferred from the North Coast Fish and Game Squad in the Pacific Northwest to the Valley/Sierra Nevada Squad in the Sacramento Valley. What a change from the towering redwoods, Douglas fir, and Sitka spruce in a temperate rain forest with its salmon, sturgeon, Columbian black-tailed deer, and many ocean species to the heat, humidity, and agricultural lands of the Sacramento Valley with its millions of waterfowl and mosquitoes! At least, those were my initial valley impressions until I began examining more closely what lay before me on this latest adventure. I thought I had had a massive resource base to work with in the Pacific Northwest, but in fact that area didn't compare to the resources I was soon to encounter in the Sacramento Valley. I had more fish, fowl, mammals, and other wild riches at my fingertips—and, I was soon to discover, at the tips of seemingly everyone else's greedy, grabbing fingers as well.

I set out at a dead run to learn my new district. The myriad hunting and fishing seasons were ongoing or just around the corner, and I had to quickly learn the ropes or the critters would suffer. Little did I realize that even when I came to know the district like the back of my hand and worked the hell out of it day and night, the critters would still take an abnormally lethal pounding.

The vast valley was not only biologically and ecologically unique, it also included numerous population centers scattered throughout that contained many diverse and distinct cultural subgroups such as the illegal gill-net fishermen plying their trade along the rivers and estuaries; illegal buyers of wildlife in San Francisco's Chinatown; Italian communities known for stretching the legal boundaries when it came to killing ducks, geese, and dove; the commercial-market hunter pursuing ducks in the rice fields in the dark of the night; the overall hunting community with its many "counting" and "identification" mistakes; "sport" fishermen running drop lines and set lines along the waterways; and old family "names" shooting or dragging ducks in the rice fields at night to fill their freezers or those of their friends. It is a simple fact that anytime you mix wildlife and humankind, the result is major wildlife law enforcement problems. With such a multitude of sins, it was a chore for the critters just to survive human impacts, let alone the vagaries of nature.

As if that were not headache enough, I soon found that many of the people in my county were aloof and standoffish, and to a degree disrespectful, when it came to wildlife law enforcement. That is not a good situation for a wildlife officer because, even more than in any other kind of law enforcement, it is imperative that the public respects and supports the principles of a conservation program. Without steadfast support and the public's belief in conservation, one simply cannot expect to control ongoing wildlife crime.

The disrespect encountered was in part because wildlife violations were victimless crimes in the eyes of many in the historical valley communities, so they did not consider such violations to be serious. With a lot of hard work, I knew I could remedy that problem. In order to do so, I had to "blaze a trail" not only through the violators but into the hearts of the other folks in the general area. It took a little longer to address the other part of the problem, which came down to the cultural history of the area and some rather poor performances, in the eyes of my valley folks, by my predecessors.

The Sacramento Valley had long been loaded with tremendous populations of fish and wildlife of just about every kind. Early settlers subsisted on these natural resources, and it soon became a way of life to harvest and sell these great hoards to the thousands of newcomers arriving daily, looking for fertile lands, the gold fields, stands of timber, fisheries, business opportunities, a wonderful climate, or the fulfillment of other dreams. That spirit of living off the land and enriching oneself from this seemingly unending bounty had carried forward into the modern-day philosophy of many of Colusa County's gentry—it was considered almost a God-given right by some of the individuals I would run across. That deeply ingrained notion of taking what you wanted, when you wanted did not lend itself to welcoming the new local game warden with open arms and a kiss on each cheek.

The good folks of the region had little respect for many of the game wardens who had come before me. There were stories of officers who routinely confiscated hunters' game under the guise of the law and then, according to local legend, kept the seized evidence for themselves. Reportedly some officers had also found it difficult to leave "demon rum" alone, or to get off their dead hind ends and earn their keep. Officers who were considered obnoxiously mouthy specifically and hind ends in general, many hardworking locals found unacceptable. During many early conversations with the valley folk, I just listened, sorted the wheat from the chaff, and tried to learn. I soon realized there were numerous axes to grind and many more that needed burying, but in a lot of the "smoke" I did see some "fire." I realized that to succeed with any kind of conservation program or even just to confront some of the rougher elements, I would have to be everything those earlier officers hadn't been, and then some. It seemed as if the only person who could have met all the expectations of the valley folks had been hung on a cross some two thousand years earlier! So I decided to be myself, do the best possible job I could for the critters and people of the area, and let the rest go to hell in a handbasket if need be.

During those early days, I naively tried to establish friendly relations with the gamekeepers of the many duck and pheasant hunting clubs, mostly to no avail. I knew a lot of my illegal hunting problems would come from those places during the rapidly approaching waterfowl and pheasant seasons. In order to be effective, I needed to get inside those hunting operations and work at the top of my game, or the critters would end up in the crapper. It was apparent that the gamekeepers wanted to keep me at arm's length because a number of their members had a tendency to stray over the line of the law. Fact was, if they let me in on their members' illegal activities, they stood a good chance of losing their jobs for doing so. Some of the gamekeepers enjoyed the latitude of hunting on the clubs when the members were gone, which was another reason they didn't want a game warden hanging around. Others just plain hated what I stood for, hated what my predecessors had done to them, hated the agency I represented, didn't feel that a game warden was human, didn't like the game laws interfering with their God-given rights, simply didn't like me personally, or all of the above! I realized I would have to prove myself to these good folks and remind them through the long arm of the law of their conservation ethics as well as the real-life issues of the limitations of the valley's natural resources. I figured I would just have to meet my "clients" at every turn—those needing my law enforcement attention would get just that, and those simply needing assistance would get that as well. I was beginning to learn how highly the local people valued a good work ethic; a man's word, especially that of a badge carrier; and a liberal application of fairness, honesty, and consideration. Over the next thirty-two years, I was to discover that applying those principles was pure gold for a public servant, or any human being for that matter.

Using a detailed map of Colusa County, I quickly began to learn my assigned land and water areas, which meant learning every road and waterway in my district! I ran along every road, including all the little farm roads, and memorized where they came from and led to. Then I learned the names of the landowners and tried to meet them, establishing some kind of rapport during that early stage of our relationship. I made a point of learning where every hunting club was located, who the gamekeepers were, their life histories (as best as I could), who was good and who was greedy, and which clubs had reputations for the best hunting. I also tried to obtain all the combinations or keys to their locked gates. That last part took some doing, but finally, after a lot of hard work, I got it done.

Many times the bad guys inadvertently provided access to the sites of their wrongdoing. Often the four-tumbler Sesame lock combinations on the clubs' gates, because of the "slow learners" among some members, would be something simple like the numbers of a particular year, such as 1-9-6-7. Or it might be the last four digits of the club's phone number, or the date the club was founded. If it were a deer club, it might be 3-0-0-6 or 3-0-3-0, popular rifle calibers of the day. Old combination locks with some wear on the individual tumblers were easy to pick. However, I won't give that particular secret away. You will just have to become a game warden and learn how to do that one by yourself.

When a club used a key lock, I would ask for a key, hoping that their cooperation would be a step toward establishing a better working relationship. Trespassing by the "have-not" shooters was a constant problem, and sometimes I would be given a key to assist me in keeping those folks off the clubs' grounds. Most of the time, though, I was politely told to bug off. Then the devil in me would take over because I simply didn't like being told to go screw myself! I might cut a link of the chain holding the gate closed and put in one of my own locks, or take the numbers of the lock and make my own key. Sometimes, just walking up to a locked gate and looking around, I would see several sets of footprints leading to an empty beer can lying alongside the fence or a board on the ground near the gate. I often found a key hidden under that beer can or board. Sometimes the gate would be at the end of a bridge, which made access problematic, especially if your vehicle couldn't swim. ... In those cases, again, just stepping back and looking around produced many keys. I remember once following sets of footprints over the canal bank, and hanging under the bridge on the inside of a timber was the key to the gate blocking my way to adventure. I would wait for a nonshoot day (most clubs shot on Saturday, Sunday, or Wednesday in those days), then spirit away the key hidden under that can, board, or bridge, have a copy made, and then quickly return the original, with the folks on the other side none the wiser. Getting access so I could move in quickly on those breaking the laws, be they owners or trespassers, was vital if my conservation program was to be successful. It was a game that led many clubs to change their locks periodically, especially after a surprise visit by the local "tule creeper" and a flurry of citations. But I was seldom unable to gain access, even if it took using my last line of offense, my "master key" — namely, a three-foot set of hardened bolt cutters backed by a set of powerful shoulders and a tad bit of determination.

Some of you readers might be thinking that kind of activity on the part of a law enforcement officer is a bit dicey or a shade illegal. After all, if you cause any damage to property or person, you personally or your agency (or both) are criminally or civilly liable. That was why I would cut only one link of chain next to a lock. In that case, if the landowner wanted to press charges, I was personally liable for one link of chain. Also, many statutes backed by case law at both the state and federal levels grant a conservation officer the right of access to private property if that officer has a sound reason or probable cause to suspect that wildlife is being taken. If officers had to stop to obtain a warrant or permission every time they needed access to a property during a situation involving the taking of wildlife, conservation through law enforcement would be impossible. Finally, the U.S. Constitution lays down some pretty damn good wording regarding what rights a citizen of this great country possesses. It is pure folly for a law enforcement officer to disregard those rights—you will find your hind end sued clear off or placed in jail (or both); you will lose your investigation or case, and you'll be lucky to continue holding your job. ... The thinking officer will run at the edge and do everything possible to right the wrongs, but all within the bounds of legality.

Whenever I got a section of my district down pat, I moved on to another. Then I would come back and work the same areas at night because everything looks different during the hours of darkness. This took a lot of eighteen-hour days, but my kids were still little, and I had a bride whose patience was beyond compare when it came to me chasing the bad guys. She took care of the home front and let me run, realizing I was on a vision quest. But even at that level of intensity, I soon found that I was not big enough to be spread around in sufficient depth to help all the critters all the time. There was just too much going on for one man to handle. So I ran a little harder, foolishly trying to make do. My sore knees, bad back, bad ankles, and sore joints today at sixty-two years of age serve to remind me of that degree of effort and the many muskrat holes I stepped into as I lumbered across those swamps and rice fields under a full head of steam.

The county's geography and ecology didn't help. The west side of my district was semiarid and loaded with deer, elk, turkey, lion, black bear, and dove. That habitat was mostly oaks, cheat grass, and dense stands of brush, with conifers in the higher elevations. The east side was agricultural, with orchards and wheat, safflower, and rice fields in abundance. On the agricultural side, I had everything from two species of salmon, striped bass, snipe, bullfrogs, dove, sturgeon, catfish, waterfowl, and warm-water game fish to pheasants, mule deer (some of massive proportions because of the excellent habitat), and California valley quail and rabbits. No matter where I turned, I had business, and many times more business than I or a dozen of my kind could handle.

When I first arrived that summer, the deer season was in full swing. So I hurried off to the mountains and foothills to the west in an attempt to keep a lid on a district that had been without a game warden for some time. That meant herding along the run-of-the-mill deer hunters, trying to keep them in line all day long in the backcountry, many times in 100-degree heat. Then, after a change of clothing, I would stalk the dyed-in-the-wool poacher working those same areas under the cover of darkness, also in 100-degree heat. One could work twenty-four hours a day and have interesting "traffic" going on the entire time.

I still had to learn the rest of my district because bad things didn't just go away in those areas when I was absent. I had warm-water game fishing going on day and night; general recreation along the river and sandbars with the usual amount of litter during the day (it was part of a game warden's responsibility to keep recreation areas clean in those days); boat fishing on the Sacramento River for salmon, sturgeon, and striped bass; and in the fall and winter, all the rest of the hunting seasons thrown at you in one giant glob—deer, pheasants, and waterfowl being the big three. Then I still had the last vestiges of the old-time market hunter stalking the waterfowl of the valley, along with many of the locals supplementing their freezers from the masses of feeding waterfowl in the dark of night. Suffice it to say, there never was a dull moment and after my first year in the valley, averaging sixteen-hour days from July until the first of March, with only a half a day off for Thanksgiving and one day for Christmas. And that was after working Christmas Eve's shooters!

Bear in mind that this all took place before the regulated eight-hour days the state and provincial conservation communities now operate under. In my opinion, restricting a conservation officer to an eight-hour day is stupid. The poacher doesn't work an eight-hour day but is an opportunist and will take from Mother Nature's larder around the clock. One who is trained in wildlife law enforcement and knows what needs to be done finds the restriction of an eight-hour work day (seven hours in parts of Canada) really hard to swallow, much less understand. The Fish and Wildlife Service pays its officers an additional 25 percent of their base pay to work unlimited odd and unusual hours. That move precludes any violations of the Fair Labor Standards Act and allows those officers free rein to pursue those who need pursuing. The states and provinces limiting their officers to an eight-hour or less work day would do well to follow the Service's lead. I am acutely aware of the financial hardships it would place on those organizations, especially after twenty years' experience as a senior manager for a three-quarter-million-square-mile area, but I have yet to find any hurdle so great, financial or otherwise, that it couldn't be surmounted. The resources of North America are limited, and with the increasing populations and the collateral recreational pressures on plant and animal communities, the states and provincial organizations need to take serious heed of what the future may bring. Working fourteen- to sixteen-hour days is a little extreme, but it is that or watch "Rome" burn.

That first year, during the heat of the day when killing was at a lull, I would take time off from the deer-hunting areas and head for the foothill dove areas or the valley floor to learn more of my district before pheasant season dropped on me with a roar. On one occasion, I chanced to be working on the west side of my district in an area in which I had seen a lot of dove alongside the roadways feeding on the abundant mullein seed or resting by the score in the trees or power lines. Stopping in the 100-plus-degree July heat by the California Division of Forestry fire station on the Leesville Road, I got out for a drink of water from my ice chest.

Taking a deep drink, I was surprised by the soft thumping sound of at least two shotguns to the south. I froze and listened carefully. Sure as hell, there they were again! Two quick shots and a trailing shot, apparently coming from a piece of Terrill Sartain's property on which he ran cattle and had a deer-hunting club. Running the sound of those shots through my mind, I ruled out anyone target practicing with a heavy rifle or handgun—the sounds were too muted to be rifle fire and lacked the soft *pop* of a pistol. Dove season was closed, and people usually didn't hunt the abundant California ground squirrels (the only other current open season) with expensive shotgun shells, so off I went to investigate. Soon I arrived on the Leesville Road side of a small intermittent creek on the west side of Terrill's land. Knowing there were no crops in the area that dove would flock to, I opted for the creek area, where I knew the dove would stop to drink. Quietly stepping out of my patrol truck, I stood there in the intense heat and listened. *Boom, boom ... boom, boom!* I could clearly hear the shooting along the oaks bordering the creek about one hundred yards away but couldn't see any vehicles or shooters. I vaulted the barbed-wire fence along the road and trotted across the fields of star thistle and dove weed, mindful of the area's ever-present rattlesnakes. Soon I was on the upper portion of the creek, and within moments I spied through my binoculars a short, stocky man with a Browning AL-5 shotgun gunning dove as they dropped out of the trees into the small pools of water along the semidry creekbed for a much-needed drink. *Boom-boom,* and a slowly drifting puff of gray feathers marked the deed and the spot into which a dove had flown, never to fly again. The lad strolled over to the dead dove, lifted it out of the creekbed, and placed it in his game bag. Without an apparent worry in the world, he continued walking along the creekbed in my direction. Farther down the creek, I could hear the heavy thumping sounds of another shotgun, presumably doing the same thing. Dove season didn't open until the first of September, and these lads had a jump on the season by about two weeks. It was easy to see why, though. They were in the lower end of a desolate valley, on a remote piece of private property. Few people had any business there except the land owner, and these guys must have had not only permission to hunt there but the added factor of isolation to give them the boldness of confidence in remaining undiscovered. However, I was to discover over my time in the valley that in the case of these particular chaps, isolation had nothing to do with it. Plain and simply, it was arrogance and the desire to be killing something—and the law be damned!

When the lad walked near my hiding place behind a pile of gravel covered with star thistle, I rose up and said, "Good afternoon. How is the hunting?" From the way he jumped like a bug on a hot rock, I could tell that finding a game warden way out there during his little illegal dove shoot was the last earthly thing on his mind. He just stood there as I approached, carefully reached out, and removed the shotgun cradled in his arms. His eyes searched my face as he tried hard to remember whether he had ever seen me before, and I could hear his teeth grinding in the frustration of this rather unfortunate meeting. Unloading the shotgun, I discovered it to be unplugged, or capable of carrying more than three shells. "Come on, let's go meet your friend," I said as I started walking downstream, still carrying his shotgun. *Boom-boom-boom* went three quick shots from the unknown shooter just a short distance downstream. Good, I thought; he doesn't have a clue I am even in the country. Walking around a small turn in the creek, I spotted my second illegal dove shooter intently watching some oak trees to the south. His back was turned to me, and he didn't know I was there until I was within thirty yards of him. Finally, hearing someone walking over the gravel behind him, he turned, expecting to see his partner in crime. Shock crossed his face as he looked at me, and I saw his eyes darting to the silver star on my chest. For a moment, I could see the thought of running cross his mind, but he gave up the idea as the distance between us shrank to less than twenty yards. His vehicle was parked just yards away in a small grove of trees, and I could have reached it quickly enough to stop him, so that escape avenue was not an option.

"Afternoon," I said. "Fish and Game warden; please hand me your shotgun." He just stood frozen with surprise as I walked up to him. Reaching out, I carefully removed his shotgun from his hands and checked it. It too was unplugged. Identifying myself officially once again so there would be no mistake as to who I was, I asked for and received the lads' hunting and driver's licenses. Up to that point, they hadn't spoken a single word. They were in shock at being discovered by a game warden out here in the middle of nowhere, in a district from which a game warden had been absent for months. From the way these lads were acting, my guess was that they had been doing this little illegal killing act of theirs for years and had never been caught. Their driver's licenses identified one as Wally Oppum and the other as Wes Dollar, both from Chico. Looking up at my two very quiet and obviously now pissed-off shooters, I said, "Lads, I think you have a jump on dove season this year by a week or so." Still not a word. After removing each man's birds from his game bag and counting them, I sat down on a gravel bank, took out my citation book, and started to write up their violations. At that moment I happened to look on the ground along the stream. Scattered on the gravel everywhere by the few remaining water holes, and even around my feet, were loads of safflower seed! Damn, I thought, not bait too! I got up and commenced to walk the baited area, gathering in its magnitude. As if it wasn't bad enough that these guys were shooting over one of the few watered areas that the dove could use, they were also using bait to lure the birds in greater numbers. Boy, I thought, it takes all kinds of killers! I shook my head in disbelief. Real sportsmen, these two, I thought.

Sitting back down on my mound of gravel and keeping a sharp eye on my two lads, I again got out my citation book. Both men were issued citations and in so doing I discovered that Wally Oppum worked for Terrill Sartain, owner of this property, as a farm laborer. The other, Wes Dollar, was a mortician in the Chico area. Several weeks later, they forfeited bail to the tune of $350 each. Over the years I would cross swords with both of these men numerous times for taking over-limits of ducks and dove, possession of over-limits of ducks, and taking dove and ducks during the closed season. The sad truth of the matter was that I had run into two twenty-four-carat killing sons of bitches. Subsequent information from some of my valley folks confirmed that assessment. I finally had enough when I caught Wally killing wood ducks during the closed season under the guise of herding ducks committing depredations on Terrill Sartain's unharvested rice fields. That error got him booked into the local jail in Colusa. That caused one hell of a "hoorah" between Terrill and me, but after that, unknown to many in the county, the two of us, a young game warden and a wealthy, powerful landowner, from radically different backgrounds and times, became great friends. From then on, when I needed assistance, Terrill would quietly throw his considerable weight behind my projects, and they usually got off the ground with a flourish. After taking that firm stand against the casual killing of waterfowl even when they were committing depredations on the farmers' rice fields, I began to see a change in the local attitude toward the new game warden. I don't know if my hind-end-tangling session with one of the bigger rice farmers in the area had anything to do with it, or if it was the long hours I worked for the critters, but I could sure see the beginning of a change. It wasn't the end of all my problems, but it was the beginning of the end. Whatever world Terrill and his wife, Helen, are in today, may the good Lord take a liking to both of them. They were great folks, and good friends.

When not chasing the elusive deer hunter or closed-season dove shooter, I continued to work the valley floor to learn the roads, the landowners, and the behavioral habits and life histories of the critters, especially the pheasant. I had never worked pheasant hunters before and was looking forward to the season. What a meathead I was, I later found out, to harbor such warm anticipation! I tried to learn the very best locations and favored types of habitat for every species of game in the valley. That particular year we had zillions of pheasants! They were everywhere. There wasn't a spot I covered in which I couldn't find wily pheasant galore! Every morning at daylight (my favorite time of the day), I would hear the pheasant roosters crowing by the hundreds, no matter where I was. Throughout my travels on the many hundreds of dusty farm roads, I would run across dozens of hens with their broods of brown fuzzballs running down the road, or the males all flattened out as they sneaked away into the tall, concealing roadside grasses. Once concealed, they would freeze as I drove by. It was unreal, a throwback to times past! Then came the dawn: when you have lots of critters to hunt and they are a great game bird such as the pheasant, not to mention a culinary delight, you've got problems. Little did I realize that my first pheasant season was to be a rip-snorter!

Most pheasant breeds came to the United States from China, India, and Pakistan in the late nineteenth century. They were first introduced in the Willamette Valley of Oregon in the 1870s, taking the nation by storm. They quickly found an unoccupied niche, and the rest is history. Hardly anyone who is a bird hunter will pass up a chance to hunt this elusive and hard-flying game bird. The male's brightly colored "explosion" at your feet and cackling call as it streams away at a blurring high speed is a long-lived memory for those of us who have hunted these magnificent creatures. Holding the bird after a good, clean shot and great retrieve by your bird dog on a pleasant November afternoon is an experience that is truly meant for the heart and soul. Finally, the memory of that same bird eaten shortly afterward with mashed potatoes, a light white gravy, fresh garden vegetables, and a piece of my bride's homemade apple pie never fails to remind me of a little slice of exceptional living that will never be forgotten.

Duck season was also now in full swing. Anyone who has never witnessed the madness of millions of ducks and geese mixed up with thousands of eager hunters across the golden rice fields or deep-water duck clubs of California hasn't lived! There is just something about the sounds of a soft, drawn-out *quaaaack* of a full-plumaged drake mallard easily dropping into your decoys along with a sky full of whistling wings on an autumn day that cuts to a man's very core. It is a joy reserved for those of us who have a little bit of the dreamer in our souls. Throw in the dirty business of extinction by those taking too many during the day or poaching the birds at night as they feed in the big harvested rice fields and you have a taste of the good and bad — a genuine game warden's stew! With over 350 formally recognized waterfowl clubs in my district in those days, with their inherent problems, and all the illegal night hunting hammering along in the dark, it is no wonder I was never home. Then along came pheasant season, with its thousands of dyed-in-the-wool hunting advocates, and the conservation officers would simply be crushed under the weight of their enforcement responsibilities!

California in those days, if I remember correctly, had a four-per-day pheasant limit. The birds could not be shot before eight A.M., and all hunting had to cease by four in the afternoon. The reason was to give the birds time to feed without being harassed by the pheasant hunters. The season was not that long in those days, but the hunting pressure was immense! Then there were those damn paper tags California required to be placed on the leg of every rooster killed. A small book of pheasant tags was supplied with the hunting license, and every time a hunter shot a pheasant, it had to be tagged immediately! Well, as was to be expected, there was a lot of monkey business surrounding those tags. Birds weren't tagged in the field, and if the happy hunter got them home without detection, he was free to go out and kill four more that same day. Many tried to use the same tag several times on different birds during the same day; many shot early or late and didn't bother to tag the birds because they were illegal to begin with. Then there were those who shot the birds from motor vehicles on the roads and hid their untagged birds in the automobile because there was still a legal question regarding searching a motor vehicle without consent in those days. As if that weren't enough, there were those who would reuse the tags by throwing them in the game bag and saying they fell off, or that the other dead birds knocked the flimsy tags off—and on it went. No matter how I cut it, I would have a full-blown "hoorah" just about every time I caught a pheasant hunter in a tagging violation unless I had him cold with other violations as well.

Many of the pheasant hunters in that day and age were basically a pain in the hind end—and crybabies! I don't think I ever saw such childish behavior when it came to violating the ethics of the hunt: shooting the birds on the ground as they tried to run; stealing other people's birds; taking too many; wasting birds that were wounded but not killed; trespassing on private land to kill a just-seen rooster; early shooting after purposely setting their watches to reflect the legal shooting time even if it wasn't correct; shooting a bird in front of their kids, whom they brought out to learn to hunt; shooting their kids' birds and then making the kids tag them; not tagging their birds and claiming they had lost their tags in the game bag—and on it went. To be a game warden working the "noble" pheasant hunter in those days took a lot of patience, and sometimes a bit of a hardened heart as well.

As I said earlier, this was my first pheasant season as a game warden, and it looked like it was going to be a good one. There were thousands of birds in the valley. The cover was excellent, and a quick check showed that every motel in surrounding valley communities had been booked for months for the opening weekend of the season. Driving by many a farmhouse, I was amazed at how many friends (as evidenced by the many new house trailers) the farmers had just a day or so before the start of pheasant season—friends never to be seen again until the start of the next pheasant season. ...

Opening morning found me out on Lurline Road just north and west of Colusa, quietly sitting out of sight in a small grove of willow trees. Having to drive a marked truck put me at a disadvantage. Sure, it had some deterrent effect as long as I was in sight, but drive off and the critters better look out! That morning I had picked a huge fallow field just north of where I sat, with a lot of harvested cropland surrounding the area. I figured I would work it on foot, looking like any other hunter (hunting gear, shotgun, and all), moving in and among the sportsmen to see how they behaved. By daylight there were thirty-three vehicles parked along the road near my place of concealment, with many more as far as I could see up and down other stretches of Lurline, all parked near their favorite fields. I could just imagine what the rest of my district and county looked like! Being brand new and unknown, I figured I could strike many times before the lads realized there was a rotten apple in their barrel of pheasants!

The habitat surrounding me was great, and I don't think I had seen so many pheasants anywhere else in my district. There were so many that I only wished I could hunt them on opening morning as well. But such is the plight of the conservation officer. When hunting is at its best, you had better be out there working because that is when the damage is being done to the birds, and when you need to be "making money" for your agency, teaching those who are misbehaving a little lesson in ethics.

Not forty yards from me, a dozen folks got out of their cars parked along the road, crossed to the north side of Lurline Road, and entered the tall weeds of the fallow field I had singled out to watch. No big deal—except they were thirty-six minutes too early. In those days the local judges made us give the early and later shooter the benefit of the doubt of a cheap watch by giving them ten minutes either way (not a practice followed everywhere, mind you, so don't get trapped). However, a chap who strayed past that ten-minute grace period bought the entire "farm," or the time by which he exceeded the legal boundary. I had set my watch that morning by the time in the sheriff's office, so I knew my time was the real McCoy. The lads entered the field in a line abreast, quickly jumping four pheasants, all roosters. I knew they intended to signal to any other hunters by their presence that this was their area, so don't barge in. However, walking into a field full of game before legal shooting hours can be an unwise thing to do. If you have just one trigger-happy shooter who is tempted by the presence of game, he will often start off the early shooting, and the rest of the world will blow up! Well, *blow it up he did* as two graceful roosters got up in front of the sixth man in the line, and he let both of them have it. The explosion of the shotgun caused at least a dozen other roosters, already nervous because of the noise of humans walking in their field of weeds, to leap into the air in front of the other hunters. Soon the air was filled with small clouds of drifting, swirling, brightly colored feathers, evidence of the presence of a live rooster just moments earlier.

Grabbing my cite book and heading out at a dead run, I trotted into the middle of their line, yelling, "Game warden; stop your shooting. It is not legal shooting time as of yet." My reward was to have at least another dozen shots go off before I got all my shooters corralled! When all was said and done, I had twelve individuals from Colusa for shooting thirty minutes early. Every one of them had at least one untagged rooster, and two had a closed-season hen as well. From the few minutes of elapsed time between their entering the field and my entrance, I would walk away with twelve citations encompassing twenty-six violations that eventually totaled $1,200 in fines! That doesn't sound like much today, but keep in mind that the average salary in those days was $10,000 per year or less!

I hurriedly began the business of citation issuance and seizure of the birds, ever mindful of the tremendous barrage of shooting going on all around me. Not wanting to miss a chance to capture any of the bad guys, I wrote like a banshee, then ran back to my patrol truck carrying eighteen evidence pheasants with the shooting sounds of hundreds of gunners taking it to the pheasant, now that legal shooting time was upon us. Throwing the birds' broken bodies on the passenger-side floorboard, I cranked up the truck and took off down the road to the west side of the fallow field, where no one would know me. Again I ditched my patrol vehicle, this time in a duck club parking lot, and headed out on foot. Within ten minutes, I was onto a group of five gunners for whom a bird came down every time a gun barrel went up. By the way these lads were shooting, they had been there before and knew exactly what they were doing. Anytime you see a hunter or group of hunters working over the resource like that, you want to hang close because it is often just a matter of moments before they stray over the line. Working along the weedy edge of a shallow canal, I kept them in sight as if I were another hunter working off to one side. Then, as if on cue, they got together and, walking rapidly, disappeared into a dry canal bed not thirty-five yards ahead of me. In the short amount of time I had been watching this bunch, I had seen them kill eight roosters that had risen in front of their guns. They had been shooting before I got there, so I surmised that they had many more in their game bags and were good candidates for over-limits. When they walked down into the dry ditch, with numerous looks over their shoulders, I became even more suspicious. Why intentionally walk out of sight into a ditch when you are having a great hunt unless you had something to hide? I waited a few moments, thinking they might be crossing over to my side of the canal to continue hunting. Nothing. After a few more moments, I went forward to investigate.

Walking up to the spot where I had seen the group disappear, I began to hear voices over the constant shooting going on around me. All the lads were in the bottom of the canal, counting out their pheasants. They hadn't seen me yet, so I kept walking toward them like a rube hunter. When I was almost upon them, they heard me busting through some brush, and several of the lads attempted to throw their hunting coats over a smaller pile of pheasants off to one side. I said, "Hey, guys, looks like you got a few of the damn things. I can't hit my hind end with a paddle, but I'll keep trying." I kept walking as I spoke until I came even with them on the canal bank and could see that not one of their pheasants lying on the ground in plain sight was tagged. I discovered over the years that not tagging in the heat of fast and furious shooting was typical. Everyone was so intent on getting all their birds that they didn't tag them until they were done or, in many cases, saw the game warden approaching.

Figuring I would have some fun at their expense, I said, "Say, you lads have quite a few. You wouldn't mind sharing some, would you?"

They looked at each other as if to say, "Who is this dingbat?" Finally one of the lads said, "Sure." He removed one of the hunting jackets on the ground, which turned out to be covering a small pile of roosters, took out four badly shot-up birds, and tossed them up the bank at my feet. I guess he figured I would get the hell out of "Dodge" by walking away with my new-found "limit."

Thinking I would have a little more fun before blowing my cover, I said, "Hey, these are really badly shot up. How about giving me some of those nice ones by the other coat that aren't so badly shot up?" How is that for brass? I thought.

With that, a young man scrambled up the bank and gathered up all the pheasants just thrown to me, saying, "All right, asshole, how about no birds?" With that, he jumped back down the bank with my four beat-up birds and threw them back on the pile. Then they all stared at me as if to say, "Don't you have something else to do besides bother us?"

Walking down the canal bank, I jumped across the muddy bottom to confront the now puzzled lads. Taking out my badge I said, "Game warden. How about I take all of them since they are not tagged in accordance with state law, plus it appears you have a few too many." You could have heard a mole pass gas in a windstorm with that revelation of silver held in front of their eyes for all in the bottom of that ditch to see.

One guy, who turned out to be a kid named Carl from Williams, kicked the entire pile of pheasants under his hunting jacket into the shallow water of the canal and swore up a blue streak. The rest just stood there in shock. As I got things under control and made Carl go in the water to retrieve the birds he had kicked, I discovered that all of them were at least one pheasant over, and none of the birds were tagged. I issued citations all around for the over-limits (from one to four over) and the untagged birds, all the while sitting in the bottom of the canal where no one else could see what was going on. It turned out my lads were hunting on an uncle's land. Suffice to say, they were all pissed and more upset with themselves for being so easily picked off by the new game warden, a man they had never seen before, than for their poor hunting practices or ethics. … They felt a little better and managed a few laughs when they discovered I had issued citations to twelve other chaps before I got to them. They wanted to know if I was going to tell anyone I had caught them. I said no; my citations were a matter of public record in the Justice Court, but I had no intention of blabbing as to who I had caught. That seemed to settle them down a little, and two weeks or so later they forfeited a total of $750 in bail without a whimper. As I was soon to discover, many in the valley took pride in violating the game laws and not being caught by the game warden. Getting caught breaking the game laws by the local "tule creeper," as those of my ilk were sometimes called, could lead to a lot of humiliation and goading by one's peers. As a side note, I went on to catch every one of those lads breaking the wildlife laws at least once more during the following seven years that I worked in the valley. So much for learning from experience.

Loading the game bag in my hunting jacket with twenty pheasants, I grabbed the remaining nine by their feet in one hand and headed back to my truck, leaving my Williams lads to head for home with a set of long faces and a whale of a tale to tell about their first meeting with the new game warden—who coincidentally was the size of a small whale. On the way to my truck, I ran across two hunters who obviously didn't know me from Adam. Seeing me approaching with a full game bag and a large hand full of pheasants, one of the lads just whistled. "Brother, did you have some shoot or what?" the short one said.

"It makes our measly five birds look kind of wimpy," said the other. They didn't say anything about my apparent enormous over-limit but were just awed by my numbers of birds. I guess it takes all kinds, I thought as I approached the lads, laid down my birds, and identified myself. If nothing else, those birds made *great* cover! Both lads had not tagged a single bird, and twenty minutes later I had cited both of them and seized their five birds as well. Now I had a *real* bunch of birds and, after issuing the lads their citations, made a bee-line for my truck to reduce the load a bit. I spent the next forty minutes drawing birds so they wouldn't spoil in the warming day. Once done, I tossed them onto the floorboards and front seat of my pickup to cool out, washed my hands with my drinking water, and decided I had better head for some fields to the north in order to spread some more cheer around the county. I figured the lads from Williams, whom I had seen stop twice to talk to nearby groups of hunters and point toward me, had let the cat out of the bag, and if I wanted to catch anyone else breaking the laws, I had better find greener pastures elsewhere. I don't know what it is about telling people when a game warden is in the area, but those of us in law enforcement have all had that experience. We are doing our level best to see that the tradition of hunting is continued for all, and yet those just busted will advertise our presence through public discussion, making our job more difficult. It does nothing in the long run but ruin their sport and that of others. Go figure. …

Driving by a gun club just off Lurline Road on San Jose Road, I saw four lads coming out of an old shed on the back side of the property. Without a backward look, they walked quickly toward an adjacent unharvested milo field. The building looked like an old boathouse and wasn't near any living accommodations where I would have been subject to curtilage (search and seizure) issues, so ditching my vehicle (in the shade of a bamboo thicket so the birds wouldn't spoil), I headed toward it on a lightly traveled and heavily overgrown farm road. Working through the willows, I made my way undetected to the old boathouse. Taking another look at my lads, now hunting their way across the field, killing a lot of pheasants in the process, I ducked into the shed. It took a few moments for my eyes to adjust to the reduced light, but there in front of me, hanging from some nails on a rafter, were four limits of rooster pheasants, all neatly drawn and cooling. It was such a shame, all of them being untagged. … Taking a quick look through a hole in the boards of the shed, I could see that my lads were going to hunt north, up the east side of the milo field, cross over to the west, and then hunt back to their secret at the boathouse. Then it would be an easy walk back to the Black Jack Duck Club, where their cook would finish cleaning and preserving the birds. *Boom-boom-boom—boom-boom* went the guns of my successful hunters as they worked their way across the milo. I began to grin. There would be nothing like a good old-fashioned homecoming when they entered the boatshed only to find the local game warden waiting—and *guarding* their birds for them. ... Or would it be like a homecoming in the "woodshed"? The shooting got louder, and they were soon close enough that several times their shot rattled off the tin roof of the shed. Finally I could hear happy voices and much laughter. From the sound of it, they had each limited once more, and this time it had taken, according to one booming voice, just eighteen minutes to kill sixteen birds! "Let's hurry up and get some lunch and these birds taken care of so we can hit her again this afternoon. If we don't shoot our milo patch for an hour or so, other birds from the surrounding areas will seek out cover in there where it is undisturbed, and we will have another hell of a shoot," said one voice.

We shall see, fellows, about that afternoon shoot, I thought. ... We shall see. ...

Coming through the doorway, the first fellow turned to talk to his fellow violators behind him, and when he turned back around I wasn't two feet away, sitting on a sawhorse in plain view. *"Holy Christ—god-damn,"* he yelled as he spun around, knocking down one of his buddies as he roared out the door and ran a dozen yards or so down the weed-choked farm road before he realized he had dropped his shotgun and limit of pheasant back at the shed!

"What the hell? Who the hell are you?" bellowed the fellow picking himself up off the dirt after being run over by his buddy.

"State Fish and Game warden," I said pleasantly enough. I could afford to be polite, since I was sitting on a sixteen-bird stash and from what they were carrying it looked as if they had another sixteen. Soon they had settled down after their scare. Sending greetings around to all along with my identification, I then issued four more citations for over-limits and untagged birds. My fellows, all Italians from Richmond, were pretty glum, especially when I informed them that I had overheard their conversation about hunting the milo field again in the afternoon. "Not something you want to do, lads, in light of your double limits of birds already taken," I said with a stern look. No one said a thing, all realizing they had said enough already. Finishing my first ticket book, I commenced filling out a new one with information on my chaps from the milo field. Soon I was on my way with another load of thirty-two rooster pheasants for my vehicle. Damn, I thought, this working the pheasant hunter is a lot of fun, and pretty easy. In a matter of just a few hours, I had apprehended twenty-three shooters for a total of forty-six violations! Love this Colusa County and the opening day of pheasant season for the cherry patch it was, I thought.

Over the next two hours I checked another twenty-seven pheasant hunters, and every one of them was perfectly legal. ... So much for the cherry-patch theory! One group of twenty-seven hunters I checked was hunting on Link Dennis's property. They were relatives of Dennis's with a bunch of their friends out of Maxwell, and not one violation did I find. As I was eventually to learn, Link Dennis did not approve of wildlife violations by anyone hunting on his lands. I would later befriend many of those folks, and one of them, Tim Dennis, four years later became my deputy—one of very few deputy federal agents in the nation, and a damn fine one! When the two of us went after violators, we caught them. I don't remember *ever* losing any cases in which we doubled up going after someone. Tim was not only a great friend but a damn good catch dog as well. I miss those days. ...

Later that morning working almost due north of Williams, I noticed a lad at quite a distance on a motorbike driving slowly down a farm road alongside the interstate. He had a shotgun across the handlebars of his bike and stopped every so often to shoot at something on the ground to his front. He would motor up to the thing just shot and put it into a saddlebag on the far side of his bike, then continue down the farm road. I couldn't tell what he was shooting, but I suspected that they were running pheasants. Speeding ahead of him and getting out of sight, I set up an interception by some machine barns north of his probable exit route. Waiting until he was alongside one of the shed openings, I stepped out in front of him, no more than ten feet away from the front of his motorbike. Seeing me holding up my badge, he gunned the engine and tried to drive by, only to have me grab his bag over the rear wheel and jerk him to a resounding stop. It turned out he was a lad from Williams hunting pheasants on his dad's land. Unfortunately for him, he had six roosters and three hens in his bag, and if I hadn't grabbed him when I did, there was no telling how many more he would have killed. As I wrote up this lad for an overlimit of roosters, possession of closed-season birds (hens), taking game birds with the aid of a motor vehicle, and untagged birds, I heard a truck drive up behind me. Turning, I saw a stocky farmer getting out of his truck and striding over to me like he was pissed I was on his land. "What's up, son?" he asked, looking at the boy still sitting on the motorbike with a long face.

"I am getting a citation from the game warden," the young man responded.

"What for?" the farmer asked loudly.

"Taking too many birds and a few hens," the boy answered lamely.

Since I hadn't been asked any questions, I just kept writing, figuring the man would talk to me when he was damn good and ready. Sticking out his hand, he said, "Afternoon, Officer, I'm Dave Johnson. And who are you?"

"My name is Terry Grosz, and I'm the new Colusa game warden," I said as I stood up from my kneeling position and shook his hand. In light of the number of cool welcomes I had previously received from the local populace, his warmth was quite a surprise.

"Damn, you sure are a big one. Are we so bad here in the valley that they have to send us giants?" he asked.

"Not really," I joked. "I'm the runt of the litter, and they just happened to drop me here for the duration."

He gave a big friendly grin, then turned to his son and said, "Throw your bike in the back of the truck, boy, and be careful you don't scratch it. I want it to fetch the best price possible so you have some way to pay off these tickets. Then follow your bike into the front seat of that truck and mash your ass in it! We have a few things to discuss on the way home." Finishing my citation, I walked over to the truck and had the lad, who had turned eighteen on that very day, sign, making his birthday complete. Handing him his copy and an evidence receipt for the birds, I turned to walk back to my truck, only to be intercepted by Dave. "Terry, whether you know it or not, you just did me a big favor. I don't condone the illegal killing of wildlife and never have. I have done my level best to keep Rick on the straight and narrow, but he seems to be marching to his own drummer ever since his mother died. You don't know my son like I do, but the look in his eyes tells me this experience has scared the hell out of him and really gotten his attention! I will keep working on him, and in the meantime, if you catch anyone on my land breaking the laws—and I do mean anyone—you cite the hell out of them. I want something for my grandkids someday, and killing it all off today is no way to insure that they have something to enjoy in a few years."

He shook my hand again, and that meeting ended in a cloud of dust as Dave and Rick headed down one of the many dusty farm roads back toward Williams. I would bet a month's pay that was an interesting ride home for Rick. Over the next few years, I met Rick in the field numerous times, and he was always straight with the law, as were all the hunters he was with. We got to be friends, as much as a local farm boy and game warden could be in the atmosphere of the valley at that time. I lost touch with him when he went off to college and I was promoted and transferred to North Dakota. It had been a long and tiring day, and I had sure expected a lot more guff than I got from Dave over the matter with his son. Receiving the opposite treatment felt pretty damn good, and that moment kind of gave me a little boost, making me ready for more.

As an aside, in 1995 my secretary came into my office one afternoon and said an "old friend" was in Denver and wanted to stop in and see me. I said, "Send him in." To my surprise, in walked Rick Johnson, only this time instead of being on a motorbike with a bag full of illegal pheasants, he was in a U.S. Air Force uniform, and the only "birds" I saw were the eagles on his shoulders signifying the rank of colonel!

"Good afternoon, Terry," he said as he walked smartly over to my desk and warmly shook my hand. We passed the afternoon talking about old times as old friends will do, and I discovered that he was *the* boss on an air force base in Utah. It turned out that his base processed a lot of military surplus, and before the afternoon was over he had arranged for my officers in Utah to screen some surplus military hardware before anyone else got the chance. I ended up using the fruits of that opportunity rather successfully on a large covert operation ongoing in the region at that time—at no cost to the Department of the Interior. I understand that Rick's kids now hunt pheasants on his dad's land. It seems that Dave's wish came true in more ways than one. ...

Getting back into my patrol truck and realizing I had spent not one ounce of time on the north or east side of my district, I headed that way to "show the flag." Passing a farmhouse on the east side of the River Road as I headed north out of Colusa, I noticed several house trailers and a dozen or so cars parked around the residence. I also noticed a gang of men standing out back under some walnut trees cleaning a mess of pheasants in a couple of fifty-gallon drums about the same time they noticed the game warden driving by. Whipping my truck around, I headed back to the crowd in the hopes of finally meeting the landowner (I had tried two times previously, unsuccessfully) and maybe checking a few pheasants as well. Man, there were ten sets of eyes on me as I drove past the house to where all the action was by the two cleaning drums. I had whipped the truck around so fast that no one, even if they wanted, had time to vanish or hide any illegal evidence. Stepping out of the truck, I said, "Afternoon, gentlemen; looks like you lads did rather well this morning." There wasn't much return to my greeting, and I could see why. There were piles of rooster pheasants everywhere, and first of all, hardly any had been tagged! Second, it looked as if a few of the lads, as evidenced by the large piles of pheasants at their feet, had done a little too well! Ignoring the obvious for the moment and trying to be neighborly, I said, "Is there a Pete Cook among you lads?" Pete was the landowner I had been trying to meet for several weeks. His lands butted right up to some of the finest hunting in the county, and there were several good farm roads leading right past his house that I could use to secretly enter those areas—that is, if he and I could hit it off and I could trust him to not report to his neighbors when I coursed through his lands en route to theirs.

"I'm Pete," said a dark-complected, stockily built man with a heavy shock of black hair as he stepped away from the barrel-cleaning crowd. "What can I do for you?"

"Well, I needed to first of all meet you and introduce myself as Terry Grosz, your new game warden, and then ask if I could use some of your farm roads to access the lands to the east of your properties?"

"Well, let's go inside where we can talk, and I'll get us some coffee," he said as he shook my hand and then put his hand on my shoulder to turn me toward the farmhouse.

Now I was caught between the devil and the deep blue. I had seen a lot of illegal birds and knew that if I left, all would appear to be legal upon my return. I felt that Pete, in order to protect his hunting friends, was trying to shepherd me away to give his clientele time to square away the obvious. I also suspected that if I didn't go with Pete but attended to the illegal pheasant business at hand, my request for access across his property might be denied. Damn, talk about a rock and a hard place! Turning away from his hand on my shoulder, I said,

"Pete, the first thing I need to do is check these lads and their pheasants. You as well as I can see that we have a few problems with birds not being tagged. That probably ought to be addressed before someone in this crowd does something foolish like hiding the birds or the like." Looking him in the eye, I could see the helpless resignation that comes from trying to help one's friends and falling noticeably short.

With that, I moved over to the fellows cleaning the pheasants by the first drum, identified myself, and asked if I might check their hunting licenses, tags, and birds. There was a little mumbling before the lads started reaching into their pockets for their wallets. As I checked each lad's license, I checked his birds as well. I could see three fellows around the second cleaning barrel casually dumping pheasants into the mess of feathers and intestines in their barrel. They would stand as if picking a bird, and when they thought I was not looking at them, would gently drop that bird into the barrel, where it would quickly sink out of sight, and quietly pick up another. When they felt I was again occupied, they would repeat the process. It would have been a perfect trick if I hadn't been watching. I let them do their thing, all the while recording in my mind, as they dumped their obvious over-limits, who was doing what.

The six lads on the first barrel all had their hunting licenses in order and had limits of birds. However, five of them had not tagged their birds, and I pointed that out to them as a violation for which they would be issued a citation and have their birds seized as evidence. That created a lot of grumbling, especially when I took all their birds and laid them off to one side. I then took each man's hunting license and laid it on his pile of birds for later matching of the shooter to the birds when I issued citations. Then I turned to the set of lads still cleaning birds by the second barrel. By now they had their licenses out for me to review, and all were in order. However, to a man, they had not tagged their birds, in part because of my close proximity! Pointing this out to the group, I was again met with silence. I then asked the lads to step back and, facing them with the barrel between us, commenced to lift whole, uncleaned pheasants out of the barrel, laying them at my feet. After taking thirteen birds over and above their legal limits of four each out of that barrel, I walked over to the lads and said, "While checking the other lads, I saw you three out of the corner of my eye dropping extra birds into the barrel in an attempt to hide your over-limits. How many did each of you drop?" Silence! I repeated, "How many did each of you discard into the barrel?"

There was more of the silence thing, but finally one lad raised his hand as if he were in school needing to go to the bathroom and said, "Five of those birds are mine." He really did look like he needed to go to the bathroom about that time. With the cat out of the bag and with their buddy folding to the law, the other two admitted to the other eight. All the time this series of events was going on, I tried to keep an eye on Pete to see how he was taking it. He just stood there and coldly looked on. He looked pissed. Returning to my nearby patrol truck, I got out a couple of new citation books (only twenty to a book in those days) and began to call the lads over one at a time with their birds and licenses so I could use the hood of my truck as a table. When all was said and done, I had written eight of the ten fellows for untagged birds. And had written the three lads who had dumped the pheasants in the barrel for over-limits as well. In the process, I seized forty-five more birds to add to the pile already in the truck.

Finished with the paperwork, I walked over to Pete, who had been silently standing by a walnut tree, and asked if he had any pheasants. "Cheeky bastard, aren't you?" he slowly said.

"I get paid to be thorough by the license-buying community and just thought I would ask," I said.

"I don't shoot the damn things very often, just let them live on the place so my friends can have a few," he said.

"OK," I said. "I take it those remaining four tagged birds laying by the barrel are yours?"

"Yes, they are."

"OK. Then how about that cup of coffee?"

"Like I said," he said, "cheeky."

With that, he turned and went inside the ranch house, and I followed, leaving the other men standing around their barrels trying to figure out why God was so mad at them. Nonetheless, Pete and I somehow hit it off, and I used his access roads many times over the following years both as a state Fish and Game officer and as a federal agent. I never caught Pete in any kind of questionable activity, and I never again had any trouble on his property regarding pheasants. I guess one time for him and his friends "in the barrel" was enough.

While "visiting" with the lads on Pete's property, I had occasionally heard two shotguns on the river side of the road, maybe a few hundred yards north. After finishing at Pete's place, I headed north driving along another dirt road leading up onto the Sacramento River levee in an attempt to locate that shooting. Sitting up on the levee, I used my binoculars to scan the prune orchards to the west and saw two men walking through the grass. Both had shotguns, and they were carrying several pheasants each. Dropping off the levee in my truck, I headed toward them, driving slowly through the orchard in order to reduce my dust trail. When they became aware that I was driving up to them, they quickly laid down their shotguns and birds as if nothing had happened and continued walking away. I stopped by their shotguns laying behind a tree and hit my siren. Man, you talk about getting their attention! I could see the whites of their eyes from thirty yards away, *through the backs of their heads!* Both rather sheepishly turned and walked back to me as I gathered up their old Winchester model 12 shotguns and five pheasants. As it turned out, neither had hunting licenses, and the birds were untagged as well. Both were barely able to speak English, but between their poor English and my atrocious Spanish, I got the citations issued. They were both farm laborers, and I happened to know where they lived. The landowner had several old house trailers and a shack or two drawn up in a sort of compound where about seven very poor Mexican families lived. Both of my fellows were currently employed by that landowner and expected to be for the next six months, so I just issued citations instead of booking them into the Colusa County jail as I would have had to do if they were transients. When I seized the pheasants and tagged them, I could see the disappointment in their eyes. I knew those birds were probably meant for their next family meal, but that was the way it was. I also seized their shotguns and told the lads that the guns would be returned when they paid the fines. The guns would be kept at my home, and they could arrange to meet with me to retrieve them when they could show me a receipt from the Colusa Justice Court indicating that the fines had been paid. They agreed and went off at a fast pace to their compound. I think they figured I would ask for their green cards next, and I suspected they had none. Returning to my pickup, I realized that the pile of evidence birds was beginning to crowd me off the front seat. I had birds stacked from the floorboards up to the window and all across the seat!

This first experience as a game warden in pheasant country was turning out to be a good one—if you were a game warden and not a pheasant. I had never seen such a tendency to violate as I had experienced that day. It seemed that the spirit to take all one could was everywhere. And I had checked fewer than seventy-five people out of maybe five thousand that were hunting pheasant that day in the county!

Moving north, all the while burning daylight, I checked another thirty or so hunters on Terrill Sartain's properties, including some of his famous movie-star friends such as Andy Devine and Roy Rogers, without incident and then crossed the river on the Princeton Ferry to the north-central portion of my district. Moving west on the Princeton Highway toward the Sacramento National Wildlife Refuge, I spotted a line of hunters moving across a large fallow field heavily overgrown with tall weeds on the north side of the road. Stopping along the highway, I took my binoculars and counted twenty-three people in the hunting party. From the sound of their shooting, they were having a good hunt. Getting in among those hunters without being discovered was not going to be easy. The country all around was open, and there was no place near them where I could leave my marked patrol truck and walk in undetected. Again and again, I ran a battle plan through my mind only to shelve it as unworkable. Finally I decided to wait until the line arrived at the bottom of the field next to the highway and then speed right in among them. It wasn't the best plan because they would see me coming for the last hundred yards or so and start to fix whatever needed fixing, but I had no other choice. Being new to the district, I still hadn't learned all the back ways to sneak in on people, nor had I developed intelligence sources of informants and public-minded citizens to tip me off in advance. In the current instance, the critters and I paid the price.

Watching my group of hunters, it was plain that the field was lousy with pheasants. I estimated that for every bird they flushed within gun range, at least half of them fell, filling the air with puffs of brown and tan feathers. Then I noticed another group of seven hunters who popped up in my binoculars at the bottom of the same field near the highway where I sat. I had no idea where they had come from, but they were now lined out along the bottom of the field to cut off any pheasants wise enough to run ahead of the line of hunters coming from the north. I discovered later that the second group had been dropped off earlier by the hunters in the field. I also learned that this pheasant hunt was an annual family affair.

When the gang of hunters coming from the north got to within the last thirty-five or so yards of the south end of the field where it met the Princeton Highway, the air suddenly became alive with hundreds of pheasants. Many of the birds had run to the end of the field and then, hearing the blocking hunters, held until the last moment. When the noise of the line from the north got too loud and disturbing, they flushed. For about two minutes it looked from my vantage point as if someone had turned over a beehive! Pheasants exploded from the weeds at all points of the compass, and the heavy shooting now turned deadly earnest, sounding like a line of musketry on the field at Gettysburg on that fateful July day so many years before. The air was full of swirling, falling birds with puffs of feathers from solid hits drifting in the wind until the feathers, drawn to earth by gravity, hung up in the tall weeds. It was amazing! I had never seen such a killing field, all legal, mind you—at least until the game warden got there and sorted things out. The northern line of hunters finally shot its way to the blocking hunters to the south, and, shooting together, they merged. Hunters and dogs were running everywhere, picking up the dead and running down the wounded birds. Shouts, gestures, laughter, and yelling at their dogs was the word of the day at that moment. Realizing that now was the time to go, while everyone was preoccupied with the chaos of the scene, I poured the coal to my vehicle and steamed their way. True to form, my hunters just ignored another vehicle driving down the Princeton Highway until I got within fifty yards of the happy crew. Then many stopped and looked at the rapidly approaching vehicle, soon recognizing the seal of the great state of California on the door! Soon I could see them talking excitedly to each other, and soon they gathered into clusters, hurriedly tagging their pheasants and exchanging birds with each other in cases of over-limits.

Pulling into a turnout next to them, I quickly stepped out of my truck and managed to walk right up to nine hunters before they could rearrange their birds or escape. I could tell from the looks in their eyes that they couldn't believe what they were seeing! Since they knew who I was by the markings on the truck, I dispensed with the usual identification routine and began gathering up hunting licenses, having the lads pile the birds at their feet after removing them from their game bags. In that short period, when the birds had exploded from that final thirty yards of cover, all but three of the nine men I had in tow (seven from the blocking line, two from the north line) had taken limits of pheasants. The remaining three had nice over-limits of five each! Telling the lads to stand by their birds, with their licenses in hand (I had written each man's number of birds on the back of his license), I quickly headed into the field to check the other hunters, who were making themselves scarce. Many who had come through the field from the north had begun rapidly walking back to where they had parked. Others began to run, telling me they had a lot to hide and would just as soon not share their secrets with me! Out of that group of twenty-three hunters who had driven the field from the north, I ended up with only eight! The rest just walked away from me, knowing I had my hands full and couldn't follow them without losing those already in tow. Fifteen out of at least thirty hunters! Welcome to your first day of pheasant season, Terry. Nothing like hitting a group that size of shooters who were less than honest or respectful of the law. Writing off those who were rapidly running or walking out of my reach, I headed my six "newfound friends" south to meet with the nine still waiting for my return. Those nine couldn't run because I still had their hunting licenses in hand.

Talk about a sullen bunch! I sure had one when I got them all together. There was gloom and doom all around instead of the spirit of happy killing that had predominated before my arrival. They were not so tough when it came to dealing with one of their own kind rather than an unarmed pheasant. Checking all the hunting licenses and driver's licenses, I found I had a crew from the Princeton and Butte City areas. Many of them with the same last name, and I later found out that more than a few of their kinfolk had run afoul of the Fish and Game laws in the '30s and '40s with night shooting and sale of ducks. It was beginning to look as if family bonds and lawlessness ran pretty deep together in some instances. Of my current crop, not a single lad had tagged his pheasants! Two didn't have hunting licenses, and four had over-limits! By the time I get this straightened out, it will be noon tomorrow, I thought. Repeating my procedure of calling the lads over to the hood of my truck with their birds, I began the paperwork. By the time all was said and done, I had written all fifteen! All for untagged pheasants, two for an additional charge of hunting without a license, and four for over-limits as well. In the process, I seized sixty-one pheasants. I could just imagine what could have been seized if I had had some help quietly waiting by the cars at the north end of the field. By now those cars were streaming out of the area in clouds of dust on every available road, and you could bet your bottom dollar they weren't coming my way! After finishing with my fellows, I took the remaining drivers to their vehicles on the north end of the field and after searching their vehicles for any extra pheasants let them go their ways. Watching the dust of those departing vehicles, I thought, Well, you certainly introduced yourself to a prominent historical family in your district this fine day.

Grabbing a cold drink and an apple from the cooler in the back of my truck, I commenced gutting a mess of birds that I thought would never end. When I finished, I washed my hands and arms once more with the ice water from the spigot of the ice chest. Grabbing another apple to keep my big guts from eating the little guts, I headed south toward Delevan before I ran out of daylight and pheasant season closed for the day. The air was still full of the sounds of shotguns bringing the elusive pheasant to ground, but the shooting wasn't as heavy as before. However, my sense of urgency was still there.

Coming in on what I was later to come to know as Newhall Farms, I spotted four chaps hunting far south of the Delevan Road in a harvested rice field. It took me some time to find a farm road leading to them, and then I was stopped by a cable gate for which I had no key. I could see by the fresh tire tracks that a vehicle had recently gone in on the road. Standing up in the back of my truck with my binoculars, I soon spotted a vehicle partially hidden behind a large mound of dirt several hundred yards away. Not wanting to cut the lock in order to drive in, I figured I would use "shank's mare" since their vehicle was only a short distance away. Pulling my truck off the road, I grabbed my citation book and binoculars and headed for the vehicle, suspected as belonging to the four hunters still about three-eighths of a mile away. Realizing it was almost the end of shooting time for pheasant, I decided against walking out in the field and checking the lads, figuring I would just stay put at their vehicle. That way, if the lads were in the wrong, they would walk right up to me and I would be among them before they knew it.

Crawling up on a mound of dirt and lying down, I began to watch my four hunters. I had only a poor set of 7×35 binoculars (left by the previous Colusa game warden), but I watched my chaps hunt as best I could. Several times I observed them shooting at what I assumed were pheasants because of the low trajectory of the shooting and then continue walking along the rice checks for what appeared to be more birds. Soon it was four o'clock, the legal time to stop hunting pheasants, but you wouldn't have known it by the sounds of shooting all around me! For a good thirty minutes more, the shooting continued as if there weren't any quitting time. However, my four guys were walking back to their vehicle, so there wouldn't be any citations here for late shooting. Not wanting to be discovered before they reached the car, I slid down behind the dirt bank and waited for the sounds of voices to tell me they had arrived. About twenty minutes later I could hear them, and then I heard the lads opening up the back door of their vehicle and figured it was time to make an appearance. Stepping out from behind the mound, I said, "Evening, gentlemen; Fish and Game warden. How was the hunting?"

Suddenly I froze, as did my four hunters! I couldn't believe my eyes! They were the same four hunters I had caught earlier in the morning at the old boathouse by the Black Jack Duck Club for over-limits and untagged pheasants! I don't think they could believe their eyes either. They just stood there looking at something they sure as hell never wanted to see again. In their hands were the pheasants they had just taken. Not over-limits this time, mind you, but every one of the lads had at least two and one had four roosters! Since they had already taken over-limits earlier in the day, the birds they now held just added to that misery. I finally said, "It's obvious you lads didn't get enough of this hunting thing this morning, eh?" They didn't say a word, still in shock at seeing my miserable carcass once more. After all, what the hell can you say when you pulled the ripcord and your parachute didn't open? I requested that they unload their shotguns, which they did. Taking out my citation book, I said with a sigh, "You guys know the drill. May I see your driver's licenses once more, please?" Normally, I would have just used the information out of the citation book since I had recorded their illegal actions once already this day. However, that filled-out citation book was back at my patrol rig, and I was using a new one. Writing out the citations on the hood of their Suburban, I discovered that one lad had two, two of the lads had three, and one had four pheasants. Additionally, they had not learned the tagging lesson from that morning's experience, and all the birds were once again ... untagged. I think we were all shaking our heads at the turn of events. What were the odds of my finding them twice in one day? As they drove off after I finished, I couldn't help but think, there go four losers. I guess they figured to hell with the game warden, they would go hunting in the afternoon if they wanted. Not being complete dummies, they had changed hunting areas, knowing that would throw the game warden off. Hell, they were even wearing different clothing than they had worn that morning! As I said, losers—or God was really pissed off at them. Gathering up my twelve evidence birds, I started the long walk back to my patrol truck.

That walk gave me time to come to think about just how unfortunate the critters really are if the folks taking that resource aren't inclined to obey the laws. It was pretty obvious that my predecessor must not have worked the hell out of these chaps in order to keep them more in line. Either that or the very healthy population of birds that year was abnormal, causing normal men to fly off the handle of ethics and common sense and kill as if they were making up for lost time. Amidst the late shooting going on around me, I decided not to fall into that trap of sitting back and letting things take their course. I was young and had a good woman to patch me up and send me back to the wildlife wars so the animals would get what I had to offer in the form of all-out protection. There were lots of kids who needed to see this resource miracle, and there was only one way to make that happen. That was to ride the lads stepping over the line, "rapping their fingers" until they learned or the critters were all gone. I opted for the former.

Back at my patrol truck, I again cleaned my evidence birds, throwing the guts into a weed-choked canal alongside the road. Better to let some form of critter feast that night than throw them into the garbage can at home. Then, washing my hands once more, I lowered the tailgate, sat down, and watched events unfolding around me. The air was full of the sights and sounds of thousands of waterfowl leaving Delevan National Wildlife Refuge and, like a living tornado, funneling into the adjacent rice fields to feed, unmindful of the trauma the pheasants had just undergone. They were hungry, and little else mattered. I smiled at the bounty, slid my hind end off the tailgate, closed it, and got into my truck. I didn't have the time to sit there and enjoy Nature's feast that evening, I still had work to do.

One of the first things I did when I moved to Colusa County was to get the names and addresses of those folks, old or unfortunate, who needed a little extra help. That information came from many sources, including the social workers and sheriff's office. Taking that list off the visor of my truck, I began making the rounds, delivering pheasants seized that day from those who couldn't follow the rules, count, or, even worse, give a damn. You might ask how I could get rid of evidence before court, and that's a good question. I had worked out a deal with the county attorney that in "slam-dunk" cases, in order not to waste the game, I could give it away while it was fresh to those in need. I would take pictures of the evidence, take a sample of the critter, a tailfeather in this case, and then give the meat away. I also obtained a receipt from the party receiving the game.

I had a ton of pheasants, so it took a while. I remember one couple, Tom and Sada Yamamoto, whom I had met earlier and knew liked pheasants. I drove up to their little home and had them pick out six pheasants to eat. Sada was a tiny lady and very carefully picked out six pheasants as instructed. She took three that weren't too badly shot up and three that were really shot up. "Sada," I said, "why don't you pick six really good ones?"

She turned to me and said, "Mr. Grosz, there are other people out there who need them too."

What a princess, I thought. She did not work, and her husband was a farm laborer, certainly not making a fortune. I removed the three shot-up pheasants from her hands and replaced them with three big, fat ones. I will remember the smile from that little lady to my dying day.

Heading up to the east side of my district, I pulled into the compound holding all those Mexican families. Soon my truckload of pheasants was surrounded by excited children. Hearing all the excited voices, the parents, including the two men I had cited earlier, came out to look at the pile of birds in the back of my truck. "You folks take three birds for every member of your family," I said. At first they were reluctant to do so, but with a little encouragement, they all dove in, making my pile of evidence birds a whole lot smaller. As everyone happily moved off with their bounty, the men I had previously cited came over and thanked me in their broken English. One had tears in his eyes. From that day forth, I saw to it that those folks didn't suffer from want of evidence meat, especially in light of all that I seized over the next seven years. It was surprising how much information came to me about illegal activities that were happening on the east side after that. ...

Hind end dragging and all, I continued north to the home of a black man who worked as a laborer for Terrill Sartain. I didn't know the man but knew he had a huge brood of kids and, in order to care for them, worked double shifts for Terrill. Neither he nor his wife had any college education, but he was seeing to it through his unreal work efforts that every kid of his went to college. Every one of those kids was eventually sent to college by this man and his wife. Stopping at the cluster of shacks where this family resided, I cleaned out the rest of the pheasants (still a hell of a pile), giving them to a deserving and hardworking man and his family. Talk about happy—he wasn't very big, but he sure gave me a "man-sized" hug. To have meat in one's diet is great, but to have pheasant is even better, and I figured that if they had that many healthy kids, the missus must be one hell of a cook.

The next day I was up and out of the house before daylight. Picking another area off Four Mile Road, I ditched my truck among a collection of farm machinery, crawled up on one of the harvesters for a better vantage point, and sat there to drink in my blessings. The air was November cool, and I could hear many whistling wings of the duck and goose passing overhead. I would soon be back in the saddle enforcing the laws pertaining to those species, but for now I would stay with the pheasant hunter until we both ran out of steam. As the sun came up, I could hear roosters crowing, welcoming another day. There didn't seem to be as many as there had been the day before. I was sure many of the dumb ones were no longer alive, and many of the wiser were holding their beaks shut until things quieted down. I couldn't blame them in light of the ton or so of lead shot fired at them the day before. ...

That second day of pheasant season was like the day before but not as hectic or rewarding in terms of the number of citations issued. Many of the birds had left for deeper cover, like that on the national wildlife refuges that dotted the valley, or had moved onto private property, where they were not disturbed as much. It doesn't take Nature long to figure out where and when to run and hide. The key is to have a place to go to when times get tough. When they don't, extinction is next in the line of their evolution. Numerous shots to the south soon pulled me from my place of concealment and into another day's soon-to-be adventures.

Looking back on my young days as a game warden in the valley and my first pheasant season, I have to marvel. I wrote fifty-three citations involving seventy-five separate violations and seized 176 pheasants that first day. Another thirty-one citations involving fifty-two separate violations and 103 seized pheasants soon were to follow on the second day of the opening weekend of the pheasant season. Total fines for that two-day period exceeded $10,000 in my two justice courts, and that was in the days of $25, $50, and $100 fines!

Never in my life had I expected such an assault on the wildlife as I discovered that opening weekend in November so long ago. Nor did I expect the level of the behavior of the American sportsman to be as low as it was. However, I was maturing and growing in wisdom as each day passed, and I began to look at my profession, the wildlife, and their odds of survival in a much different light. Everything is finite, and it seemed as if the human race were constantly racing to see where that end point was. In the case of the world of wildlife, I guessed I would just have to find a way to intercept that direct line-of-sight path of destruction chosen by most unthinking humans. I was going to have to see if I could bend their paths of evil intent just enough so that others yet to come could marvel at the greatness of the land's gifts. If not, the final "reward" for such stupidity isn't far away.

two

Crunch

THE HARSH RINGING of the kitchen telephone on the afternoon of a rare day off jangled me out of my moment as a cook. Ignoring the ringing in the hope that my wife would respond, I continued working on my special turkey-breast recipe consisting of meat thinly sliced and marinated in clam juice overnight, making the deep-fried product taste like abalone, a gastropod culinary delight. The stark reality of the third ring made me stop dredging the marinated meat in raw egg and spiced cracker crumbs as it announced the obvious unavailability of my bride. Grabbing the phone with a hand covered in cracker crumbs, raw egg, and sticky clam juice, I said in a somewhat agitated voice, *"Hello!"*

The caller was none other than my close friend from Yuba City, California Fish and Game Warden Bob Hawks, or the Digger Indian as I respectfully called him because of his California Indian heritage. "What are you doing tonight?" growled the familiar voice.

"Well, thank you for the greeting and salutation," I retorted, knowing Bob's penchant for always running on a short fuse.

"Screw that crap," he predictably replied. "I have a problem over here and need some damn help."

Good old Bob. He never changed, just kept right to the point—abrupt, some would say. Sensing his urgency, I quickly forgot my displeasure at being interrupted. Bob was a very good friend and a damned good "catch dog." If he was calling, he truly needed help, and I was just the son of a gun to provide the desired assistance. Changing gears into my serious mode, I said, "What's up?"

"Spotlighters," growled the familiar, terse voice. "I have a bunch of spotlighting sons of bitches working the Sutter Buttes behind locked gates and am having a hard time catching them."

"What happened to the rest of your Fish and Game squad—why aren't they helping you?" I asked.

"They can't be bothered," said Bob, sounding out of patience.

"Sounds like they are too damned lazy to work, if you ask me," I said without thinking it through. Bob's grunt confirmed my pointed comment about the work ethics of my former Fish and Game squad members before he could think it through either. Taking a moment to reconsider the issue, I realized that those wardens had been good men when they were younger, but now most were aging and had pretty well played themselves out mentally and physically in the rigors of the profession. I quietly made a point of asking God's forgiveness for my haste to chastise these officers, realizing that there but for the grace of God go I.

It was summer 1970, and I was still a wet-behind-the-ears Fish and Wildlife Service U.S. game management agent. I had been assigned to the Martinez Office near San Francisco and was responsible for federal wildlife law enforcement for the northwestern half of northern California. I loved the new profession, but the office location, and to some extent the work area, was the pits. Crowded highways with traffic up to your eyes; people everywhere (you even had to stand in line to use the public restrooms); population centers crowded bumper to bumper; and at night, because of the city's lights, you could not see the stars. Add to that the constant din of a city day and night, the ever-present howling of police sirens, the grinding, crashing sounds of garbage trucks at daybreak as you tried to sleep, and the polluted air, and it was easy to understand a country boy's displeasure.

As if that were not enough, during my first week in my office in the basement of the Martinez Post Office, protestors against the Vietnam War threw a firebomb, meant for upstairs, that crashed against the side of the building, bounced, and went off in my basement walkway, frying everything in sight. The postal folks were really good about this problem, cleaning up the mess within a week and repainting the front wall of my office a soft pink in the process. That was all a guy my size needed—a pink office! The following week went one better. An overhead sewer pipe chose to rupture during one of my absences, covering my office with three feet of human effluent from the upstairs bathrooms. In the several days before I returned, this mess did wonders for all my files, low-lying equipment, evidence guns, and wooden office furniture. This time the postal authorities were not as efficient in the cleanup, and I found myself not wanting to spend long periods of time in my still dank office, especially on warm summer days. ... So much for the welcome mat at my new duty station!

I had always sworn that I would never work in a big city. I had been born and bred a country boy and was used to Mother Nature's pleasures. However, when Jack Downs, the Service's agent in charge in Sacramento, offered me a game management agent's position in a city, I discovered that I could not turn down the professional opportunity of a lifetime. There were 178 game agents in the nation at that time, and joining those august ranks had been my dream since my college days at Humboldt State. So much so that I had engineered my college courses and state Fish and Game warden career so that if a game management agent position ever opened, I would be well experienced, mentally prepared, and professionally competitive. That dream became reality after Jack's supervisor in Portland fired an agent in Sacramento who had been thrown in jail for contempt of court for telling a judge in a personal civil matter to "stick it."

For the better part of the next two years, I lived and worked in the Bay Area, enforcing federal wildlife laws. Aside from having to live in a metropolitan area, the complexity and diversity of the work was a new experience that benefited me greatly. However, I could not sell my home in Colusa because of high interest rates, which had risen from the normally advertised 4 percent on a thirty-year loan to the then unheard-of 13 percent. So I had to leave my family behind to address my duties some one hundred miles away. As a result, I found myself home in Colusa no more than two days a month. Now my wife, in addition to teaching full time and providing a good home life for my children, also had to be Dad. A damn good one, I might add, but no long-term substitute for the real thing. When I was home, I usually had a backlog of family assignments and home repairs facing me far in excess of the allotted forty-eight-hour period. Hence my impatience at being bothered on those valued days off.

However, I was cross-credentialed by the state of California (that is, I still carried a state Fish and Game commission) and occasionally worked cases and investigations that were purely under state jurisdiction. The bottom line was that agents worked with their state Fish and Game counterparts, as time permitted, in order to maintain good working relationships. It was a smart move professionally because, as is still the case today, Fish and Game wardens were the first line of defense in wildlife law enforcement. Being that first line against the hordes of violators, they tended to find themselves overwhelmed because of the sheer magnitude of the job. Any assistance they got was greatly appreciated and generally returned in spades, aside from the usual pissing matches (as in any profession) between game wardens and agents who had zero personal tolerance for each other. Though I had left the California Department of Fish and Game in May 1970, my roots and friendships there ran deep, and I still had a strong loyalty to those hardworking state officers.

That was the case now. I was a federal officer, and spotlighting was a state enforcement issue. However, Bob never asked for assistance unless he really needed it. He was a gruff little bastard, harsh if need be but an excellent wildlife officer who made life hell on wheels, horseback, or afoot for Fish and Game violators in his district. He was my kind of man, and I felt comfortable working alongside him because of his work ethic and professionalism.

Bob's impatient voice hammered through my mental wanderings: "Well, are you going to help me or are you going to piss backward like the rest of my squad?"

Bob always did have a way with words, I thought as a smile crossed my face. "When and where?" I asked.

"How about tonight, eight P.M., my house?" Bob's short, clipped phrases told me this problem really had him amped up, and the bad guys were in for a real treat if he caught them.

"You got it," I said. "What do I need to bring besides the usual equipment?"

"Just bring your ass and a good set of handcuffs," he replied curtly. "If I get close to these deer-killing son of a bitches, they are going to the bucket forthwith!"

"That gear I have, and I'll see you later," I responded.

Bob said, "Thanks; see you tonight" and abruptly hung up. Holding the cracker-crumb-covered phone, I thought, That is just like that damn Bob. He had a bee by the tail and was just about to make it into honey. Oh well—back to my cooking. The oil was hot, just like my friend, and it was time to render my culinary masterpiece for my two sons, who ate like baby robins, and "Mrs. Dad."

When I arrived at Bob's house in Yuba City, I was met by his lovely wife, Lynn. Lynn really had her job cut out for her in being Bob's wife and best friend because Bob was a hard charger who rarely spent much time at home. This lack of home life is characteristic for any *good* wildlife officer's husband or wife nationwide. However, she had a pretty good handle on him and seemed to get what she needed in spite of Bob's hard-driven schedule. I gave her a big hug, telling her that Bob better not see us together like this. Bob, who stood within earshot watching us, only grumbled something unintelligible as he headed back into the house. Keeping an arm wrapped around Lynn as I escorted her to the house, I said, "I hope that wasn't a bad word he just uttered." She grinned, knowing just how unprintable it had been, and we entered their kitchen. Bob beckoned me to sit down at the table, and I drank a glass of cold tea as we went through the typical briefing for the upcoming detail. Sitting down across from me, Bob took a deep drink of iced tea, looked at the half-empty glass in his hand for a moment as if it were a short bass for which he was about to issue a citation to a hapless fisherman, then set it down with a thump and began speaking with a grim yet determined look.

It seemed that Bob had been receiving information daily from an irritating informant concerning a small group of poachers who had been spotlighting deer in the Sutter Buttes. Bob had pinched this informant in times past, once for an illegal deer, and now the shoe was on the other foot. It seemed that every time the informant phoned to find out how the investigation was progressing and learned that there had been no success, he bit off a chunk of Bob's hind end. Bob had heated up a little more each time until now, at a distance of six feet, you could have melted a gold ingot in the direct heat he was emitting. As I said, Bob was a good catch dog—as long as no one beat him with the bone. ...

The Sutter Buttes, for those unfamiliar with California geography, are the smallest mountain range in the United States. They are located in the heart of the Sacramento Valley, a few miles northwest of Yuba City. At one time this small set of mountains was home to mule deer, bighorn sheep, tule elk, and grizzly bear. On that particular day in 1970, they were home to only mule deer, an abandoned ground-to-air missile complex, and the silence of early California history. The native plants of the Buttes have long been overgrazed, and as a result the landscape consists mostly of hard volcanic rock, a few stunted oak trees, and that invasive plant species from Russia indicative of an overgrazed range: cheat grass. The area was also very hard to reach, being surrounded by private farmlands and behind locked gates. But once the hunters were there, the killing was good because of this isolation and the abundance of deer that made the area their home. The deer habitually fed out into the surrounding rich farmlands during the nights because cheat grass is a lousy food source, and then rested in out-of-the-way places in the Buttes during the day. The living conditions were perfect for wild animals until humans came along and dipped their sticks into that pool of life.

Bob told me his information indicated that the deer were being taken by several area outlaws using a spotlight, and the meat was being moved into local markets, with some being sold as far away as San Francisco. Since it was illegal to sell wild venison in California and the meat had a distinctive taste, the informant said it was being sold primarily to Chinese or Italian restaurants because the spices and sauces of those styles of food preparation were the best way to hide the flavor, and the wide selection on the menus created a demand for large amounts of meat. Pretty damn clever I thought, but not as clever as the ringleader. The person in charge of this operation almost seemed to have the good Lord on his side. He was a practicing minister in a local church who used only his own parishioners as drivers and holders of the spotlight and the rifle in order to maintain operational security. The group used an old, beat-up, unregistered military-style jeep (a vehicle they could abandon in haste if threatened with capture) to shoot their deer, and once the carcasses were skinned, cleaned, and processed back at the church's basement kitchen, they used the church bus to transport the meat to their buyers.

Damn fine cover, I thought. Who in their wildest dreams would suspect a man of the cloth as a serious poacher or stop a church bus on suspicion of containing contraband? Using God as top cover has its distinct advantages. But those of us in the business long ago learned that the "good, bad, and ugly" come in coats of many colors. *No person or profession is exempt from greed and ego.*

Bob and I left his house in the humid heat of the darkening Sacramento Valley summer evening. I had been given a white Rambler American (a model that is no longer manufactured) as a patrol car and told Bob in no uncertain terms that we would use it for the night's escapades. He looked over at my piece of vehicular junk, then looked at me and asked, "Why?"

"Well, first of all, it is unmarked. Second, if you drive with those damn short legs of yours [Bob was about five foot nothing], I won't be able to fit in the front seat of your patrol car. And last, look at that piece of crap you're driving." In those days, Bob was driving a Chevy Chevette, with a one-horsepower engine and a top speed of one micron per hour. I continued, "In a chase you won't be able to catch them, and if you do, I won't be able to get out of your car in less than a year to give you a hand. Also, my vehicle has a 390 with a four-barrel and will fly if need be. It doesn't have any brakes under the best of conditions and is made from pot metal and plastic, but other than that, we will have a fast set of wheels." Bob realized the truth in my words and smiled as he walked over to the federal vehicle, tossing his gear into the backseat.

Bob wanted to check salmon fishermen at Chandler Station because he wanted to wait until later in the night to head into the Buttes. That area was a popular night-fishing spot, especially for salmon snaggers (people who used illegal-sized treble hooks to snag fish in the body as opposed to legally hooking them in the mouth). Chandler Station was an irrigation pumping station off the Sacramento River that often had a few king salmon backed up behind the tail race. For some reason the salmon would get confused by the chemicals in the waters (salmon migrate back to their birth waters by following that water's chemical signature, or smell) and would leave the Sacramento River and head up this channel, ending up behind the pumping station. To show the extent of migrational confusion that sometimes existed in the Sacramento River, I had even discovered salmon in flooded rice fields reaching almost to the town of Maxwell. The salmon had gotten turned around and ended up in the backwaters of a quiet rice field miles from the river, where they would suffer mammalian predation or some other violent ending.

The salmon is a remarkable fish with a unique migration pattern and life history. In those days, the Sacramento River and many of its tributaries had spring and fall runs of king salmon. Overfishing by sport fishermen, illegal gill netting, accidents such as those already described, commercial overfishing in the ocean, pollution, snagging, predation, dams, and loss of spawning habitat due to logging and other poor land practices have all but ruined their former greatness. *If they aren't already*, those Sacramento River salmon populations should be totally protected, in my opinion. In some cases they have gone from populations numbering in the millions to just a few hundred. Enough is enough! They need to be left alone until they return to a healthy percentage of their former greatness.

Quietly parking a short distance away from the Chandler Station, we watched three fellows fishing in the tail race through our binoculars. None of them appeared to be snagging salmon, but Bob said, "Let's go down and check them anyway." I drove to the fishing site, parked the car just above the fishermen on the canal bank, and turned off my engine. Because our vehicle was like any other on the road, they acknowledged our arrival with nothing more than a quick backward glance and continued fishing. After a while, Bob and I got out of the vehicle and, dressed like civilians, visited with the men for several minutes as fishermen are wont to do. Then, still sensing nothing out of the ordinary, we identified ourselves and checked them for compliance with the state's fishing regulations. They were all legal and wanted to chew the fat now that they knew our identity. We still had time to burn before we wanted to be in the Buttes waiting for our spotlighters, so Bob and I obliged.

Our fishermen had been drinking, and after a short while of warming up to us, they began showing off card tricks and the like. As each man tried to outdo the others for their special audience, I noticed that one fellow always seemed to be in last place. Finally he couldn't take it anymore and, feeling he needed a "10" for his next performance after his buddy's coin trick, said, "You think that was a great trick—watch this." With that, he walked over to where their Coleman lanterns were arranged on the stream bank to provide illumination for their fishing, took a gas can, and filled his mouth with the white gas normally used to fuel their lanterns. Not heeding our quickly uttered words of caution, he took out his cigarette lighter, blew out the raw gas with gusto, and lit the lighter at arm's length. No biggie—the typical "fire-eater" act you see in any circus. Well, what followed was not typical of any circus act! His entire head and right arm blew up in one huge fireball, *whoosh!* Jesus, we were stunned as he dropped to the ground and started rolling toward the water. Bob and I sprang to his aid, only to arrive too late as he rolled off the bank and dropped down three feet into the water of the canal tail race with a tremendous *ker-plush!*

He came up a moment later, and the fire was out. Bob and I helped him crawl out of the water and up onto the bank. "Boy," I said with a devilish grin, "that was some trick." The human fireball wasn't amused as he walked over to their ice chests and began rummaging for some butter to put on his burned skin. Finding some, he began to rub it all over his head, right hand, and arm, which were rapidly turning flaming red (no pun intended).

"Shouldn't you go to a hospital?" Bob asked.

"Nah," the lad retorted in a tough-guy sort of way. "I'll be all right."

Bob and I got back in our patrol vehicle, shaking our heads. With a friendly wave good-bye before someone tried to top *that* trick, we continued down the dusty canal road toward other fishing areas. Once out of earshot, we laughed until I thought we would split a gut. Between tears of laughter, I said, "Can you believe that? It's a wonder that guy didn't kill himself." Although Bob and I felt it really *was* the best trick of the evening, we had to shake our heads in disbelief. However, it provided us with a lot of chuckles as we checked several other groups fishing in the vicinity of the Chandler Station.

Not finding anything worth looking in on, other than a surprised couple from Colusa making love in the back of a Chevy station wagon, Bob and I backtracked. Passing the human fireball's camp, we were surprised to see the men loading their gear and starting to leave. We learned that the human fireball had decided he needed to go to a doctor after all. One look at his horribly burned face, arm, and hand told the story: he was a red, blistered, and swollen mess! His half-cooked face was now showing the extent of the damage. There wasn't an ounce of hair left on the front of his head, including inside his nose. His eyes were almost swollen shut, and his ears were twice their normal size. His nose was the size of a small football and as red as if he had been on a forty-year drunk. His right arm had swollen to the size of that of the old cartoon character Popeye. If he didn't end up requiring skin grafts, I would have been amazed. Oh well—so much for the winner of the trick for that evening. ... As the old folk expression goes: "Sometimes you eat the bear, and sometimes he eats you."

Bob and I finally headed toward the Buttes, driving through a ranch whose owner was sympathetic to our endeavors and wouldn't report the game wardens' late-night entry to his neighbors. Sitting at the edge of this property where it adjoined the Buttes' foothills, I turned off my headlights and cut the taillight switches so that if I hit the brakes, the brake lights would remain off and we would not give away our position. Those switches also cut off the backup lights. This strategy would later cause us a mountain of heartburn. But I am getting ahead of the story. We sat there quietly for about twenty minutes to let our eyes adjust while watching the slopes of the Buttes before us for the telltale bluish pencil-thin spotlight beam of poachers. All was as dark as the inside of a dead horse and quiet as a slow, deep-running stream.

Once our eyes had adjusted, I began to drive slowly in first gear down the numerous dirt roads at Bob's direction. We kept our windows down so we could smell any dust hanging in the air, which would announce recent travel on the same road by another vehicle. We covered the entire road system on the southwestern side of the Buttes, to no avail. It was as quiet as a mouse pissing on cotton. Bob and I slowly moved over to the northwest side of the Buttes and commenced our sweep of the known deer concentration areas on that piece of landscape.

The reader needs to keep in mind the inherent danger in driving without lights in the dark on unknown roads. For instance, we might have run off the road, hit an obstruction in the middle of the road, run over a porcupine (bad for both the tires and the critter), driven over a cattle guard in which the guard had been removed unbeknownst to us for repair, or hit a black Angus cow lying in the road. Finding a poacher who was also running without lights was always a rude and metal-rending surprise as well. It was even more fun the next day explaining what had happened to your vehicle to your supervisor, especially when the agency did not condone running without lights! But if you want to catch the big dogs, sometimes you have to run with the pack. ...

The night air was beginning to cool and if it hadn't been for the serious nature of this outing, it would have been a great evening for two old friends, discussing old times and reliving great memories. However, like many of the best-laid plans of mice and men, it was not to be.

Moving uphill on a road that passed through several dense stands of drought-stunted oaks, Bob and I suddenly spotted the beam of a powerful spotlight about sixty yards ahead of us on the same road! It was shooting almost straight up into the air, as a spotlight will do when working a steep hillside. I hurriedly attempted to get closer so we could hear shooting—or better yet, witness the spotlighters casting their light on or illegally killing a game animal. Bob and I quickly laid out our plan for the approach and arrest once we had the fellows in our clutches, figuring we would work in behind their vehicle for a proper car stop. As is often the case when one messes with a man of the cloth and his friend God, things can go into the toilet in a hurry … and did in this particular instance!

Breaking over a small hill, still running without headlights, Bob and I saw a military jeep immediately below, moving slowly away from us. We could plainly see that the vehicle had three occupants because they were illuminated by the spotlight's backlight. One of the men was standing in the back of the jeep, sweeping the spotlight across the area to the west, while the gunner sat expectantly in the front passenger seat, eyes glued to the point of light, hoping for a killing shot. They weren't more than forty yards away, and if they were to turn and look back, they couldn't help but spot my glaring white elephant of a patrol car in the soft black of the night. Damn! I thought. We had figured the spotlighters were over one more hill and were not prepared for the situation confronting us. Just moments before, we had agreed to drive to the back side of the next hill and stop just below the hilltop. We were then going to run to the top and peep over with our binoculars, hopefully catching the bad guys doing a dirty deed. Then we would run back to our car and storm over the hilltop like the cavalry, catching the bad guys with hat in hand and critter on the ground. Well, as the reader can see, we were a day late and a dollar short. …

Holding my breath in the slender hope that they would not look back but would proceed down the road in their current direction or hurry up and kill a deer in our presence, I slammed on my brakes. But it was not to be! Without warning, they abruptly turned the jeep and began driving uphill toward us. All the while, they continued working the spotlight beam in and out of the gullies to the east, looking for the blue shine of a deer's eyes. Bob and I were in a quandary. There was no place for us to go to get out of their way or sight. Numerous lava boulders were scattered throughout the surrounding cheat-grass fields and alongside the dirt road, so if we blindly drove out across those fields in an effort to hide, we would more than likely tear out the undercarriage before we had gone fifty feet. Plain and simply, we were trapped! God had just made our little game of cat and mouse more interesting. ... If we couldn't get the hell out of there, we would have to make a head-on car stop, the most dangerous kind because the bad guys can see you as well as you can see them. Not wanting to be in that deadly enforcement position, I began to back up as fast as I could. Try that sometime in the black of night after you have lost the best of your night vision from a set of lights before you. You will find that you don't move too fast, especially without the aid of backup lights—and we didn't. I managed to get back over the lip of the hill and was thinking about doing a power turn in the road and disappearing in that direction, hoping to get another chance at a from-the-rear approach.

Over the hill they came, happily shining their spotlight into every gully, totally unaware of our presence because they were concentrating on looking for deer. I continued backing up as fast as I could without leaving a trail of dust, but the spotlighters' headlights were almost upon us! An instant later their headlights illuminated our darkened, slowly retreating patrol car, and they immediately stopped. With much shouting, they tried to back up out of sight of the darkened vehicle sitting in the middle of the road before them, as if hoping maybe *they* hadn't been seen. I could see the man standing in the back of the jeep hang his spotlight cord over the roll bar, with the light's beam swinging wildly in every direction, pick up a rifle, and quickly try to unload it. Well, the cat was out of the bag and there was no sense in sticking our heads in the sand like a couple of dingbats, so after them we went.

Turning on the headlights and siren and with my powerful engine roaring, I raced forward in an attempt to cut them off before they got over their surprise and fled the scene cross-country. Seeing our vehicle storming down on them, the driver of the jeep realized that going backward was not the way to race an oncoming patrol car. He slammed to a stop, shifted gears, and, confirming my worst fears, plowed off the road to his left in a cloud of dust. The ground was so rough that everyone in the jeep was bouncing all over the place, hanging on for dear life. Plain and simply, he was trying to use his vehicle's higher ground clearance against ours as he raced across the rock-covered terrain, hoping to escape to the east. I could tell by the way he was bouncing around that it would be pure folly to pursue the same course, so I carefully started angling across the grassy slope, picking my way around the rocks, in an effort to cut him off. The jeep driver quickly discovered that he was blocked on the north side by a large, dense stand of scrubby oak trees that prevented him from turning in that direction and escaping back down the road. He continued to storm eastward, bouncing and lunging over the rocky terrain while his passengers frantically hung on. Racing and jolting along through the rocks, the driver saw that he was now blocked from going farther east by a deep ditch running north-south. He quickly turned south and ran along the ditch bank, only to find an old stock corral now blocking his path in that direction. This turn of events forced him to turn back to the west, toward my onrushing patrol car. Trapped by the trees to the north, a ditch to the east, a heavy pole corral to the south, and our car to the west, the driver made a split-second decision to force his way past us.

Bob, figuring the jeep had to stop or ram us head-on, opened his door and dangled his feet out. He was hoping that as we slowed, he could vault out the door and be on the fellows before they could use their rifles on us or unsafely unload them. The jeep's driver, seeing that I was not going to turn aside, tried a desperate move. He started to cut between me and the set of corrals. There was just enough room for him to escape if he hurried, so he gunned it, shooting forward. If he was successful, he would escape because it would take me some time to turn around while the jeep continued cross-country in four-wheel drive. It was a good plan because I couldn't tail him in my sedan with its low clearance and two-wheel drive. Seeing this move and knowing that Bob had his legs dangling out the door, I made a fateful decision. No two ways about it—if their vehicle swung by the passenger side of my rig, it would hit Bob's open door, smashing it shut, which would have crushed both of Bob's legs just below the knees. *No way!* I thought. If this clown wants a "hoorah," then I am just the person to give him one—and a damn good one at that! No one, and I mean *no one,* injures a partner of mine! Waiting until the last moment, I swung the steering wheel of my car hard to the right as I power-locked the brakes, sending my right front end into the path of the on-rushing jeep. My vehicle skidded to a stop, but the jeep driver attempted to power through me. *Crunch* went the two vehicles in a bone-rattling collision, punctuated with flying headlight glass, grill parts, and dirt! The spotlighter standing in the back of the jeep damn near flew over its roll bar and into the front seat. Bob hit the soft padding of the dash hard because he wasn't seat-belted in anticipation of a fast exit. He quickly rebounded and darted out of our vehicle at a dead run with his sidearm drawn. The other driver, recovering from his impact with his steering wheel, quickly jammed the jeep into reverse, trying to back away. Escape was key in his mind, and the whirling tires kicking up clouds of dirt over the hood of my vehicle and the objecting over-revving engine made that point clear to everyone on that hillside. However, the two vehicles' front ends were locked together, and having Bob's 9-mm Browning pistol screwed into his ear and Bob yelling, "State Fish and Game warden; you are under arrest," certainly took the starch out of the driver's spine. He quickly let off on the throttle in resignation.

I flew out the door into the cloud of dust as soon as I could put my vehicle into "park." The fellow in the passenger seat of the jeep, later identified as the preacher, was busily trying to jack a round into the chamber of his rifle. He succeeded just as I got to him, and with a wild-eyed look of fear and anger, he focused on me! However, a fast horse he wasn't. Reaching out at a dead run, I grabbed his rifle with my right hand, pushing the muzzle up and away, and simultaneously grabbed his right arm with my left hand, jerking him out of the jeep at an adrenaline-induced speed. He landed face first in the dirt at my feet in a powdery explosion with a loud *ummmph!* I disarmed him in a second while Bob had the other two covered with his sidearm. With things now under control, we unloaded the jeep's occupants and sat them down in front of the undamaged, still glowing left headlight of my vehicle.

Investigation of their jeep didn't produce any illegal game but did produce two loaded rifles, a possible violation of the Fish and Game Code, which prohibited loaded firearms in a motor vehicle on a way open to the public. However, most of the Buttes were under private ownership in those days, and one could in fact have a loaded firearm in a motor vehicle on private land (I don't know if that is still the case today). We sorted this out later and discovered that they had in fact been on a private road; hence no violation.

After a quick conference with me, Bob advised the three men that they were under arrest for violation of the Fish and Game Code's trespass laws: they did not have permission to hunt on the property (we discovered later that they had cut the locks on the gates to enter the area), and since they didn't have any illegal game in their vehicle and we had not seen them cast a light on a game animal before our abrupt meeting, they could not be charged with anything else. It wasn't the way we would have liked to handle the charges, but any port in a storm as long as it is legal when dealing with boneheads involved in a knowing violation. The three men were sullen and said nothing as they tried to recover from their surprise encounter. Bob continued, "You fellows are going to be handcuffed, searched, and transported to the local jail in Yuba City. Any questions?" Again silence, so Bob and I searched the men, finding nothing out of the ordinary, handcuffed them, and sat them back down in the dirt.

I now surveyed the damage to my plastic-and-pot-metal, purchased-from-the-lowest-bidder government patrol car. It was a mess! The right front fender was crushed back into the leading edge of the passenger door with such force that I was surprised Bob had even been able to get the door open. I guess being amped up has a way of overcoming such difficulties. The hood was wrinkled and wouldn't open, the right side of the bumper was broken off and hanging limply in the dirt, and the entire front end had been pushed back about half an inch. Also of course I had lost my right headlight, which had certainly seen better days.

I recalled the picture in my mind's eye of Bob's feet dangling out the door. Had those chaps smashed into that door at the speed they were traveling … my thoughts drifted away from that picture and returned thankfully to the view of a smashed patrol car rather than smashed or amputated legs.

Fortunately, the engine and radiator were all right, but I sure couldn't go anywhere until I got my smashed right fender off the tire! Looking at the little military jeep, I was surprised to find that the only damage to it was a bent license plate! Damn, no wonder we won

World War II. ... Said a lot for the Rambler and the company that made it. Maybe that was one of the reasons they went out of business a few years later.

I took a set of monster bolt cutters out of my trunk (at least it still worked) and walked back to the front of my car. Using the bolt cutters, I cut off the part of my right front fender that was smashed against the tire. Leaving the cut-off part of my front fender still wrapped around the jeep's bumper, Bob and I loaded our prisoners into the rear seat of the patrol car. Crawling under our vehicle, I wired up the bumper so it wouldn't drag on the ground, and we were ready to go. We put the poachers' rifles and spotlight in my trunk for safekeeping and started out for the Yuba City jail.

Not knowing if my car would make it to the city, I called the sheriff's office on the radio and described the night's events and my vehicle's condition. The dispatcher said she would send an officer to meet us on the main road circling the base of the Buttes. As we drove along the dirt roads, I noticed that Bob wasn't as grumpy as he had been earlier. To his way of thinking, we had his bad guys. True, we hadn't managed a spotlighting or illegal deer violation, but we had them for trespassing, and Bob was content. He knew the chances were that the deer poaching would stop once this charge was adjudicated, and Bob could then put his enforcement energies elsewhere. Also, the backbiting informant would be satisfied because Bob had done his job in fine style. All in all, it was a good night's work on behalf of the critters and Bob's ravaged hind end.

After booking our prisoners, we headed back to Bob's house for something cold to drink and an early-morning snack. Lynn met us at the door and said, "I knew you two would get into some kind of devilment tonight, and that feeling was confirmed when I heard you calling the sheriff's office on our police scanner."

Bob patted Lynn on her last part over the fence and with a big smile said, "How about something cold to drink?"

Lynn gave him a kiss and scooted off to the kitchen. Bob took off his pistol belt, settled into a chair, and said, "I knew if you and I got together, we would get it done."

I grinned, reaching out to slap his outstretched hand, and we said in unison, "The Gold Dust twins." That nickname had been given to us by Captain Jim Leamon when I was still a Fish and Game warden in honor of all the money we brought in as a result of a few days and nights of some unusual and unique efforts that led to some very unlikely cases (as described in the chapter "The Gold Dust Twins" in my first book, *Wildlife Wars*).

Our Buttes spotlighters each paid $500 for the error of their ways but did no jail time. The high cost of their fines for a trespassing violation, which usually ran around $100, surprised Bob and me. We later found out that the judge and the preacher were not the best of friends: hence the man of the cloth got his day in court—or was it penance? Who says justice is blind? In addition, the judge ordered them to forfeit their rifles and placed all three men on probation for three years.

Some time later, Jack, my immediate supervisor—and a damn good one I might add—had the damage to my pot-metal car surveyed by a body-and-fender man. The estimate came out at $857! Not bad for a patrol car that cost only $1,000 new. The preacher and his jeep had only a bent license plate, and I had major damage to a vehicle that weighed twice as much. Figure that one out. Jack decided that no one was going to wham a federal officer or his patrol car without paying the price, so he went after the driver of the jeep, whose insurance company, after much foot-dragging, paid the $857 to the government for repairs—and, in essence, the error of the insured man's ways. The minister was later removed from his church by the embarrassed members of his flock for his poaching, and his deer killing in the Sutter Buttes stopped then and there!

I haven't seen Bob in years, and I wonder if he still remembers the wild ride he took that night. Come to think of it, maybe God wasn't "flying top cover" for the minister and his cohorts that night after all. Or maybe He was there, but for different reasons. Thinking about it in the quiet of my study many years later, I remember my lightning-fast decision to take that jeep head-on, thereby saving Bob's legs, which he put to use in a long, successful career in wildlife law enforcement for the state of California. That thought must have come from somewhere or someone. ... Maybe God *was* "flying top cover" that evening—but for the other side.

Bob and I are retired now, and we both survived all that the wildlife wars could throw at us. In retrospect, it seems as if that "top cover" continued over the following years for two wildlife officers, doesn't it? As I said, we will take it any way it comes, just as long as it is legal.

three

Marsh Madness

THE COOL AUTUMN AIR rolling softly through the open windows of my patrol vehicle felt good on my body as I sat silently watching the unfolding early-morning drama. Borne on that air came the faint, pungent smell of alkali dust raised by numerous vehicles hurriedly moving around me. I could hear vehicle doors slamming and the distinct *clunk* of johnboats being offloaded and, once launched and filled with hunting gear, softly bumping into each other as they slowly twirled at anchor in the marsh. Those sounds were spiced with colorful swearing over mashed knuckles as the loading of equipment continued, along with the occasional barking of hunting dogs, happy to be out from the confinement of their kennels.

Truck, my dog Shadow, and I were sitting on Tule Lake National Wildlife Refuge at the edge of a dike bordering a large marsh. It was two-thirty in the morning, and as far as the eye could see rows of headlights were streaming into this hunting area, leaving plumes of acrid alkali dust for those following too closely on the same roads to "enjoy." The marsh was currently home to several hundred thousand migrating ducks, geese, shorebirds of every kind, hundreds of expectant hunters, and a lone U.S. game management agent assigned to enforce the wildlife laws—a task made hopeless by the sheer masses of waterfowl and humanity flooding into the area as they terminated their migrations from the arctic or their nearby motel rooms.

I was a young man in 1970, and it was an exciting and vibrant time to be alive. It was also the opening morning of waterfowl season in northern California and my first as a game management agent for the U.S. Fish and Wildlife Service. "Tule," as the refuge was colloquially known, is a Pacific flyway waterfowl staging area immediately south of the Oregon border in north-central California. It was the ancestral home to hundreds of thousands of migrating waterfowl, other water birds, and numerous endemic marsh species. Tule first saw the Native Americans, who took little and left much for the morrow, followed by the Europeans who took everything, leaving faded memories of better days gone by for those yet to come. During the white settlers' occupation, much of the great marsh was drained, burned, and then turned by the steel of sod-breaking plows pulled by teams of sweating horses. Many of the great hordes of migratory birds were either killed by the locals for food, killed by market hunters and shipped via rail in barrels by the thousands to faraway commercial markets, or found themselves flying elsewhere because of the dramatic loss of habitat. No more came the great migrations heralding the change of seasons, and without much of the marsh's microenvironment, with its natural percolation of waters into the surrounding soils, the adjacent lands soon took on a more arid appearance. After countless seasons of plowing, much of the reclaimed lands sacrificed their ten thousand years of topsoil to the winds. With this loss of topsoil and its remaining water-holding capabilities, the lands became a vast dry-land farming operation. The end result was hardscrabble conditions that ultimately took the "smile" off the lands as well as the wildlife and their human communities.

Fortunately, some of these drained lands were purchased and reclaimed years later. To these scarred lands were added permanent dikes, water impoundments, and canals, creating a stable water base, only this time under the caring hand of the U.S. Fish and Wildlife Service's national wildlife refuge system. It wasn't as magnificent as in times past, but this remnant of its former greatness facilitated what was left of the once massive waterfowl migrations. This natural avian phenomenon slowly returned as the birds recognized the partial restoration of their ancestral home. As they returned, so too did the semimigrant sportsman, in increasing numbers to witness the feathered spectacle darkening the skies. This return of the marsh and fall migrations ultimately provided a sport of kings in the hunting and a myriad of gourmet delights for the table. This pattern continued for the next fifty years.

I was watching this instant drama through sleepless eyes after sitting in my truck all night. Such is the price paid when there are no empty motel rooms near the vast surrounding grain fields and the marsh because they were all rented a year in advance by an eager hunting public. Being young, I was happy enough to be in the front seat of that truck, and I doubt I could have slept in a bed anyway because of the excitement of being there in the swirl of life, making history as a member of a "flying squad." "Flying squad" in that state and federal wildlife regulatory agencies used to assemble large numbers of officers in zones of high sportsman use and concentration such as the opening morning on Tule. The thinking was that if there was a law dog behind every bush, those tending to break the law would become more restrained.

I had been assigned to work with a group of senior state and federal conservation officers who had experienced this type of "flooding the zone" activity many times before. They were *very* good at what they did for a living, and I was eager to claim my share of that enforcement heritage. However, I soon discovered that it was accepted by more than a few that newcomers such as myself had a lot to learn and would not be as successful a partner as an older, more seasoned officer. Plus, many of us rookie unknowns had not established extensive agency or personal friendships with those senior officers. So we younger officers found ourselves shunted off into marginal work areas or hooked up with senior officers of questionable reputations until we had proved ourselves over time. That was simply part of the code of the old conservation law-dog society in some parts of the West, especially in the federal service. I was terribly disappointed. I had hoped to be assigned to a sage, instructive senior officer so I might glean many of his hard-earned "man-hunting" traits. This type of training is often the best way to cut across time-consuming learning experiences and skip reinvention of the enforcement wheel.

Having had few mentors early on because good ones were few and far between, I had learned the hard way, through numerous long days and blind alleys, that success in working waterfowl hunters, especially the violating members of that subculture, was based mostly on the keenness of one's senses and a strong work ethic. You had to understand the weather, migration patterns, land- and water-use patterns of the fish and wildlife, the animals' life cycles and histories, human behavior, and those "voices" from within directing you toward a particular individual or activity. The more you honed those senses through learning, the better you were at enforcing laws and protecting critters, until for many of us it became almost an ethereal science. Once the "tips of the trade" were learned, it was not uncommon for an officer to bypass many hunters in the field until that inner compass pointed to a certain individual or group needing attention. Those of us blessed with this innate ability found that up to 70 to 80 percent of the individuals isolated by such means tended to be in violation. To many officers such as Frank Simms, Joe Oliveros (God rest his soul), Jack Downs, Frank Kuncir, and Kash Schriefer, catching became easy because of the guidance provided by the learned inner self and associated senses. There is no way to explain this phenomenon in the very best officers, but after you have caught your fifteenth person in a row in one day based on those senses, you realize that it is a very real force to be reckoned with and hearkened to. The second part of the formula for a good waterfowl officer, work ethic, is almost self-explanatory. Hunters taking waterfowl are out and about during every hour of the night and day. Controlling that kind of traffic, especially those walking on the "dark side," requires long hours of work and sleepless nights. It also means the officer may relegate his or her wife or husband to the level of "second love" and ignore the other members of the family until the work is done. Sometimes that takes thirty years—as in the present case! Enough said. ...

It became readily apparent upon reviewing the assignment roster that no one was comfortable working with a rookie like me, with only four months' unproven federal service. I had four excellent years' experience as a state Fish and Game warden, three of those in a major waterfowl district, but apparently in the eyes of most of the federal officers selected for the Tule flying squad that amounted to nothing more than a pinch of puppy shit. The senior officers had friends with whom they planned to work and special work areas they favored. Their plans did not include dragging along an unknown and teaching him their personal tricks of the trade. Sometimes such practices went to the extreme. For example, one afternoon on Delevan National Wildlife Refuge in 1970, Agent Bob Norris introduced me to another agent named Marshall Dillon. Yup, that's right—Marshall Dillon was his God-given name. Crawling off the air boat I was using to pick up dead and dying birds infected by botulism, I stuck out my hand in a gesture of friendship and recognition of a brother officer. Marshall Dillon just stared at me from under the brim of an immense bull rider's hat without removing his hands from his pockets. After an awkward moment of silence, he said, "Are you that young college kid Jack Downs just hired?"

"Well, there are days I don't feel so young anymore [hell, I was thirty years old at the time], and my college days seem like a distant memory," I replied, "but yes, I am."

"We don't have any use for your kind in the ranks," he said slowly, his dark eyes never leaving mine. With that, he turned and walked back to his vehicle, leaving my hand still extended and unshaken. Starting up his patrol car, he drove off without a backward glance. As I said, a different breed of cat in those days.

I never forgot or forgave those isolation practices as I worked my way up through the ranks over the next thirty years. I made a point of working with younger officers every chance I got, sharing knowledge I had gleaned from experience. If for some reason I could not spend time with those officers, I saw to it that a senior officer was assigned to accomplish this transfer of ideas and field information. The sooner an inexperienced officer was up and running, the sooner the critters got a little more much-deserved survival time. Once the new officer was effectively on his own, you could turn your interests elsewhere, and now the enforcement arm would be coming at the bad guys from two directions!

After getting over my initial disappointment and remembering that I had over four years' experience with the state of California to guide me, and *damn good experience at that,* I gritted my teeth and set my sails into the wind. I didn't want to join the "also-rans" but wanted to be at or near the head of the pack in numbers of citations and show them, especially Jack Downs, my new supervisor, that *I was worth keeping!* Jack had recently hired me away from the California Department of Fish and Game, leaving me in my home state, which was a hiring practice not routinely followed. Usually a new agent was moved to another state to avoid the petty politics between the losing and gaining agencies that followed such a transfer. But Jack needed experienced officers to work the waterfowl-hunting and illegal night-shooting fraternities in the Sacramento Valley. I was a known and proven entity in that arena as a state officer, so he brought me on as a regional hire (no longer done; all hiring is now done out of Washington, D.C.). Of course, there were the usual critics on such matters as regional hires returning to their state of origin, and I didn't want to give them any fodder based on my performance. I knew how to work wildlife violators and figured I would just push myself harder in order to attain my goal of beating the socks off those whom I considered great officers but set in their ways. One sure way to do that was with a handful of quality citations sufficient to choke a horse. Boy, it didn't take me long to join the "arrogant" department normally reserved for senior officers, did it?

In keeping with my new goals, I spent ground and canoe time in and around the marsh to which I had been assigned. Knowing that the best violations would be where the birds and people generally mixed it up, I set my plans on being in the middle of such a "game warden's stew." Soon it became obvious that many of that year's birds (juveniles—dumber than a box of rocks) were located in the Tule Lake marsh, just south of the refuge headquarters. I say many, but that was a relative term. The Tule Lake system was holding at least a million birds that year, so no matter where you looked, there was shooting potential beyond one's wildest imagination! However, for the concentration of birds I had in my area of the marsh, I intended to offer what protection I could.

The air was literally darkened with skeins of the graceful pintail duck, noisy mallard, and trilling white-fronted goose in the mornings and evenings when they left the protection of the refuge to gather up some grits in the surrounding harvested grain fields. All of these species were considered top-of-the-line species for eating. Interspersed throughout this mix were tremendous numbers of the speedy green-winged teal, tight flocks of wigeon, drab gray redheads still changing into their winter plumage, secretive gadwall, a few princely canvasback, and sprinkles of about every other kind of waterfowl species known to God. It truly was a time of plenty, making a dreamer like me realize what the "good old days" must have been like before they were ruined by our forefathers.

To patrol the marsh successfully required a shallow-draft boat and a lot of hard work with a paddle. Being young, I was not averse to the hard work associated with using a sixteen-foot Grumman sport canoe in a marsh. Hard work had been my lifestyle since I was nine years old, and I didn't see any reason to change at that late date. I noticed that many of the senior officers were hard drinkers who favored staying out late to see if they could deplete the local bars of their "John barleycorn" supplies, not to mention rounding up any unattached ladies or stray soiled doves. It was almost as if this generation of law dogs, realizing they were nearing the end of their era, wanted to live every minute of it to the fullest before the clock of history stopped ticking. They also favored working the big wheat or barley fields, places where they could comfortably use their vehicles and spotting scopes, keeping physical labor to a minimum. Not all of the officers were of that ilk, mind you—there were other crazies like me, but many of the older ones preferred the short chases if they had their druthers. Regardless of their actions and occasional hell raising, they protected the resources when doing so was not even a gleam in many other conservationists' eyes. In the process, broken, worn-out bodies, lousy equipment, and all, they did one hell of a job! In fact, I believe that many of the birds we see in today's wilds are there because of the efforts of those rugged conservation officers of yesteryear. After years of reflection, I now realize that I was staring into the face of history when I was walking the ground with men whose footprints in time are represented by the animal populations of today. The American people and their children owe a great deal to those hardworking men, most of whom have now traveled across the Great Divide.

Putting my "sitting in their backyard" theory to the test, I spent the afternoon before the opener in the marsh with my dog Shadow and the Grumman. I was not disappointed. Everywhere, and I do mean *everywhere,* the open water was full of resting waterfowl, unsuspecting of tomorrow's trials. They hadn't been shot at for almost a year, and the next day would bring a lot of surprises and stilled hearts, I thought as I otherwise silently enjoyed my passage. Returning to my launch site, I anchored my canoe alongside the levee and returned to my nearby truck. Realizing I was already at one of the best places (central to the anticipated action) to launch in the morning, and not wanting to compete for launching space with a bunch of eager hunters, I decided to stay overnight in the field, guarding my spot and canoe. Sitting down in the dusty barley stubble next to the levee, I opened up a Coca-Cola, lit up a strong Italian Toscanni cigar, and leaned back against the truck tire, drinking in the afternoon's soft breezes and deep blue, cloudless sky. Shadow lay down beside my legs, and soon her snores and foot movement told me she was where all good dogs go on a lazy afternoon, chasing a slow-moving rabbit across a never-ending sea of grass. I watched the constantly arriving skeins of ducks and geese, first announced as small dots on the northern horizon. Soon those dots grew into various species, ultimately gliding in on tired wings as they sailed into the marsh from the latest leg of their migration. On they came, and if I used my binoculars, the glasses would be filled with even more "dots" arriving from the north. Bird migrations are truly one of God's miracles. It is too bad that most folks living where such phenomena occur never enjoy this spectacle because they don't take the time to "see."

Throughout that evening and into the next morning, the marsh filled jug-full with every type of duck and goose known to Tule, dominated by the pintail, mallard, and white-fronted goose. The pintail's beautiful fluting call and the hen mallard's harsh quacking filled the air as they traded back and forth across the darkened skies in confusion over the increasing and disturbing human activity surrounding the marsh below. Those sounds, coupled with a clear northern California sky filled with a passel of stars, a front moving in from the northwest, and a Morgan-silver-dollar-bright moon over the marsh, made for a moment that wasn't far from those known in older times. Incorporated into this natural canvas was the now constant "Where am I?" trilling calls of the white-fronted goose as their numbers exploded into the thousands. Arriving overhead all night after migrating 1,500 miles from Alaska, they too must have marveled at the human activity unfolding below after their quiet summer nesting on the tundra.

The noise from constantly arriving migrants, other marsh bird calls, and marsh gas smells of methane continued to be interrupted by the increasing crescendo of human activities up and down the levee as far as the eye could see. Vehicles now lined the dike almost bumper to bumper, with their crazy-quilt array of occupants waiting for the much-anticipated beginning of the day's events, still hours away. It had been almost nine months since many of these folks had had the opportunity to participate in the wildly popular sport of hunting waterfowl, and it seemed that the pent-up emotions of all those months were displaying themselves in "coats of many colors" in these last few hours before the dawn. Barking dogs, blinding dust rising in clouds as vehicle after vehicle thundered by on the levee road, headlights aimlessly illuminating the skies and the harvested grain fields as they rolled over the rough terrain, voices shouting aimless commands, the clanking of boats being readied for the coming ritual, dog fights, more dust, and the occasional sound of the spinning wheels of a vehicle stuck in the soft dirt of a surrounding field produced a hellish din. Ah, humanity, I thought. It brought so much to a quiet, cool autumn morning in the marsh. ...

Thinking back to my quiet arrival several days before, I smiled a tired, dusty smile. Traveling east on state Highway 161 that day, I had noticed about ten thousand hopeful hunters camped along the road berm near Lower Klamath Lake. That is right: *about ten thousand!* They were camped bumper to bumper for miles, using every sleeping device known to man. What a zoo. People were sleeping in expensive recreational vehicles right alongside poor souls lying in dirty blankets on the ground next to their vehicles. A fancy cooking setup designed to roast a whole hog was juxtaposed with a cast-iron skillet skillfully supported by a couple of rocks over a fire of sagebrush twigs. Dogs of every lineage dotted this line of humanity, from beautiful Labrador retrievers to canines of questionable genesis. I decided I did not want to patrol that area of the marsh as I grimly visualized the pandemonium that would be associated with such a mass of unkempt humanity. Moving on, I headed over to the old Fish and Game building where many of the state and federal officers were to bunk. Finding few beds comfortable enough for a carcass my size, and with an assignment allowing me a fair degree of latitude, I went on to the harvested wheat and barley fields to the east and the adjoining marsh area to the south. By moving farther into the hinterland in quest of a little more peace, dignity, and quiet, I hoped to find hunters who, feeling secure in their isolation, might just cross over the line in the sand drawn by the hunting laws of the land. Sometime later, the dog and I set up our little camp in a freshly harvested barley field right next to the marsh. I figured I could experience at least a little of the natural marsh essence without the human clamor crowding out the very air I had to breathe. I was soon to be proven dead wrong!

Hunting over a marsh takes a lot of hard work and planning. One needs a good shallow-draft boat, motor or paddles, a dog that knows how to retrieve ducks and geese from a boat (and knows how to get back into the boat), mounds of decoys, duck calls, hot coffee, and sandwiches that most likely will be sat on or knocked into the bilge water in the bottom of your boat by your wet retriever. This knowledge, coupled with my previous waterfowl experience as a state Fish and Game warden, brought several enforcement points to mind. A serious, hardworking hunter isolated deep in a marsh can sometimes get carried away and find it tough to accurately count the number of birds he has taken, especially if there are a lot of close-at-hand targets in the air clamoring to land among one's decoys. On the first day of hunting season, there would be thousands of young, uneducated birds—uneducated in that any set of decoys would look like the real thing, something to trust and drop into. Many of these birds would become a meal for the man who pulled the trigger or the mink that would ultimately retrieve their carcass if it ended up crippled and lost in the dense marsh. Those circumstances made for great over-limit opportunities, which was the type of case I preferred to work; hence my site preference that day. However, I soon discovered I was totally unprepared for the scope and degree of activity that was to follow.

The noise and dust were beginning to get to me as my place of "peace and quiet" filled up with the racket of those who little knew how to appreciate the magic a marsh possessed for the soul. Knowing I would not get any more sleep in my pickup, I decided I would move into the marsh earlier than I had planned. I would be in a better position to pick a quiet central place so I could watch as many hunters as possible when legal shooting time arrived. Until that moment arrived, I could sleep in the bottom of my canoe, with the added pleasure of waterfowl quietly bobbing around me. Putting my gear, water, and food into the canoe, I loaded Shadow in the bow and without any further fanfare unlimbered my paddle and pushed off into the marsh around three in the morning.

Jesus, did I ever start a "land rush" by the dingbats who had already ruined my quiet time! Everyone along the dike must have been jealously watching to make sure no one had the advantage in going into the marsh early. As soon as I pushed my canoe from the marsh's edge, folks along the entire dike took that movement as a signal, and the rush for a good shooting spot was on, despite the fact that it was still about three and a half hours before legal shooting time! Bedlam ensued. Flashlight beams by the dozen wandered aimlessly along the marsh canals, almost turning night into day with their reflected light. Boats clanked and motors roared to life. The noise of engine cavitation from many motors drowned out the sounds of other madly racing boats colliding, equally lost and outside the index of common sense. Mixed into that soup of idiocy were bellowing shouts, swearing, the thumps of gear being hurriedly and heavily dropped into boat bottoms back at the dike, more deep *clunks* heralding loaded-boat collisions, more swearing, and dog fights by the score echoing up and down the levee before the toothy antagonists were loaded into boats to join in this swirl of marsh madness with the rest of the "sooners." As if that were not enough, thousands of ducks and geese aroused from sleep in their marsh home by this invasion of "sportsmen" took to the air in alarm. Confused, they began flying around like cannon shot at Bull Run, adding their plaintive calls and whirring wings to the increasing din of this newly created hell. Sensing that my sleep-in-the-canoe plan had just landed in the toilet, I picked a large clump of tules, dragged my canoe into them so I wouldn't get run over, and just sat observing the knotheads swirling around me. God, it was a revelation of the primal-idiot elements of human nature.

By three forty-five A.M., except for the occasional lost soul, the hundreds of boating "sportsmen" seemed to be expectantly located where they wanted to be for the morning's shoot. I could still hear an occasional shout or the clattering sound of an outboard plowing through someone's decoys and the resultant hollering, but generally, except for the clunking sound of a thermos being dropped in the bottom of a boat echoing dully across the marsh, the hunters were quiet. The waterfowl were trying to reenter their marsh haven from every angle on the compass. Flights of ducks and white-fronted geese whistled noisily to and fro, trying to find just the right place, only to find it occupied by a boatload of people or full of bobbing decoys. Canada geese, the most intelligent as well as regal of the geese, wisely wrote off the marsh as a bad idea and headed off into the early-morning skies, honking their disgust. Ducks plowed into the waters next to decoys and swam expectantly into the sets looking for company, only to meet the painted-on blank stares of their newfound "friends." The pungent smell of methane gas had been overridden by the penetrating smell of gasoline and oil from the hundreds of outboards that had just churned the serene marsh waters into a smelly soup.

The combination of hunters in shooting positions before legal shooting hours, thousands of ducks and geese returning to their marsh in close proximity to the waiting guns, humans' predictable lack of control, and a little wisp of the devil in all of us made an explosive mixture with potential lethal results for the migratory residents of the marsh. I held my breath. Staying legal and not early-shooting the birds as they whizzed by (legal shooting time was one-half hour before sunrise) would be no easy feat. There were always hunters of questionable ethics who could ruin a perfectly good duck hunt, and after witnessing the "grand entrance" that morning, I didn't have high hopes for many quality sportsmen in my area. To compound things, the bright moon made the low-flying waterfowl highly visible and tempting targets.

Realizing that the fragile marsh peace might not last, I pulled my Grumman back into the water, reloaded my dog into the bow, and slid onto the cold metal seat, where I sat quietly expecting the worst. I had worked many a good duck hunter in years past, those who held their fire until it was light enough to shoot and identify the birds whizzing by at speeds in excess of forty miles per hour. But all it took was a greedy few to turn the shooting area from serenity to madness in a heartbeat. After what had already occurred that morning, I believed that the really good sportsmen would have distanced themselves from this crowd. I wasn't far off in my estimates.

At three fifty-six A.M., far to the north, I heard the faint *thump-thump-thump* of a shotgun being discharged. The temptation was just too great, and that chap couldn't wait, I grimly thought, hoping one of my colleagues was near at hand to put the grab on that early-shooting idiot. Let's hope the folks in my part of the marsh didn't pay any mind to that sound, I thought. A quick look at the luminescent hands on my watch revealed that legal shooting hours were still over two hours away! Here was some damn knothead opening up the waterfowl season under the light of an almost full moon. I continud holding my breath and fearing the worst, and the devil rewarded me accordingly.

A flock of about a thousand startled mallards flew over the marsh not thirty-five yards above the water, making a roaring *swooshing* and wing-clattering noise heard by all. With that and the three shots to the north, the whole goddamned marsh blew up! It seemed as if every gun in the marsh that morning, and there were hundreds, had just been waiting for that chap on the north end to start shooting. I guess those boneheads felt that if "Joe" could shoot that early, it must be all right for them to start shooting as well, and since others in their part of the marsh had opened up, it must be time for everyone to shoot. And so they did, with gusto!

Unless you have experienced this kind of situation, it is hard to appreciate, much less describe with sterile, one-dimensional words. It must have sounded kind of like the moment when several thousand Union soldiers at Gettysburg, lying five deep behind a stone barricade, rose up and commenced shooting at Picket's men during that famous charge. Only instead of one shot from a musket, everyone in my marsh fired at least three times from their modern-day shotguns.

I tried hollering at those closest to me who were blazing away for all they were worth, telling them that shooting time was still hours away. I was rewarded with the continuing deafening roar of hundreds of shotguns going off, the whir of hundreds of thousands of desperately flapping wings from surprised birds, a face stung by falling shot from a shotgun near my position, all wrapped up in this ultimate display of humankind's conservation ethic! *That did it!* Off Shadow and I went into the "wildlife wars" amidst the constant *ping* of lead shot off the side of the canoe or the stinging *thwok* of pellets flying into my unprotected face. If these knotheads were going to shoot early, then they had better plan on a little law enforcement as part of their daily "bag limit," I grimly thought. Unfortunately, "little" was the operative word in the roaring marsh that morning!

By the time I got to my first shooter, he had already killed and retrieved two pintail ducks with just the light of the moon as an aid! I identified myself, told him he was shooting early, which was a violation of state and federal law, and requested and received his hunting license. Quickly turning the license over, I wrote on the back in ink the number of shots I had seen him take at waterfowl, the times he had shot, and the number of ducks killed (hunting licenses were made of paper in those days and were clear on their reverse sides). Requesting and pocketing his driver's license, I returned his hunting license (he needed to keep it on his person if he continued to hunt during the legal shooting hours yet to come), I told him when legal shooting hours commenced and to knock off any more shooting until then. I instructed him to meet me in a nearby parking lot at ten A.M. There I would record the needed information and return his driver's license.

I figured that way, he could still get in a short morning hunt between the beginning of legal shooting time and when he had to leave to meet me. The surprised shooter tried to argue that everyone else in the marsh was shooting early, so he had thought it was legal. My cold, moonlight-illuminated stare and explanation that I was off to catch every one of those folks early-shooting let him know "that dog wouldn't hunt!" Moving to the next set of early-shooting violators (a group that included almost everyone in the whole damn marsh), I repeated what I had explained to the first fellow and continued on to the next, and the next, and the next for a solid hour without break! Most of the hunters were just around the next bend of tules with their decoy spreads in open water not thirty yards away. That arrangement made for almost instantaneous access and contact with the next group once I had finished with the previous violator. To make sure no one tried to mark out what was written on the backs of their hunting licenses, I "doubled up," meaning I would take the driver's license and hurriedly write the last name from that in my pocket diary, then code in shorthand what I would need for any future legal action. For example, I would write, "Jones—1-PT-401-2." That meant shooter Jones shot one (1) Pintail (PT) at 4:01 (401) A.M., shooting twice (2). The rest I could reconstruct later, so off I went to the next shooter, who was happily blasting his way into federal court as well.

The moon was now partially obscured by light clouds from the fast-moving weather front, but the shooters continued to fire at the ducks and geese confusedly flying overhead or landing in the water next to their decoys. It reminded me of a feeding frenzy, though it was easy to understand this behavior with the air so temptingly full of birds, many flying in great flocks of a hundred or more no higher than ten or twenty yards over the shooters' heads. Plus, everyone knew the first couple hours of shooting would be the best as far as filling one's game bag. It was during those moments that the waterfowl were at their most inexperienced regarding the deadly moments at hand. After that they would be more wary, flying higher and becoming tougher to decoy and shoot. It was obvious that everyone in the marsh that morning intended to get their share before the birds wised up and got the hell out of "Dodge."

I was struck by spent shot several dozen times, was hit on the head by a dying gull (thank God it wasn't a goose), had one duck and later a white-fronted goose fall dead straight into my canoe (both of which my dog promptly claimed as hers), and saw numerous dead or wounded waterfowl fall within arm's reach. It was pure carnage, and there wasn't any sign of letup! I finally put away the paddle and started my outboard so I could get around the marsh faster, reaching more shooters before legal shooting hours arrived. If these chaps were going to kill *my* waterfowl so blatantly, then they could expect to have their day ruined as well as part of their shooting experience. I too now found myself in a feeding frenzy.

Several times that morning I had to stop and just let the shooting go on around me as I caught my breath. There was so much going on, often at such low levels that anyone out in the open water literally took their lives in their hands. Keeping that danger in mind, I tried to interpose clumps of tules between me and the shooter until the last possible moment. Then I waited until I could hear my targeted shooter reloading his shotgun. I would gun the outboard, turn on my flashlight and holler as I swung into view. Even with that precaution, I ended up with welts all over my face and hands from low-flying shot! And I wasn't the only one. Shadow yelped several times as she caught loads of spent shot standing in the bow of the canoe, and many of the shooters I contacted complained about being hit with falling shot as well.

Pretty soon I had so many seized ducks and geese in the canoe that I didn't have very much freeboard, making any further running around in the marsh somewhat dangerous. To avoid being sunk by the combination of the weight in my boat and a wake from one of the wild men roaring around picking up crippled and dying waterfowl, I started leaving my evidence birds in the hands of the illegal shooters for later confiscation in the parking lot. I indicated those bird numbers by species on the backs of the hunting licenses and in my diary as well. When we met in the parking lot, I would seize those ducks connected with the violation and add them to my growing pile of evidence birds. Still the early-shooting mania continued—and so did I.

Those readers who do not hunt should understand that there are several very good reasons for state and federal laws prohibiting early shooting. The animals need some down time without shooting interference to rest, preen, and get something to eat. In the days of old, when fewer folks lived in North America and before the advent of protective conservation legislation, birds were shot or trapped around the clock. With lots of wildlife, not many shooters, and plenty of habitat, that kind of killing was felt, but not as much as in today's world. With today's restricted habitat, reduced bird populations, increased numbers of shooters, and better guns and ammunition, unrestricted shooting would force many species into the black hole of extinction. In addition, there are many more species and sex restrictions today, and shooting in the dark precludes identification before the trigger is pulled. There is also the issue of crippled birds who escape into the dark, only to die an agonizing death from their wounds or, unable to fly, in a terrorizing moment fall prey to the flashing teeth of a hungry predator. That is not the kind of loss a wildlife manager can justify or sustain; hence the regulation of shooting hours so one can see what the shooter is doing. There is also the issue of safety. Most hunters now wear some form of camouflage in the wild, and the inability to see each other during poor light conditions in the field is a setup for many tragic situations. Last but not least, shooting early does not meet the conservation ethic of a fair chase. Those who are true sportsmen do not subscribe to such illegal practices and in every breath condemn those who do.

Legal shooting hours finally arrived, and even though I had cleaned up a number of violators, I was thankful for the light. There were still thousands of ducks and geese trying to land in the marsh, and the shooting continued hot and heavy. By eight o'clock, because of their early-shooting success, many of the hunters had begun to leave the marsh with their limits of birds. Most had shot early, but since I hadn't seen them shoot, they were free to slide. Under law, an officer has to observe a violator take or attempt to take a protected species. Without such eyewitness evidence, it becomes next to impossible to prove the violation beyond a reasonable doubt in a court of law. However, I wasn't done yet. I started working on those possessing over-limits and hoping to slip by without being checked in the isolation of the marsh. I apprehended nine hunters with over-limits by nine-thirty.

I had told the folks apprehended for early shooting to be in the parking lot by ten A.M., so I had to leave my over-limit pursuits and head my canoe in that direction. Once back at the dike, I unloaded ninety-one ducks and geese, along with seven gulls and other shorebirds I had found lying in the water, into the back of my unmarked patrol truck. There were several hunters on the same levee not twenty yards away who had limited out and watched with keen interest as I unloaded my huge pile of birds. They did not know who I was since I was dressed in hunting clothes, and not one of them said a damn thing about my obvious "over-limit"! So much for the hunter ethic when dealing with *some* individuals in the fraternity. Loading my canoe on the overhead rack, I boarded Shadow, grabbed a cold Coca-Cola, cranked the Dodge into life, and headed for my designated parking lot.

I was met by several dozen hunters who all had one thing in common: long faces. Stepping out of my truck, I took my ticket-writing gear and put it on the hood. Looking over the sea of waiting faces, I could see lines of dusty vehicles coming from the marsh toward the parking lot and wondered how many of those chaps would turn out to be mine as well. Reaching into my game bag, I retrieved a handful of driver's license and started calling out names. Each violator stepped forward and handed me his hunting license with the violation inked on the back. Comparing that to my hasty field notes, I filled out a field information form (we didn't issue federal citations in the field in those days) for every person I had contacted that morning before returning both of his licenses. If the hunter was holding evidence birds left in his care, as I had indicated on the back of the hunting license, I seized and tagged those birds. I briefed each man on the court's administrative process, answered any questions, and then moved on to the next violator. They were starting to stack up in ever-increasing numbers. Most were of the long-faced and embarrassed variety, interspersed with a few grumblers regarding their loss of hunting opportunities on opening day. Their words rolled off my tired back like water off a duck. Life is a series of choices, I thought, and they had made the wrong ones that morning. My hardened feelings were reinforced as I viewed the growing pile of evidence ducks and geese in the back of my pickup. Those critters sure didn't get much of a choice. So it was tough if many of my new-found clientele were unhappy.

This activity went on until three-fifty P.M. as more errant hunters arrived, filling the parking lot to "take their medicine." By the end of the episode, I had filled out sixty-eight field information forms for early shooting, three for taking protected species (gulls), and another nine for over-limits. Surprisingly, I didn't write a single ticket for an unplugged shotgun or for not having a federal duck stamp. It was obvious that these chaps were basically good people who had just gotten carried away with the excitement of the moment when the marsh blew up. I don't remember how many birds I seized that day because I failed to record the number in my diary in any understandable fashion. Suffice to say, it was a pile. ...

After finishing (everyone showed up for every license I held), including drawing all the birds in lulls between citation issuance so they wouldn't spoil, I tiredly began checking other hunters leaving the neighboring wheat fields after their day's goose-hunting exploits. Continuing into the evening, I worked late shooters and had some success, catching a commercial party of six on Sheepy Ridge, led by a paid hunting guide (though I did not catch the guide, who was a fellow Humboldt State College wildlife management graduate), shooting almost thirty minutes late at the hordes of mallards flying low and overhead from the refuge en route to the tasty grain fields.

With that, I finished my day and headed for the state Fish and Game cabin, where many of the state, refuge, and federal law enforcement officers had already gathered for a dinner that was being prepared courtesy of the California Department of Fish and Game. I met Agent-in-Charge Jack Downs, and after we had shared information about the day's successes and plans for the morrow, he assigned me to work with Carl Gruener, a newly arrived agent from the regional office staff in Portland. Jack didn't seem surprised at the large number of citations I had written that day, just amused. Hell, I wasn't amused! I was dead-assed tired, hot, dirty, hungry, and somewhat embarrassed on behalf of the hunting fraternity for the stupidity it had exhibited that morning. Jack didn't say anything about my "woofing," just grinned at his tired troop and wandered off to drink with other, less hot-under-the-collar officers and swap tales from the day.

It seemed that everyone had done quite well catching bad guys that day. No one was even close to my eighty-plus numbers, but several of the teams of officers had thirty or more citations to show for their efforts. Jack Downs and his partner had made it a point to follow goose shooters from the fields to the picking facilities in the nearby town of Tule Lake. They would watch the successful hunters bring in their three white-fronts (a daily limit), leave them for picking and cleaning, and then hustle back to the field to kill some more before the birds

wised up and retreated back to the safety of the National Wildlife
Refuge. For the benefit of the reader, the white-fronted goose is a seed-
eating species (seeds are 80 percent or so of their diet) and therefore an
excellent table bird. Many hunters know this and prize the white-front
accordingly. Jack and his partner would follow the successful hunting
party back to their field and decoy set and stake out their "double-tripping" (killing a limit, depositing them out of their possession, and then
going back for a second limit the same day) shooters at a discreet distance. They would watch the shooters (notice I don't call them hunters
or sportsmen) kill their second limit of white-fronts. Then Jack and his
partner would move into the field, stop the killing, and collect the information from the shooters for later issuance of citations. Afterward
they would go back into town and seize the birds that group had
brought in earlier, completing the evidence circle. Jack and other teams
of officers repeated this process throughout the day, filling out many
field information forms in the process.

Jack's odd response to my morning's battle in the marsh was explained later in the evening as we all sat around drinking good
whiskey, relaxing, and enjoyed the camaraderie that wildlife law enforcement officers share after a good day in the field. Several Oregon
state troopers arrived at the cabin, and Jack rose to greet them warmly.
Jack had been an Oregon state trooper before coming to work for the
Service, and it appeared that these officers were old academy class-
mates or friends. As the whiskey flowed, the troopers took off their
shirts and went off duty. Many tales were told that evening of times
past, but one statement in particular caught my attention when one of
the troopers said offhandedly, "How did I do this morning?"

Jack or another agent, maybe Bob Norris (after thirty-six hours of
no sleep and a fair amount of good whiskey, added to the passage of
more than thirty years, I am not sure who said what), said, "Great,"
then pointed to me and added, "Tiny there really scored big from
your efforts—eighty-six if I am not wrong."

Overhearing my nickname, I looked at them questioningly. They
laughed long and hard at my bewildered expression. I thought I
would like to be in on what was so damn funny, since I obviously was
part of it. Another trooper, who had remained silent until now,
turned, introduced himself, and said, "How *did* you do? Was your
catch for the day really eighty-six?"

I said, "Well, I caught a passel of early shooters among my other violators today. I was doing fine in the marsh until some damn knothead opened up on the north end way before legal shooting time. After that I had to work my tail end off just to hold the line. Somewhat unsuccessfully, I might add."

He said, "Well, I guess that old black magic still works."

The group of agents and troopers privy to the "inside cards" in the conversation laughed again. I waited out my pointed questions with persistent looks at Jack, trying to figure out what the hell was going on. The laughter continued until finally with a twinkle in his eyes, Jack (or whoever) said, "What time did you hear the first shots this morning?"

I said, "About three-fifty-six."

"How many did you hear?"

I answered, "Three. What is with the twenty questions?"

Jack and the trooper laughed again, and Jack said with a knowing grin, "What do you think of the dipstick who shot early?"

I said, "I would really like to get my hands on that crank handle! He caused my entire marsh to blow up. Once he shot, I had to work my tail end off the rest of the day and forgo my plans to really work those taking over-limits! Hell, I never got out of the stinking parking lot until about four o'clock because of all the field information forms I had to fill out, not to mention all the ducks and geese I had to gut to avoid spoilage."

Jack looked long and hard at me with his trademark grin, then pointed to the tallest of the troopers and said, "Here is your 'crank handle' shooter, Terry. Have at him."

"What?"

"Yeah, here is your shooter." I looked at him and the trooper with questions written all over my face. Jack continued to explain the mystery: "Every year when we take a task force of officers into this area, we end up with a lot of early-shooting problems, which are getting not only worse but harder to control. If the Refuge folks would limit the number of hunters they let in the area [numbers are now limited], it wouldn't be so bad. But until they do, we will have many thousands of people trying to kill the excellent eating, grain-fed duck and goose any way they can. I guess the shooters feel they have spent so much money to get here, they want that amount back in duck and goose meat and don't mind breaking the law to achieve those aims. So we just have the trooper drive along State Line Road in the wee hours of the morning, stop, get out of his patrol car with his riot shotgun, and shoot several times into the air to clear out the cobwebs from the barrel. If anyone is tempted to shoot waterfowl early, that usually smokes them out and makes the catching easy."

An understanding grin began to slowly form on my now not-so-bewildered face. I couldn't believe it! As a first-timer to the "flying squad," I hadn't been privy to their little historical trick and as a result had fumed all day about that first early shooter and his lack of ethics. For the rest of the evening all I could do was shake my head at the turn of events and my resulting "good" fortune, colored though it was by my newfound knowledge of the early-shooter "assist" department.

I have matured enough over the subsequent years to smile a wry smile instead of a grimace over such matters. My long-ago rancor about the run-of-the-mill sportsman's lack of ethics is gone. I have seen that deficiency exhibited by many over the years. Not all, mind you—hell, no! But still, more than there should be from the hunting and fishing fraternity, based on the principle of fair chase and the conservation ethic. I have come to accept the problem for what it is. I have frequently heard state Fish and Game directors, high-ranking wildlife officials in the federal government, or leaders from the National Rifle Association who have *never really been there* proudly proclaim that there are just a few bad apples in the hunting and fishing fraternities. "Not more than 5 to 10 percent of the total," they commonly expound. Many of them continue with, "By and large, the majority of the hunting and fishing fraternity are fairly good, honest, and moral folks."

Based on my thirty-two years in the field at the state and federal levels, I think that notion may be hogwash. I would bet that if the truth were known, at least 40 percent of the so-called sportsmen can at any time, given the right opportunities, act like coyotes. Anytime they feel they have a green light and a chance to get away with taking a few critters outside the law, they will do so. That is basic human instinct and nature. Humans are predators as well as scavengers, and damn good ones at that! Unfortunately, those actions become a major part of the problem of the illegal loss of wildlife in this country. Now, many truly good sportsmen who are wincing at what they just read or, not believing it, will attribute these grumblings to the cynicism of an old, burned-out conservation officer. I too am a sportsman, and will be until the day I can no longer go afield to bait a number 6 hook or pull on a fleeing sage grouse with my 10-gauge. I also do not like what I just wrote! I like it even less because I experienced it firsthand, day after day, for many a year! But before you boil over, ask yourself when you were last hunting or fishing and *didn't* see something illegal, such as a fisherman using live bait in restricted waters, catching an over-limit of fish for his kids or wife, shooting dove over a baited field, killing an over-limit of band-tailed pigeons because of the isolated areas they frequent, shooting a pheasant in the weeds from a highway, early- or late-shooting waterfowl after a day of poor hunting, killing an extra elk for a buddy in camp who has a license but no elk, possession of a loaded firearm in a motor vehicle, shooting from a motor vehicle, littering, and so on!

I have worked long and hard in just about all facets of wildlife law enforcement, nationally, internationally, covertly, and overtly. As a result of those labors, I know very well that as long as ego and the almighty dollar are involved in any form, such as high license fees, ridiculous guide or outfitter costs, miscellaneous expenses (motels, oil, gas, food, gear, sale of critters, etc.), and trespass fees, along with many other frustrations such as acres of public lands "locked up" by cattle or sheep ranchers, thereby reducing opportunity and further crowding sportsmen on the few public lands open to hunting, wildlife conservation will lose. If I were a betting man, I would hold the loss of wildlife taken illegally by the normal hunting and fishing public to be just as serious as the numbers taken by dedicated poachers or commercial-market hunters! There are many more run-of-the-mill hunters and fishermen out there than the serious class of poachers. If just one million duck hunters, salmon fishermen, big-game hunters, trout fishermen, dove hunters, and the like in North America took one extra animal a year for their buddy in the hunting party or themselves to sneak home ... I rest my case. And, there are many times that number of licensed hunters and fishermen in North America! Not all are outlaws, mind you—far from it! But enough are to make a difference with our resources. If the folks holding the "thin green line" apprehended one-tenth of 1 percent of the serious poachers, they would be doing *really* well. We catch even less than that of the general run-of-the-mill poacher! With only about ten thousand conservation officers in North America, what do you expect? It's pretty sad, isn't it?

The one thing I have seen that gives me hope is the return of some youngsters to the time-honored sports of hunting and fishing. For years young people, for whatever reason, had all but disappeared from these pursuits. Now I see a small return of those eager faces, boys and girls, that were absent for so long from the joys to be found in the autumn fields and streams. I hope they will learn to respect the "soul" of their sports and fiercely protect it. However, when I look at some of their teachers, with their limited knowledge and understanding of the outdoors and what it has to offer and questionable ethics, I wonder whether that lofty goal of true understanding can be achieved. Damn, why does every sword have two sharp sides, not to mention a point?

The trooper with his "early shooting" that day at Tule was to prove one hell of a way to get the job done. I never again approached that number of tickets in one day for early-shooting migratory waterfowl. Since most of the folks I checked in the marsh that day were ten to fifteen years older than I was, I imagine most have crossed over into that great marsh in the sky. And for those few remaining, the receipt of a citation so long ago for a decided lack of good judgment is certainly a long-lost memory. As for the birds in the air and marsh that day, they are all gone, and it is unlikely that anyone will ever see such numbers and majesty again. The marsh—well, it too has seen better days. And my own better days have slipped off to where all good memories go at this time in one's life. I can only hope that my life as an officer was dedicated to a good cause and helped the resources in some small way so those yet to come can appreciate many of the same outdoors thrills I enjoyed.

It is hard to beat the unexpected bugle of an elk thirty yards distant in a patch of golden-leafed aspen, the whir of wings underfoot from a cackling rooster pheasant as he sails away to another hiding place, the swirl of a fish where your bait just entered the water, the fluting call of a flock of pintail announcing their arrival among your decoys, the unique smell of a fresh-fired shotgun shell, or the distinct taste of a cold venison sandwich shared with your faithful dog on an autumn afternoon. If I did *not* make a difference, then I guess I will become nothing more than an echo in time. Looking at the world of wildlife today and all of its continuing and expanding problems, that "echo in time" notion often doesn't seem too far wrong ... *damn!*

four

A Casket Full of Ducks

IN THE FALL OF 1970, an informant from Butte City called as I was sitting on my front steps trying to cool off after mowing what felt like ten acres of lawn. In an excited voice she said, "Mr. Grosz, Mr. Grosz, you have to get out on I-5 [a north-south interstate in western Colusa County], you have to get out on I-5, very fast, very fast!"

Recognizing the voice of an informant, I replied, "Taiko, whoa, settle down. What is the problem?"

Taiko impatiently replied, "Wes Dollar is bringing down ducks. Wes Dollar is bringing down ducks, lots of ducks. All are picked and cleaned; you must hurry, hurry! They are going to Chinatown to Lin Ming's restaurant. You must hurry or you will lose them. They killed on Turley Ranch last night in a big drag [illegal shooting of feeding ducks on the ground of a harvested rice field, usually at night], all picked and cleaned now, so hurry! They left an hour ago, and only now was I able to get to a phone. Boss made me clean up the picking facility and dump the guts in plastic bags so no one would know. They cleaned over 150 ducks at our club's picking machine and loaded them into ice chests and a big plastic bag. You must hurry." From the strident tone and urgency in Taiko's voice, elements lacking in our usual conversations, it was apparent that she knew what she was talking about. It was also obvious that this normally quiet and reserved young woman *was on a mission!* For whatever reason, someone had really wound her up, and she was going to finish it!

Wes Dollar, a well-to-do mortician from Chico, had a reputation dating from the late 1940s as a commercial-market hunter who killed ducks at night and sold his product to the Chinese markets in the Sacramento and San Francisco Bay areas. However, he had the luck of the Irish, having been missed by federal undercover officers stalking numerous waterfowl market-hunting rings in northern and central California during the heyday of that illicit gunning period. He was also very keen at learning a lesson from what occurred around him, especially when those "guns" who frequented the commercial-market-hunting blood sport ended up in jail. Regardless of the circumstances, Wes was savvy like a fox and gutsy like a slaughterhouse as he carefully continued his avocation.

For years after the arrests and jailing of many of the market hunters because of those earlier covert operations, commercial duck-hunting activity became a lot more cautious or went even further underground. But those arrests and jail sentences of a handful didn't stop the illicit gunning activities entirely because it was such an accepted subcultural way of life in those days, and heady in the thrills department for those seeking a rush. Those were still hard times for folks of the soil trying to make a living, good law enforcement was few and far between, and the markets for a well-prepared duck dinner were just too lucrative for the black-hearted to ignore. Instead of selling to any commercial buyer holding a handful of green or the unsuccessful visiting duck hunters in the bars who might be federal undercover officers, many now concentrated on selling to trusted sources. Understandably, this system made interception and apprehension by understaffed and poorly funded federal agents extremely difficult. That situation was exacerbated by the fact that the "killing fields" were being flooded with a new generation of shooters. Sons, nephews, and cousins of the old commercial gunning community, whose founding members were often still dealing with prison sentences, began hitting the rice fields at night in numbers that strained the state and federal officers' abilities to hold the line against this wanton form of slaughter. However, many of that class of shooter, cognizant of those serving jail sentences for the illegal *commercial sale* of the duck, killed instead for their winter larders and those of their friends. The night shooting and dragging was still illegal under the Migratory Bird Treaty Act and terribly destructive, but a change for the better was in the wind! The vicious market hunting and crippling still occurred, but not in the same magnitude as before as the taste for a store-bought duck dinner began to wane. However, with this new rush of shooters, assisted by nearly criminal congressional neglect in funding for the

Fish and Wildlife Service, hundreds of thousands of ducks and geese still disappeared from the rice fields of the Sacramento and San Joaquin Valleys into every known form of cookery and eatery. Favorite disposal points included Chinese markets and restaurants, Italian restaurants, Knights of Columbus and Elks Club formal gatherings, the mafia, the Chinese Tong Society, brothels, and gambling establishments from Reno to Chicago. To this day the American people still cannot fathom the loss; even more tragically, they know little or nothing about it!

In regard to that magnitude, I knew an old market gunner in the Princeton area of Colusa County who had kept a diary of his shooting excesses since he was eleven years old in 1909. We became friends of sorts, and through that unique relationship of hunted and hunter I had an opportunity while sharing a drink with him in my home one afternoon to see that fabled diary. He was complaining about me missing too many of his competitors in the fields at night! An old man, he was pissed because I was missing many of the younger gunners, which meant he had to work harder to find an undisturbed flock worth shooting. The fact that he knew the details of my nighttime enforcement activities made me wonder how many others I must have walked right by in my meager attempts to corral night shooters. It also makes me wonder how many of them with the right mental bent could have "smoked" me right then and there.

Through the spring of 1969 (he wouldn't let me see his 1970 entries), that diary recorded his killing in Colusa and Glenn Counties and sales of 36,173 ducks and geese to businesses in the Sacramento and San Francisco Bay areas! Almost all the recorded species were mallards and pintail (there wasn't much market for geese in those days). When I asked what happened to all the lesser species he must have killed with the mallards and pintail, he replied, "Just left them where they dropped. They weren't worth the bother of picking up and selling." I asked about the fieldful of cripples left after a shoot, and he said he never went back for fear of apprehension. However, he would let several needy families know where a "drag" had occurred and they would go pick up what cripples they could for their personal consumption. His monetary subtotal for the ducks in the diary exceeded $100,000 — and those were the days when a dollar meant something!

After a lot of pleading on my part, he agreed to give me the diary upon his death. "You can find it under my bed along with my shotgun and its extender," he said with a teasing grin. In 1974 I was promoted and moved to North Dakota. In the heat of a major wildlife war protecting the wetlands in North and South Dakota from illegal drainage by the dirt farmers in their rush to "feed the world," I forgot about my friend. He died in 1975, and I didn't learn of his passing until months afterward. I immediately contacted his daughter regarding the diary, with thoughts of placing it in the Smithsonian Museum. His daughter, not realizing the historical significance of such an item and thinking it was just an old ledger full of useless numbers, had tossed it into the garbage while cleaning out his home for resale! Thus went a piece of Americana, just like the ducks, dates, and dollars documented inside.

I befriended other commercial gunners who knew Wes Dollar and learned that they believed the concept of increased caution after the apprehensions of many of their counterparts was lost on him. From the very beginning, Wes had been extremely cautious and sold only to buyers known to his father (also a mortician and commercial-market hunter), thereby evading the federal dragnets. Hence, Wes continued at his normal killing rate, basically free of concern about federal intervention because of those historically trustworthy and closed-mouthed family buyer connections. Also, he wasn't as greedy as most. He was gainfully employed, and when the word got out that the feds were in the valley in dangerous "flying squad" numbers, he would lie low until things cooled off. Once he felt that the feds were no longer an issue, back into the fields at night he would go with his model 11 Remington auto-loader with a homemade magazine extender (increasing his shell capacity to eleven rounds), and the killing and selling would recommence as if nothing out of the ordinary had occurred.

From the time of my arrival in Colusa County in 1967, I had heard whispers about the mortician from Chico and his insatiable appetite for killing and selling the duck. Most of his illicit activity occurred in neighboring Butte or Sutter Counties, agent Bob Norris's district, so I didn't get too excited since I had more work than I could handle in my own district. But Wes's opportunistic lust for killing took him many places, including Colusa County on occasion, and when it did, we frequently crossed swords. I apprehended Wes several times in

1967 and 1968 for taking over-limits of ducks and dove, shooting dove over a baited area, and closed-season hunting, but I had never caught him in a really unique case like the situation Taiko had just described.

Taiko had been providing me with information for over a year regarding many illegal happenings on the northeast side of my district during waterfowl season. Her information had always been accurate, especially in regard to names of the subjects, times, locations, and types of illegality. As a cook and clubhouse manager for a less-than-honest Butte Sink duck club, she had the opportunity to witness a lot of monkey business, especially since club members and their guests frequently asked her to pick, clean, and package their illegal ducks and geese for transport home. Taiko disliked those who openly violated the conservation laws and didn't appreciate being dragged into the dirty work of preparing the unlawfully taken waterfowl for a bunch of arrogant, wealthy game hogs. Also, I discovered after she came to trust me that many of the club members made passes at her, an attractive single mom, or even openly fondled her when they had a few too many drinks under their belts. That sexually abusive behavior put her in an awkward position. She was dead set against such behavior but in need of a good job in order to support herself and her daughter (her husband of thirteen years had been killed in a farming accident). The duck club work paid well, including tips, and provided much-needed medical, board, and room benefits. So she put up as best she could with the rotten behavior of some of America's wealthiest, but it carried a sting.

As I said, she had a thing against shooters who took more than their share, especially if they were some of the chaps who insisted on harassing her. One day I happened across her the day after another bad evening of being grabbed at and fending off lewd suggestions. I was making a routine check of the duck club in which she worked. I came into the club while most of the members were still out hunting and inspected their hanging facility (a screened-in porch to hang drawn waterfowl for cooling) and then their massive kitchen in case I had missed anything from the previous day's shoot. As it turned out, I had missed a tray containing a large over-limit of duck breasts. Sensing my "miss," when the other help wasn't looking Taiko caught my eye by pulling out a flour drawer in the walk-in pantry that held the tray of illegal duck breasts. Realizing what she had done, I gave her a quiet nod of thanks as she hurried back to her sink of dirty breakfast dishes as if nothing out of the ordinary had occurred. As soon as she was in the clear from the prying eyes of the other kitchen help, I "discovered" the ducks and promptly seized them. I also made a mental note of her assistance for a later run at possibly enlisting her as an informant on a duck club that gave me nothing but fits.

A short time later, the "sportsman" responsible for the over-limit of duck breasts in the pantry, "Doc" Pinski, arrived back at the club-house with another limit of ducks, not knowing I was there. After the proper greeting and salutation, we had a little chat regarding his lack of ethics and inability to count. I made sure he was aware that I had been checking the ducks in the hanging facility and had "chanced" to see their Asian American cook trying to hide a tray of duck breasts from a previous day's kill in an effort to "protect" some club member from the law. I let the shooter think I had questioned Taiko as to their origin and that she had said she did not know whom the ducks belonged to. However, I pointed out that he had foolishly left a note on the tray requesting her cleaning and packaging services, with his name and room number, which, I lied, she had tried to hide in her hand. I had recovered the note from the housekeeper (another smokescreen) and had been able to connect the ducks to him. Since he had even more ducks in his possession with the current day's over-limit, I was taking the appropriate legal action. All Doc could do was sputter and glower at me, and Taiko escaped without even a backward glance by my errant shooter because of the smokescreens laid down in my conversation. In fact, Taiko told me later that for her efforts to "protect" him, he had tipped her $50!

Incidentally, my son Special Agent Rich Grosz and I happened to be working that same duck club during waterfowl season twenty-seven years later. Senior Resident Agent Scott Pearson from Sacramento had invited me to come into his district for a couple of weeks and work with my son in my old stomping grounds. He knew I would be forced to retire the following year because of my age and saw this as a great opportunity to allow something historical to occur before I walked out the door. His thoughts were to have a father-son special agent team (the first in years for the Service in law enforcement) working together and in the process provide an opportunity for me to teach Richard some tips of the trade regarding the outlaws and animal life histories in my old district. As fate would have it, Rich and I met Doc coming in from his deep-water duck club one morning with his hunting partner. Doc had to be at least eighty-five years old at that time. True to his nature, he was in violation, and as Rich prepared to gather the information, Doc looked up at Rich (all 6 foot 7 inches of him) and said, "What the hell did you say your last name was?"

Rich answered, "Grosz."

Doc mulled that over for a moment and then said, "You any relation to that son of a bitch Terry Grosz?" I was standing to one side and had aged considerably over that twenty-seven years, so Doc hadn't noticed me yet.

"Yes, sir," answered Rich. "I am his son."

Doc looked at Rich and after a moment of deep thought said, "Oh, great! Now I have to put up with another Grosz for the next twenty years!"

I almost fell into the water alongside the boat dock when I heard that. Here the old bastard was going on ninety and was concerned about having to put up with another Grosz for the next twenty years! That was just like Doc—he never learned. It appeared he would remain just as arrogant as the day I pinched him in 1970, and would continue walking on the dark side until he passed over the Great Divide.

The very next nonshoot day after my 1970 encounter with Doc, I visited the club when the members were away. Making doubly sure no club members were around, I knocked on the door and was soon ushered into the kitchen by the lady I was to know as Miss Taiko Sato. Standing by the door in case someone arrived and I needed to make a hurried exit, I introduced myself and said, "Miss Sato, I wanted to thank you for your help in letting me know about the ducks in the pantry yesterday." She just grinned, and I could tell it had been her pleasure. Taking a gamble based on her body language and previous assistance, I said, "Would you care to help me in the future on like violations if I *assured* you no one would ever discover your identity?"

She examined me long and hard with an intense set of dark eyes and then nodded, saying, "No one must ever know I am helping you. My daughter has only me for support, and if I lose this job because I helped you, I would be blackballed in the area by all the other clubs and never again be able to work in the Butte Sink."

"I understand," I said. "Help me, and I will lose the case before I expose you as a source of information. You have my word on it."

She agreed, and I left my business card with information on how to get hold of me when club members got to feeling too lucky and took undue advantage of the ducks and geese. Then I got the hell out of there before a field hand or someone else caught me talking to her.

Without informants' assistance in such matters, law enforcement would simply fail. It is so important to get such people involved that it is impossible to put a "price tag" on it. So when an officer has someone on the inside willing to assist, it is nothing short of a piece of heaven. … People always used to ask me what they could do, being only one person. Well, any of you who have ever felt that way should give us in the conservation community a hand. *Any kind of hand!* If you don't, you are doing nothing to make sure there is something left for your kids and your grandkids. *Your call!*

I had routinely raised so much hell on Taiko's club that I'm sure they considered me nothing short of a king-sized son of a bitch. Having an "in" on such violating, duck-killing sons of guns was nothing short of a miracle — a miracle that continued to bless me not only on that club but on several neighboring clubs as well. Taiko was a very astute observer and had a good memory for facts overheard during the many whiskey-inspired clubhouse conversations. She was also close to several other hardworking and equally abused cooks and housekeepers employed on adjacent duck clubs. Through Taiko and her conduit to those other hardworking souls, I managed to hammer so many club members that the welcome mat was never out for me on eight of the area's thirty or so duck clubs! I don't know how much money I made for the state of California or the federal government, but I know from review of one of my diaries during one 107-day duck season that the club where she worked was the recipient of eighty-four citations, bringing in over $10,000 to the county coffers (Fish and Game fine monies went to the county coffers in which the citation was issued) and a like amount to the federal court system in Sacramento. And that was in the days when fines weren't that significant, running from $25 to $150 per offense! The beauty was that those were all citations for which Taiko had provided the information against her lusty crowd. In addition, I still managed to knock the hell out of them when I surprised them in the field or the duck blinds with their over-limits of ducks and geese. With that, and with information funneled from Taiko's counterparts on other clubs, I wrote another forty-one citations in their backyards that year. In short, after that first experience in the pantry with the tray of duck breasts, when Taiko spoke, I listened.

"Taiko," I said, "how is Wes transporting the ducks down I-5?"

In her impatient tone, Taiko said, "In his hearse. He is transporting the ducks in his hearse. Hurry, hurry, or you will lose him."

I said, "I need a little more information than that. What color is the hearse [Wes had two], and you mentioned 'they' earlier. Who is running with Wes? And where are the ducks hidden? Give me a little more information on this, Taiko, because it will involve a warrantless search, and Wes can really be a horse's hind end in those kinds of situations. Besides, I don't want to catch him and then get the search thrown out because I violated his Fourth Amendment rights."

"Mr. Grosz, Wes is riding with a man named Wally and is driving his black Cadillac. The birds are all picked and cleaned in two big ice chests and a plastic sack filled with ice. And all of that is in the box," she responded.

"What kind of box, Taiko? Keep in mind I can't just search them or their property unless I have probable cause." I was beginning to get excited over the prospect of a unique case, finding myself getting caught up in what Taiko had to say.

"The casket, Mr. Grosz; the ducks are in the casket. Hurry, hurry."

I heard voices in the background as someone else entered the room. Not wanting anyone to overhear her conversation with the law, she abruptly hung up.

Damn, I thought, I could have used a little more information, but I guess that will have to do. The ducks were in a casket. What a novel idea for running a bunch of illegal ducks to the market! Who in their right mind would look in a casket being carried by a hearse? Then a smile began to cross my face: *a goddamned casket!* What a case that would make if I could pull it off. ... Taiko had always given me good information, but once she started talking she sometimes seemed to feel guilty about what she was doing, causing her to shorten her conversations to the exact point. Knowing that, I always had to hustle the information out of her or I would be left standing there with about three-quarters of what I needed. Even with that, I was better off then not knowing, so I was always pleased with what she provided. *A goddamned casket!* Imagine that!

Hanging up the phone, I hurriedly threw a clean shirt over my sweaty, just-mowed-the-lawn body, jumped into my patrol car, and headed for Williams, a small Sacramento Valley town ten miles away. The interstate ran through Williams, causing motorists to slow down, and that was a good place for an ambush, I thought as I sped on my way. Hammering down state Highway 20, I mentally ran through the facts Taiko had provided. Wally was riding with Wes. That would be Wally Oppum, Wes's close friend and another local outlaw, now re-siding in Butte City. I had tagged Wally a few times, booking him once for taking dove during the closed season over a baited area in 1968, once for night-shooting ducks on Terhel Farms during the closed sea-son in 1969, and later that same season for possession of an over-limit of ducks. If I had caught Wally that many times in such a short period, imagine how many other times he must have strayed. No matter how you looked at it, Wally was a bad hombre when it came to breaking wildlife laws. If the two of them were running together, something *really* smelled in the henhouse. Now, you just have to find out where the violation is and be able to prove it in a court of law, flashed across my mind. I tried to ignore the words *that won't be easy,* softly uttered in the back of my mind by my senior guardian angel. ...

As I arrived in Williams, I chanced to see a black Cadillac hearse pass by me, heading south. Hurriedly moving into the southward traffic stream, I worked my way to the rear of the hearse. It was Wes's black Cadillac all right. I radioed the Colusa County sheriff's office and ran the license plate for positive identification. While I was waiting for the response, I could see Wes's ugly mug looking at my obviously trailing patrol vehicle in his side mirror. He had a subtle look of recognition, but his face didn't show any concern about his illegal cargo. I could see nothing in the back of the hearse but a casket with a load of flowers on top. No probable cause there, I said to myself. The hearse didn't seem to be sitting any further down on the back springs than usual, as it might have been in carrying a heavy load of ducks, so no probable cause there either. Wes was intently watching me now through his side mirror, and Wally had turned around in the front seat to stare at me through the rear windows of the hearse. It was obvious that both men were nervous with me sitting on their tail, but that was weak probable cause at best. Pulling alongside the rear of the hearse when I got a long break in the northbound traffic (the interstate was two lanes then),

I gave the casket another once-over through the long side-viewing window. There was nothing to suggest anything but transporting a body to a piece of ground somewhere for burial, I thought disappointedly. I pulled up alongside the driver's window and gave Wes and Wally a hard once-over. Both were dressed to the nines in suits and looked the part of respectable morticians. They sure didn't look like a couple of sports who had just finished cleaning a bunch of illegal ducks. However, when I pulled alongside, they fastened their eyes on me as if I were an unwanted ghost, resulting in Wes almost running off the road! Dropping back behind the hearse, I thought, well let's talk with these guys and see what develops because I am not seeing anything out of the ordinary here regardless of Taiko's information.

Here goes another session in hell-raising with letters to the governor, congressman, and Jack Downs, my supervisor, I thought as I turned on my siren (I didn't have a red light on the patrol car in those days in an effort to keep it looking like any other civilian vehicle). The hearse slowly pulled over, and I noticed the two men looking at each other as if to ask, "How does he know?" At least I knew Taiko had been right if their looks spoke of their guilty actions. But I still had a legal mountain to leap relative to the probable cause needed to search the hearse and casket. These rascals were street smart when it came to the Fish and Game laws, and I had my work cut out for me if I was to legally conduct my search and not burn Taiko in the process. Well, nothing ventured, nothing gained, I thought as I stepped out of my vehicle.

Walking up to the driver's window, I identified myself with my badge (even though they knew who I was). Wes said, "I know who you are. What the hell do you want, asshole?"

That was a damn good question, I thought, since I didn't have a *real* hook or line in my bag of "possibles" for this fishing expedition. Because I didn't have much to go on other than Taiko's word, which I had sworn to protect, I tried the "George Custer" approach. "Gentlemen, I just received word from the sheriff's office that a black fisherman [I lied to throw them off Taiko's trail] observed the two of you cleaning and loading up a large bunch of ducks into ice chests, placing them in a casket, and then leaving the White Mallard Duck Club in this hearse. That fisherman called the sheriff's office with your license plate number, indicating in the process that the two of you had

at least 150 ducks in those ice chests. The sheriff's office informed me
that upon leaving the duck club the hearse headed west on the Colusa-
Gridley Highway. They figured you might be working your way
across the valley to the interstate and down to the Bay Area [another
wild-assed guess based on Wes's alleged sales history]. So here I am.
That information being the case, and since neither of you is under
arrest or detention at this time, I would like to take a look at those
ducks if I may." That was about as bold a position as one could take I
thought under the circumstances. *Bold* really wasn't the word! It is
really hell when you go into a gunfight with only a throwing tomato
in each hand, if you get my drift. ...

"That black son of a bitch," sputtered Wally. "I knew we should
have run him off from fishing so close to the damn cleaning shed."
Catching himself with Wes's knife-hard looks as a prompt, Wally
quickly added, "That's a *lying black son of a bitch*," omitting what he
had previously uttered about the man being close to the duck-picking
shed. What a lucky guess, I thought, with the "black fisherman"! Well,
not really. There were a lot of black folks fishing the waterways in and
around Colusa County at any hour of the night or day. It was just the
first thing that came to mind in my effort to protect my informant.
Every little bit helps, Wally, I thought. Just keep running your trap,
and I will soon place your feet in it. ...

Wes, looking down and to the left but not betraying any other emotion, said, "We aren't transporting any ducks, period. You can plainly
see there is nothing in the back but a casket with a man's body in it."

Trying to match his bravado, I said, "Who's in the box?" He
quickly gave me the name of a man I knew had just died from what I
had read in the Colusa *Sun Herald* newspaper. Undeterred by that
"strike," I said, "Where are you taking him for interment?"

Wes replied, again quickly, "To south San Francisco, asshole. Don't
you read the papers?" Damn, my trick of trying to catch him fabricat-
ing a name and burial site hadn't worked. And I knew the fellow he
had said was in the box was actually supposed to be buried in a ceme-
tery in south San Francisco.

Undeterred, I walked to the rear of the hearse, trying to get my in-
vestigative techniques back on track, and loudly asked, "Since you have
nothing to hide, may I look inside the back of the hearse, please?" It
was another interrogation trick because any fool knew there wouldn't

be evidence in plain view. In such a situation, the subject of an investigation, realizing there is nothing to be seen and hoping to throw you off the trail, will often grant permission for the search.

Wes hesitated and then said, "Sure, go right ahead, *look anywhere you want to,* asshole, but don't plan on finding anything because there is nothing back there but a stiff." My enforcement counterparts will recognize that the language I had used in my question was crafted to further a warrantless search. They will also recognize the full legal value of Wes's "look anywhere you want to" response. I was getting tired of being called a last part over the fence but managed to keep from ripping off Wes's lips and feeding them to the nearest yellow-billed magpie. Little did Wes realize that the go-ahead he had given me was the magic words needed by a law enforcement officer in a warrantless search (at least in those days).

Opening the back door of the hearse, I took a deep breath to slow down my rapidly beating heart and looked in. I couldn't smell anything like dead waterfowl, or dead human for that matter. I didn't see any water from melted ice on the floor, and I didn't see any loose feathers such as are usually found around freshly picked and cleaned ducks. In short, I didn't see anything giving me probable cause to conduct a detailed warrantless search, so I still needed evidence.

I knew Taiko's information was correct, but I didn't have any physical clues to back it up, and I hadn't gleaned any information from my conversation with Wes and Wally. I again carefully checked the casket for any sign of "fowl" play. Nothing! Not wanting to let these lads go on down the road laughing at me without taking a bite out of their hind ends, I gave the casket and flowers another very careful once-over. Then I spied my first real clue, and first real probable cause! Lying on top of the casket were two sprays of flowers. One was roses and the other some kind of white lily. On the stem of one of the white lilies, probably the part handled by someone placing them on the casket, was a single, dried, *chestnut-colored breast feather from a drake mallard!* Doing a double-take, I could feel the start of a grin that was destined to run clear across my wind-burned puss. It wasn't much of a feather as feathers go, but oh, what a beauuuutiful feather it was! My guess was that after picking and loading the ducks, one of them had carelessly placed the flowers on top of the casket for the "selling look" before washing his hands and in the process transferred that breast feather from his hands to the flower stem. A closer look at those flowers produced another stem on the back side of the arrangement with a dried, partially bloodied fingerprint. I didn't know if it was duck blood or not, but again, my "unwashed hands" theory seemed to be bearing fruit.

Picking off the feather, I carefully placed it in the right breast pocket of my shirt. Removing and laying that bunch of flowers on the hood of my truck to save the fingerprint, I returned to what was fast becoming a crime scene. Flushed with my success, I really gave the area a once-over. Finding nothing else out of the ordinary, I started to walk back to the front of the hearse to confront Wes with my discoveries. I saw my third clue as I looked in the side window along the length of the casket. The lower portion of the casket near the lid that normally was opened for viewing *was sweating on the outside as if there were ice inside!* Damn, I thought. Terry, you dummy, why didn't you see that sooner? Walking back to the rear of the hearse, I placed my hand on the part of the casket that was sweating. Sure as God made little green apples, it was cold and wet. I could see that Wes and Wally were watching me through a tilted-down rearview mirror with more than average interest. I almost had to laugh. Their heads jammed together looking at the rearview mirror reminded me of two African meerkats simultaneously discovering a fat grub. When I slowly ran my hand across the part of the casket that was sweating, Wes's eyes went from marble size to dinner plates, showing an inordinate amount of white. ... *He knew that I knew!* Wally looked like he was in an advanced state of seasickness.

Walking back to the driver's-side door, I said, "Wes, I just found a mallard duck breast feather stuck on the flowers. Normally one does not find mallard duck feathers stuck to flowers riding on top of a casket, to my way of thinking, unless the fellow inside was one hell of a duck hunter and hunted right up to the end. Additionally, I found a bloody fingerprint on the stem of one of the lilies, indicating this guy must have gutted his ducks before he 'left.'" Wes just looked at me, saying nothing, while Wally looked straight ahead out the front window, no doubt wishing he were somewhere else. I continued, "I also discovered that your casket is sweating on one end like there is ice inside. And when I put my hand on the side of the casket, it felt very cold and wet to the touch. Now, I know one doesn't transport stiffs on ice because the embalming process takes care of the deterioration problem for a period of time. With your consent to search the hearse, the discovery of that feather on the flowers covering the casket, the bloody fingerprint on a flower stem, and the apparent ice inside the casket causing it to sweat, I need you to open up the coffin so I can look inside." Before he could get his feet verbally under him in light of what I said, I continued with my best "George Custer" imitation (keeping in mind what ultimately happened to Custer). "It appears my fisherman was correct. You are carrying iced-down ducks in the casket. Otherwise, why the cold touch and condensation?"

Wes just looked at me in disbelief and Wally continued to hold his tongue, being the coward he was. Then Wes began to get verbally abusive as he denied everything, in the process managing to call me every name in the book. He said, with a fierce set of eyes advertising that a killing was in the offing if he had his way, "I will have your job for this. Just you wait until the governor and the dead man's family hear about this invasive action on your part. You bastard, you are history."

I said, "Look, you gave me permission to look at anything in the back of the hearse, and that is exactly what I intend to do. Additionally, in my preliminary inspection I discovered the probable cause I needed, along with the information from my fisherman, to look in that casket. Now, I can call the Colusa County sheriff's office and have them send over a unit to keep you here until I get a warrant from the judge in the Williams Justice Court, or you can open it up so I can conduct a search of its contents. If I find nothing, I will apologize for the inconvenience, and you can be on your way. But if there are picked and cleaned ducks in there, as I suspect, that's a different matter. However, I am not sure how to open that thing, and I don't want to damage it, so I will need a hand from you." Wes continued to stare at me with a sick look spreading across his face. Continuing my final shot to get into the casket, I said, "Be advised, I will open it up with or without your help, along with a warrant and crowbar if necessary."

For a long moment Wes didn't move, just sat there and glowered at me through narrowed eyes as if he would love to see me at the business end of a shotgun! All of a sudden he boiled out of the hearse, damn near knocking me to the ground with the car door in the process, stomped around to the rear, reached in, and partially opened the casket's viewing lid. That done, he stepped back and let me advance to look into the box. Keeping my gun side opposite Wes because of his frame of mind, and with my hind end up in my throat, I stepped forward. Taking a deep breath, I slowly lifted the viewing lid higher for a better look. I often think back to that day and smile. If there had been a body in that box looking up at me, I would have had to shoot myself in the foot to fit the situation, not to mention clean out my shorts.

However, there in the diffused light of the hearse and the sight of one very nervous agent lay a clear plastic bag (used when they ran out of coolers) partially filled with ice and a gob of picked and cleaned ducks. Next to that bag of ice and ducks were two large ice chests, placed end to end in the remaining portion of the casket. Looking over at Wes with a smug "well, well, well" look, I discovered "pissed off" written all over his face. Grinning inside, I hoped he didn't hear my internal yell of joy at seeing the hind end of a duck and not the face of a man when the lid went up! I needed a better look, so Wes and I partially slid the casket out the back of the hearse. Then, with Wes holding the end so it wouldn't fall to the ground, I opened the viewing lid the rest of the way, exposing two ice chests along with the plastic bag of iced ducks. A quick look in each ice chest revealed row upon row of iced duck bodies. Not wanting to damage the bronze casket, Wes, Wally, and I slid the casket out of the hearse and set it down on the pavement between our two vehicles so I could remove and seize the ice chests and bag of ducks.

At that point I realized I was causing one hell of a traffic jam. People were slowing down and looking goggle-eyed at the three of us emptying a casket by the highway. I had to grin, knowing that sight had to tighten up a few hind ends for unsuspecting motorists. The traffic jam almost turned to wrecks when the motorists saw us removing a plastic bag and two ice chests instead of some stiff. That action had to sour more than one passing motorist's lunch, if not put him off food altogether!

We moved the evidence to the back of my vehicle and placed the casket back in the hearse. Requesting both men's driver's licenses, I had them return to the front seat of their vehicle while I counted the carcasses. I laid out the ducks for a count on a tarp from the trunk of my car, all 158 picked and cleaned mallard and pintail ducks (the species were easy to identify from their sizes and the color of the skin remaining on their leg joints). They were not only beautifully cleaned but all had been shot in the back, confirming that they had been taken in the fields by the common night-shooting practice of a "dragger," or commercial-market hunter. Most ducks shot while flying have wounds from shot all over their bodies, not just in the backs. Through a set of tight lips, I confirmed in my mind that they were more than likely headed somewhere to the markets in Sacramento or San Francisco.

The ducks used to mob the harvested fields in the fall and winter evenings, gathering up spilled rice grains to fuel their living furnaces for the night and day that followed. It was not uncommon to find thousands of ducks bunched together just inches apart, happily feeding across the fields like feathered vacuum cleaners. Duck "draggers," or old-fashioned commercial-market hunters, would sneak up on these masses of feeding ducks in the dark of night and discharge their shotguns into this living carpet at close range from behind the protective cover of rice checks. In their terror, the ducks would lift off from the ground like a living sheet, flying away from the exploding terror before them. In so doing, they presented their backs to the guns. That combination of circumstances made them physically attractive as duck dinners to the big city markets: there was no evidence of their having been shot because they were served breast up (purchasing wild sport-shot waterfowl for commercial purposes is a felony). Many an unsuspecting buyer of an illegal duck dinner thought he was eating a pen-raised bird.

I slowly moved my eyes from this tragedy on the tarp to the two men responsible. Knowing neither would admit to the night shooting, I said, "Gentlemen, I'm going to seize these ducks, your casket, and the hearse."

Wes exploded out of the Cadillac. "That is a goddamned four-thousand-dollar bronze casket, damn you! You can't take such a valuable item from me over a few stinking ducks."

"Wes, you are right. I can't take it, but a judge can. I can only seize it and hold it for the evidence it represents, and that is what I choose to do. Since the hearse was used as transport and the casket used to hide the illegality, they are instruments of the crime and will be seized." There was some loud grumbling about getting their property back or having to walk home, which I cut short by pointing out that the ducks discovered in the box didn't have feet to walk anywhere. So

I was sure the two of them wouldn't mind walking if it came to that. … Neither man responded to my probably less-than-professional remark. But damn it all to hell, I was pissed, and the ducks needed a spokesman. This wasn't just an issue of 158 illegal ducks (although it was that, and then some) but statistically an even greater problem. In any situation like this, half the dead are females and half are males. Had all the females lived, the following year they would have produced at least eight ducklings per brood. So in the long view, eight ducklings each from approximately seventy-five females meant we actually lost another six hundred ducks! And that didn't include those wounded in the melee who crawled off into the weeds along the rice checks and ditches to die a slow death or be eaten by predators after these two "yahoos" finished their shoot.

I suggested we return to the city of Williams to meet with Judge Gibson, local justice of the peace, and quickly settle the matter. As a federal agent, I usually took such matters to Sacramento and the federal magistrate's court. However, there was a method to my madness. Judge Gibson was not only a superb judge but a damned good human being as well. He had tried these two meatheads previously for serious wildlife violations, and I hoped those memories were still fresh in his mind. He resented "game hogs" like Wes and Wally, and I was hoping those feelings might translate into a larger fine than I could get in Sacramento from a female magistrate, a nonhunting type who had a hard time smacking someone's hands when they reached too deeply into Mother Nature's cookie jar. It wasn't the most professional way of dealing with violators, but Wes and Wally needed some real attention, and I figured Judge Gibson was my ace in the hole. That way the issue would be settled quickly, and if they got their hearse back, they would at least have a set of wheels to run back under the rock from whence they came. The looks on their faces showed they were a little apprehensive over that suggestion because the Williams judge was a tough one. However, realizing that their alternatives were somewhat limited, and even more afraid of federal court, they agreed to my suggestion.

So off we went to the Williams justice court, me in my Rambler American, my evidence in the back, and they in the hearse with a now empty casket and their dreams of ready cash and a night out on the town with their ill-gotten gain dashed. Fat, beautifully picked and cleaned, rice-fed mallards and pintail went for $3.50 to $5 per duck in those days. To put that into perspective, I made $13,000 per year at the time. So the illegal duck harvest was not a bad haul, tax free and all, if the shooters didn't get caught in the process. ...

Judge Gibson was surprised at my entry into his court looking and smelling like a bear (you would too if you had just mowed about an acre of lawn), with a vehicle full of ducks, a hearse, Wes the undertaker in one hand, and his old friend Wally Oppum of past Williams justice court days in the other. Trying hard not to smile, the judge went into his back room, put on his robe of office, and returned to the bench. I handed the court clerk my now completed state citations, she in turn gave them to the judge, and after a short review by His Honor court was convened. I presented my story, of course without the name of my real informational source, and described the stop, the duck feather on the flower stem, the bloody fingerprint, the sweating casket, and the consent to search granted by the owner and operator of the vehicle. I was careful to omit the story about my "black fisherman," hoping Wes and Wally wouldn't notice. To have used him in the case would have meant lying under oath, something I wouldn't do! The two somewhat bedraggled lads with the nice suits and a ruined afternoon presented their side of the story with a certain amount of groaning about the illegal stop and search of their vehicle. The judge, to his credit, stopped this whining with a statement that I could have taken both of them to federal court in Sacramento instead of the Williams justice court. If they preferred that degree of adjudication, it could still be realized. He sat looking at the two men, awaiting their response. It was amazing the calming effect those words *federal court* had on the defendants. They had no desire to go to federal court in Sacramento, knowing full well that Jack Downs, agent in charge for the U.S. Fish and Wildlife Service, ran a tight ship, and an appearance there might result in some jail time in addition to an even larger fine than was possible in the Williams court. Hearing no further argument, the judge indicated that the consent to search appeared to be legal, and if they felt otherwise, they should state their case. No further response was forthcoming, so His Honor proceeded with the court's business.

He asked for their pleas and then granted a short recess while the two market hunters held a desperate powwow to get their thoughts together. They soon returned and both said they would agree to entering one plea each of possessing an over-limit of ducks and one plea to transporting ducks in such a condition that species could not be determined (lacking a fully feathered head or wing), as indicated on the citations. However, they requested that they be held accountable for only half the ducks each and not the entire 158 per person, as listed on the citation (copossession). The judge agreed after a few moments of thought, realizing it made little difference in the penalty judgement (the maximum fine was $500, which would be reached in the first fifty ducks over the limit). Wes and Wally looked for my response to that little sleight-of-hand victory with catlike grins, as if to say, *Take that, you horse's hind end.* I kept my face impassive because I knew they weren't dealing with a judge who had just fallen off a turnip wagon. The two bad guys felt they had me outsmarted, knowing that the law in those days carried a maximum fine of $500 per offense. They figured they would get off the hook for a maximum of $1,000 each, full well realizing they could earn that much in just one night's killing of ducks the next time they were in the fields. So no big deal. The old judge, God bless him, got a little grin, being an old duck hunter himself, not to mention a pretty fair-minded man, and quietly accepted their pleas.

"Gentlemen, I accept your pleas, find you guilty, and fine both of you the maximum of five hundred dollars per offense, or one thousand dollars total." Wes and Wally were all grins. "Additionally, the ducks are forfeited to the court for disposition. Last but not least, both of you are sentenced to six months in jail." Those words brought Wes, Wally, and me to full alert! All three of us had a bad case of the big eye when those words reached our ears—Wes and Wally out of fear and I out of amazement. This judge hardly ever sent anyone to the bucket for a wildlife violation, so that sentence really brought us up short. He continued, "That sentence will be suspended, and both of you will be placed on probation for a period not to exceed two years, with the understanding that *you are prohibited from hunting or shooting anything, anywhere, anytime in the state of California for that period of time!*" He had never done that before, and I stood there in amazement wondering whether that kind of sentence in state court was legal. Today it is a common form of punishment in such instances. However in those days, that kind of sentence was rare and usually confined to plea bargains in federal district courts.

There was a stunned silence for a moment before Wes said, "Judge, you can't do that. Hunting is our life and passion. We won't have much of a life if you do that to us!"

The judge just smiled and said, "No, you are wrong, I just did, and if you two are caught hunting anything, and I mean anything, you will find yourselves back here spending six months in the Colusa County jail. Do I make myself clear, gentlemen? Oh, by the way, the hearse and casket will be returned to the rightful owners."

Boy, for the next couple of minutes there was the most god-awful groaning you ever heard. The judge finally got a gutful of their cater-wauling, stood up, and told them they could appeal within forty-five days; otherwise, it was a done deal. With that, he adjourned court and left the room. Wes and Wally just stood there in stunned silence. When they looked over at me, all they saw was a Cheshire cat–like grin now spreading clear across *my* face. Now the tables were turned, and everyone in that courtroom, including the judge, knew the hunt was *really* on.

Leaving the courtroom, I unloaded the ducks from Wes's ice chests into several large plastic bags for storage and distribution to the needy. Then I returned the ice chests to my now subdued shooters. Once done, I looked inside the casket one more time for any ducks I might have missed. At that moment, I realized the coffin was nothing more than a metal-shelled duck-running device, lined with a sheet of plastic so melting ice would not leak out. Turning and looking at Wes, I said, "Wes, this casket is nothing more than a metal box or casket shell that you have been using to run ducks." His eyes never left mine, nor mine his. "Be advised, Wes, that from now on, every time I see you going anywhere in your hearse with a bronze casket in the back, plan on getting pulled over and checked."

"Are you through now, asshole?" he said through a tight set of lips.

I gave him one more hard look and stepped aside, letting Wes and Wally board up so they could return to Chico. At moments like that I prayed that God would continue to understand what it was like being a rice-fed duck in a casket without any feet.

For whatever reason, I never again saw Wes in Colusa County carrying a bronze casket in the back of his hearse. Wally continued to work for an east-side rice farmer, but I never saw him with a shotgun or rifle in his possession in Colusa County until the period of probation expired. My guess is that the two of them just carried on their sordid trade in some other conservation officer's backyard. Even though I put the word out to my fellow officers, they were never apprehended hunting during their period of probation. In a way, it was good not to see either of them out and about in the fields, but as is always the case, others soon took their places, killing with a vengeance, and the beat went on. ...

When I returned to my home, I was surprised to see Taiko parked in my driveway. "Did you get them, Mr. Grosz; did you get them?" she asked anxiously.

Opening my trunk, I said, "Yes, thanks to you, all 158 of them, and both men paid a one-thousand-dollar fine each, not to mention being placed on two years' probation against all hunting in California." Taiko, now all grin, watched me unload the ducks and put them in my evidence freezer. Finishing, I turned and said, "Taiko, how do you do it? I know Wes is friends with the White Mallard's president and got permission to use your picking machines, but the picking shed is somewhat out of sight. Unless you were there, I don't see information like that just leaking out."

Taiko grinned and said, "I was asked by my boss to help Wes and Wally so they could get done with what they had to do and get out before you or some other officer came snooping along and caught them. I did as I was told, and everything was going along fine until Wes put his hands on me from behind when I wasn't looking. I slapped him away and discovered that Wally was fondling my twelve-year-old daughter! I grabbed a knife I used to gut their ducks and told both of them that if they ever did anything like that again, I would open them up like I did the ducks! They backed off and just laughed at us, but I have never been so mad. I can take care of myself, but they better leave my daughter out of this. I knew I would find you and report this if it killed me or cost me my job! My daughter is still upset and scared."

Now I knew why Taiko had seemed so determined when she called me with the original information. There had been something in the tone of her voice that I now recognized as the sound of a female protecting her young. With that revelation out on the table and a big smile over the results, she got back into her vehicle and, with a wave of her hand, drove back to the duck club to prepare dinner for the visiting members as if nothing had happened. She was one tough lady.

Taiko was finally remarried to a rice farmer, leaving the duck club and the demeaning things she had had to put up with in order to support her family. I knew her new husband. If he had ever found out what had been going on in the duck club, I doubt I would have had any culprits to mess with. ... With that went my little miracle in the Butte Sink, but in that instance I was pleased to give up my inside information for her happiness. She still sends me a Christmas card every year from her new home in Ohio, where her husband now works the family farm and life is good. Her daughter went on to college, graduated with a master's degree in wildlife management, and is currently employed as a state Fish and Game warden. How is that for God's humor?

Wes and Wally are both dead now, and it seems unlikely that either went out in a fancy bronze casket like the 158 ducks they were carrying that day. I wonder who has that bronze casket and what it is being used for today? I hope it is being used to ice down beer instead of ducks. ...

five

"Aughhhh ... Holy Mary, Mother of God!"

IT WAS CLASSIC NOVEMBER in the Sacramento Valley of California. The wind was howling, the rain drifted across the ground in horizontal sheets, and the ducks and geese were flying so low they might as well have been walking. It wasn't really a nice time to be out and about unless you were a duck hunter, but if you were, those conditions were pure heaven!

Turning south on Road G, just west of Interstate 5 in Colusa County, I let the patrol truck slowly idle over the numerous rain-filled potholes in the road so as not to make any more noise than necessary. The sun had long set, and I aided my sneak by running without lights so as not to tip off the objects of my attention. Just south of my position, at the road's end, were four parked vehicles, and just south of those were numerous duck hunters still shooting at the hordes of ducks leaving the Sacramento National Wildlife Refuge looking for a harvested rice field to load up on some life-sustaining rice. As near as I could tell from the sounds of shooting I had heard earlier from an adjacent road, I had at least seven guns working over the ducks, which were so numerous by that hour that the shooting was almost nonstop. It was the middle of the 107-day duck season in California, so the season wasn't the root of the problem. But the time at which my shooters chose to pursue their sport was legally dicey. Shooting time for hunting migratory waterfowl ended at sunset. My duck-shooting lads were still blazing away forty-three minutes past legal shooting hours, going at it as if they were trying to kill every duck in the country so that none would be left to migrate to Mexico. As the resident conservation officer, it was my job to put a crimp in their style before they really got carried away, and suffice to say, the crimp was on its way.

There are several reasons for controlling shooting hours. One is to avoid the loss of birds shot after dark, or legal shooting time. If the bird does not drop right at your side or you don't have a good hunting dog to retrieve the dead and crippled birds, such loss can be tremendous; hence the need for strong law enforcement efforts against the late shooting of waterfowl—or any migratory game bird for that matter. Another reason is that many totally protected species of migratory birds flying during the same time period will be killed as well because the shooters are unable to identify them. For bitterns, black-crowned night herons, egrets, loons, and many others, flying at night in such circumstances can be particularly lethal. Another reason is to allow the birds an opportunity to feed and rest without getting a faceful of shot in the process. Last but not least is the principle of fair chase. It simply is not sportsmanlike to take a species under undue advantage, such as darkness. The "sport" of hunting is just that—otherwise they would just call it *killing*.

Arriving at the end of Road G, I quietly parked my vehicle among the other cars and hurriedly got out with a flashlight in one hand and a pair of high-light-gathering 7×50 binoculars in the other. Heading south toward my shooters, I crept about one hundred yards to a spot that was central to all eight (there was one more than I had figured). Sitting down near the edge of a rice paddy and using the back cover of a rice check, I commenced recording the happenings in my notebook.

It was dark as all get-out with the late hour, cloud cover, and light rain, but with my binoculars I had a pretty good view of the show. The lads in the field, even though these elements were challenging, were still able to shoot quite well with the aid of nearby city lights reflecting off the clouds. Many times during winter rainstorms in the Sacramento Valley, the clouds were very low, and as a result, the little valley towns illuminated the sky with their lights. This light reflected back down from the clouds, illuminating the surrounding farm lands with a soft light. When that happened, it was possible to have enough light to continue shooting ducks for up to several hours after the end of legal shooting hours—longer if you were shooting over water because water reflects back into the heavens the light reflected down by the clouds.

Since I could not recognize individual faces or even the colors of the late shooters' clothing, I had to slip into Plan B. When I saw the forms of waterfowl flying over the darkening mounds representing my shooters, I would look for muzzle flashes pointed skyward and falling or flaring (trying to rapidly gain altitude to escape the shooting danger below) ducks. Then I would record the time shots were fired at the birds by an individual, the number of shots fired, and the number of birds killed or crippled, all while lying on the rice check writing in pencil (because it doesn't run like ink when wet). Then I recorded whether the shooter was the tallest or shortest one, the heavier set of the two, the one with a dog, the one with a 12- or 20-gauge (many times I could tell by the different sounds when the gun was fired), the one with or without a hat, the one using a pump-action shotgun (which has a certain *clackety-clack* sound every time a round is indexed), and so on. Last but not least, I recorded each hunter or group of hunters on separate pages of the notebook so I could sort out later who did what. Sometimes I just couldn't distinguish one shooter in a pair from another, no matter how hard I tried. In such instances, I would record the times and shots when *both* shot at the same time. Since both were late shooting, the times would still count toward a violation of the Migratory Bird Treaty Act. It takes a bit of work, but this kind of evidence will hold up in a court of law, providing you are able to specifically identify your shooter or shooters once they are apprehended. That process can be difficult, especially if you have eight shooters gleefully blazing away at swarms of hungry ducks, all at the same time!

However, God often helps out when the world of wildlife is getting pounded, and did so that fine evening. Instead of getting greedy, I stayed patient, all the while mechanically documenting the shooters exhibiting solid evidence of their acts and letting go those shooting incidents in which I was not 100 percent certain. After a time fewer and fewer ducks entered the area because of the shooting pressure from below. With that, the shooters (notice I don't call them *hunters* because of their illegal shooting time) began to straggle out of the field in ones and twos, passing right by my hiding place. When the first individuals were within a few feet of me, I rose from the mud, dead crawdads, and other mystery smells, quietly identified myself without the use of my flashlight, and told them to sit down and remain quiet. Knowing illegal shooters' penchant for letting the cat out of the bag, I admonished them anyone advertising the fact the law was in the field would get a quick trip to the local lockup. It was now as dark as the inside of a dead cow because of an opportune rain squall, allowing me to apprehend each shooter or set of shooters as they left the field. With the arrival of the last shooter, and with their driver's licenses in hand, I directed them to head back to the vehicles. Once there, I conducted a more thorough field inspection for the plugs in their shotguns, numbers of ducks in possession, possession of duck stamps, and hunting licenses. By now it was so damn black that I could hardly see anything and could only hear the whistling wings of thousands of ducks still looking for a place to eat, along with the occasional call of a lost soul or winged straggler.

Using the hood of my vehicle and my flashlight, I would call out the name on a driver's license, issue the appropriate citations based on the information recorded in my notebook, provide the shooter with an evidence receipt for the seized waterfowl (all waterfowl killed after legal shooting hours were contraband and therefore could not be kept by the shooter), then repeated the procedure with the next hapless soul. That particular evening it just so happened that everyone I cited was a police officer from Sacramento. All were pretty quiet until I got to a police captain who asked if I would show any "professional courtesy." Looking up from the citation book, I just fixed his eyes with mine. "Well, if you were in my town I would not write you for such a simple thing," he lamely offered.

"Captain," I said, "if you or any other officer of the law catches me in any violation of the law, I expect to be issued a citation."

There was a long moment of awkward silence, and then he said, "Do what you have to do." I did!

It appeared that my shooters had gotten together to hunt on this particular land because of their friendship with the landowner and its high duck use. It was also apparent from their quiet talk around my vehicle as I wrote out the citations that they had figured the rain and wind would keep chaps like me cozy at home rather than on hand to ruin their little duck shoot. Two of them got testy about being apprehended for late shooting and denied everything. There was no way they were going to escape, so I let them squall to their heart's content. I had been only twenty-five yards away from them as they shot, illegally killing seven ducks in the process. In fact, I had been close enough at times to hear them talk about how they hoped *that damned game warden* was stuck in the mud somewhere else that evening or they would be in deep crap.

In those days, it was $25 to be apprehended for late shooting and an additional $2 per minute for each minute shot past legal shooting hours. My shooters that evening were looking at minimum bail of anywhere from $150 to over $200, so needless to say, I had some very tight jaws during that citation-writing session, especially when they were informed about what their legal "baggage" would amount to in court.

Just as I finished writing my second chap, I heard the soft *thump* of a distant shotgun to the north. Damn, I thought as I turned to echolocate my new shooter. How can that be, it now being so dark? There were no more follow-up shots, so turning to face my next shooter, I continued writing citations for the long-faced officers of the law.

About ten minutes later I heard the soft *thump-thump* of what appeared to be the same shooter to the north. Damn, I thought as I paused again. Looking north into the misting rain and utter darkness, I tried in my mind's eye to locate the general area of the shooting. As near as I could tell, my new shooter was just north and east of the Sacramento National Wildlife Refuge. This guy had to be a pro on an area he considered more than safe, I thought, especially in light of the lateness of the hour. He was probably tucked away on some private land, or maybe it was a farmer stepping out his door to take a shot or two at the aerial masses of hungry waterfowl, then retreating back into his house to avoid apprehension. Or perhaps it was someone shooting over a watered area, in which case he might be there for a while if the good shooting continued. I hoped the shooting would be good so I would shortly have the opportunity to stand in the late shooter's little "honey hole" as well. ...

The shooter standing next to me said, "That is the fellow you ought to be going after instead of us small fry."

Without missing a beat, I said, "Small fry grow up to be sharks, and what you did here tonight is not considered minor in nature. Late-shooting waterfowl, one hour and twenty-six minutes late in your particular case, is a pretty serious offense!"

He said no more, and I resumed writing at a faster pace. This shooter to the north was starting to get my attention, and the speed at which I wrote the remaining citations showed that concern. My new late-shooting antagonist continued a series of methodical, calculated shots as I wrote the last of my eight late shooters. By then everyone was grumbling because I was not "hot-footing" after the shooter to the north but had chosen to "bother" them instead.

Finishing the business at hand, and a good evening's business it was, with over $1,500 in fines for that bit of work, I watched the last of my late shooters drive out Road G, turn onto the highway, and drift out of sight as I continued tagging evidence birds and tossing them into the back of the truck for safekeeping.

Then I just sat there with undivided attention and waited for my late shooter to fire again. He didn't wait long, and I was soon rewarded with another *thump-thump*. That time I got a better fix on his location. With that, I hopped into my truck and started flying north toward the Sacramento National Wildlife Refuge, located just south of the city of Willows, California. Pulling into the darkened refuge headquarters, I drove through the building complexes, turning north past the equipment barns and machine sheds. Running on that access road without lights until I came to the northernmost boundary of the refuge, I parked and listened. Even with the traffic noise on the interstate, I was able to hear well enough to record the next set of shots. *Thump-thump-thump* went three shots in quick succession. No doubt about it, my shooter was still farther north and east of my position. Looking at my watch, I noted the number of shots and time in my notebook as eight-thirty-three P.M., or approximately three hours after legal shooting hours! Jumping into my vehicle, I peeled out, roared back through the refuge complex, hit the frontage road at the entrance to the refuge, and zipped north.

Turning right onto Highway 162 just below Willows, I steamed east, running without lights until the road made a sweeping S-jog. Finding a wide spot off the road near a car that was broken down (as I knew from a note on its windshield) I slid to a stop. Quickly getting out of my rig and walking about ten yards from it so the noises my engine made as it cooled down would not detract from the night's sounds, I quietly stood and listened in the lessening rain. Nothing, and more nothing, for about ten minutes. Then, *thump,* one shot from a location just south of me, maybe a mile away! *Hot dog,* I thought, the trail is still hot! I knew there was a duck club not far from where I now sat, and some ponds farther south and east of their clubhouse.

Figuring that was the location of my shooter, I headed south on the muddy road leading to the duck club. Running without lights of any kind (thank God for my excellent night vision), I sneaked down the road for about half a mile and stopped. Getting out, I again quietly stood a few yards from my rig and listened. Twenty minutes passed, and hearing nothing, I began to fear my lad had stopped shooting and was heading for home or a nearby duck club. I started to get back into my truck to continue south to the clubhouse when I heard *thump-thump* again just south of my position and a little to the east. Hot damn! I thought. This lad is staying with it, and so am I! I continued quietly driving south and in a few minutes arrived at the locked gate just north of the duck club.

Quickly getting out of my truck, I grabbed my flashlight and opened the case carrying my Starlight scope. This piece of equipment was used in Vietnam to turn night into a fuzzy lime-green day, and it sure was a boon to me when used in some way after dark late-shooting cases. What made the Starlight scope such a deadly instrument in the "war" against the late shooter was that it magnified available light by a factor of fifty thousand. Even just the available starlight in the heavens or the nearby city lights made it day on the ground when magnified by that factor—making me hell on wheels for the violator.

Turning on the instrument after removing the cover from the front lens, I could hear the soft, high-pitched whirring sounds as the oscillator warmed up. Taking a quick look, I could see the duck club a few hundred yards to the south and their hunting area beyond that. Not seeing anything out of the ordinary at the clubhouse, such as a hunter or a parked automobile, I took off on foot in the direction of the last shots. I hadn't gone thirty yards when I heard the familiar *thump* again off to the southeast. Within minutes the air was full of fleeing waterfowl, with the soft *shushing* of wings and fluting calls identifying them as the regal pintail. This is it, I thought. My shooter is on this club sure as God made little green apples! Picking it up a bit now that I had a pretty good location, I jogged all the way to the clubhouse before stopping. The building and outbuildings were totally dark and appeared to be deserted. Damn, I thought, not a soul or vehicle on the site! Where in the hell is this guy's transportation? The only car I remembered was the one I had parked alongside earlier just off Highway 162. Surely my shooter hadn't come from that car. It was over a mile away! If a fellow was going to late shoot ducks, surely he wouldn't park that far away and then walk all the way back, tired and loaded down with his booty. It just didn't make sense. My mind raced as I thought over the lands around the duck club. Had a local farmer stepped over onto this land and begun shooting off his neighbor's duck ponds? If that was the case, it made my catching the shooter a little more difficult because there would be much more space and many more hiding places to cover.

Trotting the fifty or so yards south of the clubhouse, I arrived on the edge of a flooded rice field, spooking some feeding mallards out of the corner of the field. Kneeling on the levee to minimize my silhouette, I flipped on the Starlight scope once again and examined the area to the east. There were four duck blinds about two hundred to four hundred yards away, but no sign of anyone in the area. I sat down in the wet grass on the dike and waited.

Overhead I could hear hundreds of sets of whistling wings along with the occasional beautiful fluting call of the pintail, harsh quacking of a hen mallard, peeping call of the green-winged teal, or three-note call of the wigeon. Out on the duck club's flooded rice fields, I could hear the happy croaking sounds of dozens of coots paddling around in their "salad bowl." It was great to be out there in the misting rain, diminishing wind, and black of the night, pitting myself against one of my own kind.

Thump! There it was, not two hundred yards away in the closest duck blind! I had even seen the skyward burst of flame from the end of the shotgun barrel through the Starlight scope. Even through the drizzling rain, I could see a figure emerging from the blind and splashing out into the shallow duck pond by the decoys. Stooping, he picked up what appeared to be the lifeless body of a duck and returned without fanfare to the blind. I quickly checked the luminous hands on the face of my watch and saw that my late shooter's most recent shot was at nine-twenty-seven P.M., or almost four hours after legal shooting time! Man, I thought, if I catch this lad, it will take him a week of hard labor to pay the legal tab for this little late-shooting adventure.

Moving in a half-crouch down the main levee toward my shooter, I stopped where the rice check walkway left the levee and led to the shooter's duck blind. Realizing that I might spook my shooter if I went any farther, I dropped my tail end into the rain-soaked earth. He was in such a location he could run in almost any direction and be swallowed up in the night before I could catch him, I grimly thought. With that thought, I held my ground. It just stood to reason that my shooter would leave via the rice check leading to my position on the levee road since he had no reason to avoid that direction. Or so I hoped. ...

The blind holding my late shooter was about sixty-five yards away. The soft, reflected illumination of the town of Willows gave just light enough for me to make out the shape of my shooter every time he left the blind to pick up his ducks. Sitting on the opposite side of the main levee, I cranked up the Starlight scope and began to really watch my shooter. He had a squatty body, shaped like a pear; wore a slouch hat; was using duck calls to lure the night-feeding ducks to the gun; and was shooting a pump shotgun from the telltale sound it made every time he indexed another round into the chamber. As close as I was and with the Starlight scope, I could identify just about every duck that came into shooting range or fell to his gun.

I had a master's degree in wildlife management and had taught waterfowl identification for several years in college as well as to my counterparts in the state Department of Fish and Game, so I considered myself pretty good at duck identification. It now became a serious pursuit as I tried to identify every duck that fell to the shooter's gun through the soft green light of the Starlight scope. Using the size of the birds flying into the reflective, water-lit decoys, their flight patterns, any calls emitted as they swung into the decoys, or their appearance when he picked them up (for example, white-breasted bodies for the pintail drakes), I began the work of documentation for my justice court in Williams in deadly earnest. I had a judge there who was a stickler for doing things right, but if you did your job in fine style, so did he, if you get my drift. ... *Thump-thump* went the shotgun as I sat there grimly recording every bird that fell. The reflected light from the town of Willows just to the north and the low-lying storm clouds made it easy for him to shoot over water this late at night. I could only marvel at this phenomenon of the lights, the greed it caused, and the gall of the shooter. That greed was soon going to come to an abrupt end, I promised myself.

I wanted to move out, apprehend my late shooter, and put a stop to the killing, but I refrained. It didn't take a rocket scientist to realize that once he became aware of my presence as I noisily slipped and slopped along the muddy rice check leading to his blind, he would be out of there like a shot. With a sixty-five-yard head start, it would be just moments before he was out of sight and gone into the real dark of the night and rice-check weeds. So I waited, hoping he would come my way and not go out the back side of the duck blind. Running after someone in the dark of night in a flooded rice field is always problematic (as my two destroyed knees will attest today). And carrying a flashlight, Starlight scope, handgun, and all the other needed gear really has a tendency to slow one down. In short, unless you are a young Jesse Owens, forget it! I patiently sat and counted through gritted teeth as my shooter continued to kill. Soon I had counted seventeen ducks that he had killed *since my arrival!* And I was able to identify every one of them except for a pair of teal that sped into his trap, falling together back to Mother Earth for the last time. Most likely green-winged teal, I surmised, mentally reviewing the life histories of the other two species of teal found in the area. Those were the rare blue-winged and northern cinnamon teal, both of which should have already migrated south by that time of the year. It was now ten-thirteen P.M., according to my watch, and still the shooter showed no intention of leaving. His excellent wing shooting was only occasional now, as if he didn't want to bring any attention to his late-shooting activity. Of course, unbeknownst to him, he already had. …

Finally my shooter stood up and looked carefully all around. He was getting ready to leave, I thought with a grin a mile wide across my wet, weathered face. The shooter disappeared into the blind and came out carrying what appeared to be several heavily loaded duck straps (leather straps with a number of loops used to slip over the heads of geese and ducks to aid in carrying them). Standing at the edge of his blind, he stared toward the levee, where I was lying down watching his every move through the Starlight scope. He didn't move for about ten minutes, and I began to worry that he had seen something that had made him suspicious. Then he began walking out the rice check right toward me! Just as I had hoped, I thought as my heart began picking up the pace. The lamb is heading to the lion for slaughter. … Making sure I had my flashlight close at hand, I continued to watch the man through the Starlight scope as he walked closer to where I lay. I could see that he was a rather rotund chap and didn't appear to be as tall as I had earlier figured. Good, I thought; he won't be a runner, and if he is, he'll make a wonderful tackling dummy. The shooter continued coming toward me struggling under the load of ducks he was carrying and loudly slipping in the mud on the rice check. He had to stop several times to readjust the duck straps slung over his shoulders and catch his breath before continuing to shuffle my way. Finally he was within twenty feet of me and in clear sight of my normal night vision. I quietly laid down the Starlight scope and turned it off. Then I made ready to spring or run. I had already decided I would confront him just as he hit the main levee, where I occupied the high ground. He would probably pause just before stepping up onto the roadway, and I could be on him in a heartbeat. Speaking of heartbeats, mine was going a hundred miles per minute as I awaited my meeting with what appeared to be a very experienced and dedicated night-wing-shooting duck poacher.

Then it was time! Standing up, I said, "Good evening" as my five-cell flashlight beam struck my late shooter right in the eyes.

"*Ho-ho,*" my startled shooter exclaimed—and then he blew up! He threw the duck straps loaded with ducks right at me, wrapping them expertly around my head, turned, and started to flee across the flooded rice field. Surprised by his tactic, I ploughed through the mass of ducks and leaped off the levee in hot pursuit. Hitting the flooded rice field in a flurry of flying water and pumping legs, I bellowed, "State Fish and Game warden!" My hollering only built a fire under my fleeing suspect, who now *really* churned through the water like a man with a cause. I was amazed at my own speed and hadn't taken more than six or seven steps before I bore-sighted my fleeing "pitcher's mound." Hitting my stride and bracing for a collision that would be heard in the heavens, I placed a flying tackle square in the middle of his back with a sureness and velocity that came from six years of high school and college football as a defensive lineman. Suffice to say, when I hit the man with my three-hundred-pound flying form, there was a tremendous impact!

"*Aughhhh ...Holy Mary, Mother of God!*" my shooter bellowed as we collided, followed by an agonized grunt as the two of us hit six inches of water and mud in the rice field with a tremendous *ker-plush!* Quickly rolling off my chap, I grabbed him by the nape of the neck, held him down with one hand, and jerked the shotgun away from him with the other. "Don't shoot ... don't hit me; I surrender," came an emotion-filled human voice. In case he still didn't know who had grabbed him, I again told him to freeze, that I was a Fish and Game warden, and that he was under arrest for late-shooting waterfowl. He just mumbled something as he tried to get over his fright and shock at being hit with a flying tackle at ten-forty in the evening in a flooded rice field where just moments before he had happily been putting a "tackle" on the ducks in the form of number 4 lead shot!

Grabbing my still glowing flashlight out of the water, I shone it on the man thrashing about in the shallow water and about fell over. I had seen this chap before! My late shooter was none other than a popular Roman Catholic priest from a nearby town! Holy Mary, Mother of God, was right as I looked heavenward to see if a lightning bolt was coming my way. ...

"Mr. Game Warden, can I get out of this rice field and stand up on the levee? I think you broke something when you hit me. Besides, there is something to be said for not drowning in six inches of water in a rice field."

"Sure," I said as I assisted the roly-poly priest up onto the high ground of the levee. My bride was a staunch Catholic, and as I stood there looking over my catch of the day, I thought, there is no way, Terry, that you are going to haul this lad off to the bucket—especially if you want any more homemade pies or bread from that woman. It was looking as if I had better just cite this lad and gently let him go back to his flock (no pun intended). The priest leaned over and groaned. "Father," I said, "if you hadn't run from me, you wouldn't be feeling the way you do right now. You gave me little choice but to stop you with a flying tackle."

"I know," he said, "but what else is a man of the cloth to do when he has sinned in the eyes of God and the local game warden—and *one of them is only ten feet away?*"

"Somehow, Father," I said, "running away on the planet that God created is not a move that guarantees an escape, if you get my drift."

"It was dumb, and I deserve what I got, but who did you play football for? I don't think I have been hit that hard in my entire life, and by tomorrow I will be reminded of it every time I move saying mass."

"Sorry, Father; just doing my job." I grinned and began to relax. Another low groan was his only reply.

I requested his driver's and hunting licenses. With those and his shotgun, I picked up the duck straps full of ducks and, having my hands full, asked him to carry the Starlight scope and flashlight. He agreed, and once the scope was in his hands, he asked what it was that he was carrying. I explained the device and how it worked, and we walked in silence for the next thirty yards. "You know," he said after a moment, "I think God must have sent this Starlight scope to you for a very special reason." Figuring where he was going, I just let him talk. "Somehow I think this is a sign from God that I am to refrain from my much-loved but highly illegal late-hunting activities. Oh, but that is going to be so hard, since I love duck dinners so much!"

"Father, I'll tell you what. You stay out of my rice fields late at night, and I will see to it that you never want for a duck dinner again."

"You've got a deal," he said, "and I give you God's word on that. One collision like I just experienced is enough to last me for a lifetime. I am afraid if I continue and we chance to meet like this ever again, I might just get busted in half!"

As it turned out, for the next two years I did in fact keep him supplied with ducks and, true to his and God's word, never saw him in the fields late at night again, though I occasionally checked him hunting during the day on a farm belonging to one of his flock. At the end of those two years he was transferred to another parish, and I never saw him again. Somehow I have the feeling that if he is still alive, the ducks in his new parish are taking a pounding when the sun goes down and the wind and rain come up. ...

We walked in silence back to my vehicle by the locked gate, where I issued him a citation for taking migratory waterfowl exactly five hours after legal shooting hours had ended. He had twenty-six ducks on his duck strap, which put him eighteen over the limit, earning him another citation for that infraction of the Fish and Game laws.

"Just out of curiosity, Father, how are you going to pay this, being a man of the cloth and all?" I asked.

"How much is it going to be?" he asked.

"Well, I doubt any judge in the county is going to put you in jail, being a priest and all, so I would plan on it going all the way up to possibly one thousand dollars total for the offenses of late shooting and taking an over-limit."

"*Holy Mary, Mother of God!*" he exclaimed. There was a long moment of silence, and then he said, "Well, there goes my Christmas trip to Ireland."

"Sorry, Father," I said, "but that is the freight for such a pair of pretty serious violations."

Finishing the paperwork on the hood of my vehicle, I asked the good father where his car was parked. "Up on the highway," he said, pointing to the north. I just shook my head. You talk about violation-savvy. Knowing he was going to violate the law, he had parked a good distance from the illegal event so no one would be the wiser if he had to run. He may have had a good heart, but there was a small piece of it in which the devil dwelled.

"Hop in," I told him, "and I will take you to your car."

He got into my truck, with a fair amount of groaning owing to recently acquired soreness after having foolishly played "football" in the rice field that evening, and I returned him to his vehicle parked on Highway 162. As it turned out, the car with the note on the windshield faking a breakdown belonged to the church. Only then did I really appreciate how far the good father had gone to carry out his illegal sport. To confirm my suspicions and maybe drive home some embarrassment, I asked why he had parked so far away from where he was hunting. With a somewhat shame-faced look, he said it was so the game wardens wouldn't know where to look for him if he got carried away and late-shot the ducks. I just grinned, hoping he had learned the lesson that God was many people's copilot, not just his own. ...

Watching his taillights disappear as he headed home, I just shook my head. It takes all kinds, from priests to policemen, to make this business what it is, I mused. With that in mind, I wondered whether I would ever be able to make a difference and get some of this wildlife crime squared away. In light of my previous captures, I thought I stood a chance! Looking skyward, I thanked the Old Boy upstairs for my many blessings and for the successes of the evening. I think there was also a request for a pardon for citing His man of the cloth as well.

Since that time, I have run across the paths of many men of the cloth and even crossed swords with a few. But I survived to retire thirty-two years later. So I must not have offended Him too greatly by capturing some of His men when they strayed across the line He had drawn in the sand — or was it in the mud of a rice field. ...

six

Perils of the Black Brant

A THICK MIST rolled in from the Pacific Ocean, dampening my clothes and coating my face with water and salt. Continuing to look westward through squinted eyes, I was rewarded by the inky black found just before dawn, shadowed by the muted roar of the surf. Turning, I could see daylight racing across the heavens to the east like a horseman out of hell charging into the dark stubbornly holding on in the west. It won't be long now, I thought, turning back toward the ocean and hunching my shoulders as I pulled my head and neck further into the warm recesses of my hunting coat. Behind me, hunters' vehicles noisily clanked down the sandy, potholed road on South Spit like giant mechanical sand crabs. All were scurrying for that favorite place among the driftwood to await the overflight of the Pacific black brant from their ocean domain into South Humboldt Bay. Huddling further into the protection my driftwood pile offered against the offshore breeze and accompanying moisture, I patiently waited for the start of that morning's hunting season.

The brant is a pelagic species of goose, not much larger than a mallard duck. It is considered a true sea goose because of glands fixed on top of the head near the nostrils that allow it to convert ingested saltwater into freshwater. This system allows for long periods of survival on salt- or brackish water without having to come ashore for freshwater. The brant is lawfully hunted by waterfowl sportsmen in Mexico and North America and is highly prized for its meat, not to mention the gunning sport it offers because of its fast, erratic flight. The brant's principal food source along the Pacific Coast is eelgrass, a marine plant high in nutritional value. It is found in the shallow bays and estuaries of Mexico, California, Oregon, Washington, and British

Columbia—where the eelgrass has not been extirpated by pollution, mechanical oyster-harvesting operations, siltation from adverse logging practices, or other deleterious human activities. That staple fuels the brant in their exhausting 1,500-plus-mile migration from their wintering grounds in Baja California to the breeding grounds along the arctic coasts of Siberia, Alaska, and northwestern Canada. The Humboldt Bay complex in northwestern California was full of eelgrass in the early days; hence the visitation of brant on their way north to propagate their species.

Therein lay the problem: a migratory bird with an excellent reputation as table fare making its way north, the hunting season, and the "fat in the fire" known as humankind—the ultimate scavenger. One who quietly waited as the brant moved from its ocean sanctuary across the sandy spit and into Humboldt Bay to find that food necessary for egg development and enhancement of the body's energy reserves. No matter how you cut it, it was a veritable catch-22. In order to survive and continue their migration to the Arctic, they had to fly to their food source over a gauntlet of guns on the beach separating ocean from bay. The pursuit would be continued by other groups of hunters from scull boats and stilt blinds once the birds were safely in the bay. In short, in order to live, they had to chance dying on a daily basis.

My wandering mind finally rested on the reason for my presence on the sandy spit adjacent to South Humboldt Bay that breezy, fog-dampened morning in February. I was a game management agent with the U.S. Fish and Wildlife Service, which in those days was one of the nation's premier land management and regulatory agencies. Sadly, that is not the case today. The agency is rife with politics from top to bottom and continues to be a dumping ground for political hacks. True, there are many thousands of fine professionals within that agency who are highly educated, skilled, and dedicated to their professions. However, it is tough to practice what one has been trained for when political forces constantly dictate, mandate, or "muddy" management initiative. Add questionable leadership from folks such as James Watt, Bruce Babbitt, or Gail Norton, or micromanagement intervention by certain members of Congress, and no wonder many issues that could be handled through sound management practices end up going to hell in a handbasket.

My assigned district ran from Monterey, California, eastward to an imaginary point in the central portion of the state, and from there northward to the Oregon line. Everything north and west of those lines was my area of responsibility regarding federal wildlife law enforcement. Suffice to say, it would have been a monstrous workload for any ten officers, much less one. Welcome to a division within an agency that is historically grossly underfunded due to shortsighted management practices at the highest levels (in twenty-eight years of service I saw *three* budgets that were sufficient for my officers or me to do our jobs).

All other waterfowl seasons in the state closed by the middle of January in those days. Hence my presence around Humboldt Bay for the final two weeks of the brant hunting season, which ended in the middle of February. The last two weeks of brant season were usually the best because that was when the birds appeared in numbers worth hunting. Its timing also made it practical for me to put in a lengthy appearance. During the duck season, it was all I could manage working the waterfowl hunter from October through the middle of January in the areas of San Francisco Bay, Sacramento, and the San Joaquin Valley. With that magnitude of work, there was no way I could justify working the brant hunters some four and a half hours' drive to the northwest. However, once my main valley waterfowl season ended, I was able to shift my law enforcement efforts northward as the brant begin arriving in Humboldt Bay.

The brant needed someone from the federal side to help them through the hunting season. My state counterparts in the area were up to their armpits in deer and elk poaching, illegal streambed alterations by loggers, illegal commercial fishing, pollution from pulp mills, and everything in between. That meant they usually lacked the manpower to work the brant hunting scene for long. Being young and full of "piss and vinegar," I figured I was just the chap to provide some relief to my state counterparts by intervening in the local outlaws' fun, making their gambling with Mother Nature and the law of the land a little more interesting.

Fingers of daylight reaching seaward over the coast range of mountains finally won the battle with the dark of the morning. I could now see the soft swells of the dark gray Pacific breaking on the beach. Several vehicles carrying late arrivals scurried down the road to places where they could park and offload their hopeful occupants—hopeful that from the cover of driftwood along the beach they would be able to bring down unwary brant winging their way to breakfast in Humboldt Bay. Like a multitude of others over the past days, many would find that this trip would become a date with their Maker rather than the expected breakfast in a bed of eelgrass.

From the cover of my driftwood blind, I raised my binoculars and, with a quick sweep to avoid discovery, scanned the likely-looking driftwood piles north and south of my location. In that sweep, I spotted nine bunches of hunters. All were looking westward in vain attempts to spot the brant leaving their ocean haven. Glancing at my watch, I saw it would be another ten minutes before the tide changed. Thinking back to the times I had hunted brant during my college days in the Humboldt area and remembering my work as a state game warden stationed in Eureka, I knew it would be at least another forty minutes before the birds sensed the tidal change and reacted.

The brant generally feed at changing and low tides. They are not good divers and have to wait for the eelgrass to be somewhat exposed before they can feed. Hence, they wait until the tide change so they can feed on dislodged, floating eelgrass or, at low tide, feed on the exposed beds spread across the mud flats. Historically there had been great beds of eelgrass in North Humboldt Bay as well, but siltation from the redwood logging industry, pollution from the lumber mills, and mud-flat disturbance by the Coast Oyster Company's mechanical harvesting operations had all but wiped them out.

Squinting my eyes once more against the mist borne by the freshening offshore breezes, I joined my fellow "hunters" in a search for the telltale wave-hopping black skeins of brant coming for what the bay could offer that day, be it life or death. As if they had watches, the first of many skeins became visible just thirty-three minutes after the tidal change. I had to marvel at Mother Nature and her ability to read the world's subtle changes. Aware of humankind's inability to appreciate natural history, much less learn from it, I quietly thanked God for not letting humans have the same life-reading abilities as wildlife. Just imagine the carnage if man possessed the natural instincts of wildlife, and used them. …

I trailed the first bunch of twelve brant as they skimmed the ocean's swells, looking as if they might pass within gun range. Turning, they approached the spit in a ragged, fast-moving line, climbing as if they recognized the dangers among the piles of driftwood below. Passing undisturbed, they sailed rapidly into the bay. Good, I thought; that bunch is safe from the beach gunners. Several more bunches of brant now winging their way bayward mirrored those that had crossed first by climbing to altitude to pass over the spit before lowering into the bay. By this time several hunters were running from one driftwood pile to another in an attempt to find an area under the points where the last flocks of brant had flown. They knew other brant still at sea had watched the first ones and would more than likely pass over the same areas, figuring they were safe routes into the bay.

By now the ocean's airways were dotted with small skeins of birds moving landward, and I no longer had the luxury of watching one flock at a time. Turning my observations from the multitudes of birds lifting off the ocean to the shooters littered up and down the beach, I began the business of putting those in the business of extinction out of business. I noticed that at the moment my own "hunt" began in earnest, I started to shake as if deeply chilled. However, that was not the case, as I was very warmly dressed!

A flock of seven brant passed over a pile of driftwood about one hundred yards south of my position. Good, I thought. I had not seen anyone there earlier, and those low-flying brant should be safe. *Damn!* As I watched, *all seven dropped* before I heard the sounds of shots muffled by the crashing surf. Heads popped up over the driftwood pile, followed by the running forms of two humans picking up the dead and wringing the necks of the cripples. I had counted only six shots, but seven birds had fallen, which was not unusual for the easily killed brant. I had not observed these fellows earlier, but more importantly, *I had now!* The bag limit was three brant per person per day, possession limit three. With the downing of seven brant, they had exceeded the daily bag limit by one. Additionally, they had not shown any penchant to leave, instead exhibiting every intention of continuing the hunt by the way they dove back into their driftwood cover to await the next bunch of hapless flyers. Little did they realize that I was also "hunting"—and I didn't have a bag or possession limit!

By now I could hear the staccato sound of shots up and down the beach as the brant tried crossing in numerous places. They came with the determination of the B-17s over Germany's cities during World War II. Some made it, and others carrying shot flew crippled over the spit into the bay to an uncertain future—to be shot later on the water unable to fly, necks wrung once caught by boatmen, or eaten alive by harbor seals. Either way, their migration was over. Then there were those that died immediately as they passed over the popping shotguns below. As they fell, humans scurried forth to claim their prize. In some cases, there were even fistfights between two eager "sportsmen" after both had shot at and figured they had killed the same bird. The prize in such encounters was usually a black brant, a black eye, and a bruised ego.

The hunting was legal, but in a tragic sort of way. These birds were heading for the breeding grounds, and many, having gone through a lengthy courtship process, were already paired. In fact, the females were probably already in the early stages of egg development. Breaking up a pair bond through the death or crippling that came from hunting meant that if another mate was available, courtship would have to occur all over again by the survivor during the last leg of the migration to the breeding grounds. For birds that normally mate for life, that process of initiating a new courtship uses up precious energy reserves, making it difficult to arrive on the breeding grounds in top physical condition, much less in shape for egg laying and successfully raising a brood. Normally the brant start to lay their eggs *within three days* after they reach the arctic nesting areas. That speed is in large part because the arctic is a harsh land with limited summer days, not to mention a pile of predators all walking around with an empty gut after six months of winter. The birds have to get in and get out before the onset of winter if they expect to live. The brant has it down to a science—a "crash" science, but a science nevertheless. Hence, the loss of a mate in such a limited population winging northward to the breeding grounds is a small reproduction disaster.

The major impact on that life pattern was the politics of setting hunting seasons and bag limits. Hunter opportunity rather than good biology was the thinking that dictated seasons and bag limits for many species, and to my way of thinking, this one in particular. The politics of hunter opportunity, even though the brant in Humboldt Bay had declined from fifty thousand or more in the early 1960s to less than half that number in the early and middle 1970s, continued to rule management of the species. During times of low bird populations, states furthering hunting regulations allowing the take of such reduced migratory species, and the Service allowing instead of curtailing such practices, illustrated how both entities abrogated their management responsibilities under the Migratory Bird Treaty Act. Allowing hunting seasons on such restricted populations is simply turning a blind eye to the survival of a species. Most states in the nation, including especially Alaska, California, Texas, Louisiana, Maryland, and Illinois, have rushed to the trough of death in misguided attempts to please their sportsmen and fill their state coffers with "pieces of silver." Truth be known, most sportsmen would support actions to preserve a species or manage it wisely *at the sportsmen's expense.* Sportsmen for the most part are not out to eradicate a species but just to utilize the harvestable surplus, as determined through good wildlife management practices. If anyone reading these lines has trouble swallowing that statement, take a look at the seasons and bag limits on our mergansers and sea ducks. They are some of the least studied waterfowl in the world! Yet year after year the state governments recommend—and the Service blindly follows—the setting of seasons and bag limits based on very little if any credible biology or actual life history information. It is amazing what a few more dollars coming into state or federal coffers, or the "biting-sow" approach of a state or federal politician, can do to a wildlife manager and his agency when it comes to the deadly politics of *hunter opportunity.*

Shaking my head sadly, I cleared my mind of that jungle and got back to the business at hand. Several groups of hunters had already gained my attention. The two who had killed seven brant earlier had successfully positioned themselves under two additional flocks of brant, killing eight more. I duly recorded all of their activity in my field notebook in case they contested their over-limits during a trial. Those shooters were nine over their daily bag and possession limit, and from the way they shot, they were not novices at the brant-killing game. They would wait until the last moment, making sure the brant were in range directly overhead, and when they rose to shoot, one would take the left side of the flock and the other the right. That way they never doubled on the same bird, and they killed the maximum during every shooting opportunity. It was apparent to me that these fellows would kill until the opportunity to do so was removed.

Little did they know that "opportunity" was soon coming in the form of a badge-carrying chap! I figured I would sacrifice a few more brant to let these outlaws *really* hang themselves; maybe the court, because of these shooters' game-hog attitude, would remove them from the hunting scene with a stiff sentence and a hunting license revocation. Then perhaps the information about the presence of the "long arm of the law" would filter out to the rest of their outlaw brethren, making them more wary of violating the hunting regulations. By not tipping my hand right away, I would also be able to grab a few other strays feeding over the fence before my presence became common knowledge.

Another group of hunters to the north had successfully positioned themselves under several flocks of twenty or more brant as they passed over the spit. I did not have an accurate count on the numbers those three outlaws had taken because I had been looking the other way on several occasions when they shot. However, they had killed so many that they were beginning to run birds to their pickup and, from what I could see with my binoculars through a crack in my driftwood pile, stash them behind the front seat. They didn't seem to have any care for what the limit was—and for offenders like that, neither did I!

Last but not least, I had a lone hunter who had stood up and shot at a large flock of low-flying brant. The birds, seeing the shooter below, typically bunched up into a small, living ball and frantically climbed upward. The sport fired one shot into the center of that "ball," and *six birds* dropped! He stood transfixed for a moment, then frantically looked up and down the beach to see if anyone had witnessed the deed. Seeing no adverse reaction from his fellow sportsmen, he scurried around picking up his still flopping booty. It was obvious that he was a novice because a knowing sportsman would have shot at the edge of such a flock or tried to pick out singles precisely to avoid the problem my shooter had just experienced. I could partially forgive him for the error he had committed in shooting into bunched-up birds if he was smart enough to quit hunting right then and there. If he did that, and took only his limit, I would leave him with a damn good hind-end chewing and minimum fine citation. However, my shooter chose to follow the way of the wayward. He returned with the six birds to his blind, buried four in the sand to avoid discovery, and continued to hunt, thereby earning an opportunity to learn a legal lesson he would not soon forget.

Two hours into the morning, I realizing from the reduced numbers of birds leaving the ocean that the morning flight was just about over. I was now going to have to expose the nature of my business in such a way that I would "net" all the offenders, even though they were scattered up and down the spit. I figured I would start with those who appeared most likely to leave first and save the diehards for last. There was always the risk that if I got greedy, several of the bad guys would escape. However, I was close to the worst, so even if any tried to escape, a short foot race should preclude the possibility of unsuccessful captures. In those days, unlike today, for a big man, I could pack the mail like the Pony Express. ... Forming a large grin on my salt-encrusted face, I thought, those of you who stepped over the line in the sand this morning will soon have the opportunity to meet one of only 178 game management agents in the nation. And the *only* one currently working in all of northern California. How is that for the luck of the Irish when one breaks the wildlife laws?

My three shooters who had shot an over-limit (or so I suspected) and hidden them behind the seat of their pickup were showing signs of departure. Drifting their way with my shotgun under arm, as a hunter will do when looking for a better shooting location, I positioned myself where I could intercept those fellows without alerting everyone else on the beach. When they walked by the pile of driftwood where I had concealed myself, carrying more birds to hide, I hissed to get their attention. Turning, they saw me sitting on a redwood log, holding up a badge and gesturing for them to come meet me in person. The look of lost souls skidded across their faces, but they complied. Gesturing for them to sit at my feet so no one else would see what was going on behind the pile of driftwood, I formally identified myself. I waited a few moments for the effect of the gold badge and the size of the holder to manifest itself like their worst nightmares and then said, "Gentlemen, I have been here since before daylight. During that period of time, I had the opportunity to watch a number of hunters up and down this beach for violations of the law. Some of the folks I have been watching were you folks. And that watching included seeing you running extra birds to the vehicle and hiding them behind the front seat." Pausing, I let those words sink in and enjoyed watching their faces register panic. The smallest of the bunch started to deny my accusation, but I cut him short with a wave of my hand. "Sir," I said, "don't embarrass yourself or make me drag you and your buddies through the sand over to your vehicle and verify what I just said. Why don't you just quietly go over to the vehicle, remove the critters from behind the seat, and without making a big show of it add them to the pile of birds in front of us. All the birds, mind you, because if I find any more stashed in your truck after you come back, I will be forced to book all of you in the nearest federally approved facility and seize your vehicle as evidence."

There was a pause, and then the oldest-looking man, realizing he was sitting not in sand but in something brown, viscous, and smelly, turned to his friend and said, "Do as he says, Brad." Brad, realizing he was sitting in the same medium, rose, walked over to their vehicle, and retrieved two large bunches of brant. Coming back from the vehicle to our pile of driftwood, he laid them at my feet. "Is that all?" I asked coldly. Brad nodded, and after looking closely into his eyes for a moment for effect I began to count the broken bodies. My three shooters had taken eighteen birds, or nine over the limit. Without further discussion, I seized all the birds as evidence (not knowing the order of kill, the courts required all the evidence in order to show an over-limit), filled out the pink slips (information forms to be used in filing charges at a later date), and gave them a mild tail-end chewing for being a little loose with their trigger fingers. Then I thanked them for being cooperative and sent them on their way. As they proceeded to their truck, I called out, "Remember, gentlemen, don't stop to tell anyone I am here or you will personally get to know the magistrate in Sacramento." They nodded and left posthaste. I watched them drive off the spit and head for home. They heeded my caution and did not stop along the way to inform any other hunters that the law was "in town." With a quick look around to assure that my previous actions had gone unnoticed, I buried the evidence birds in the sand. Then, for effect in case someone was eyeballing the situation, I stood up, acting as if I had just finished going to the bathroom behind the driftwood. No one was looking at me, so I continued the business at hand.

Turning north, I saw my lone shooter moving to his car carrying three birds and no shotgun. After looking around to make sure the coast was clear, he placed the three brant in the trunk of his car. He took another quick look up and down the beach to make sure no one had seen his actions, then returned to his blind on the beach and disappeared from sight. Sensing my opportunity, I casually walked to his vehicle, using driftwood piles as cover, to cut him off from any foolish escape attempt. Once in position, I turned and walked directly out to his driftwood pile with shotgun in hand like any other hunter. He stood up in surprise as I walked up to him and verbally identified myself. His eyes dropped to my badge, which I was holding at hip level to avoid letting others in the area discover who I was, and in that instant of recognition, he just about dropped his hind end right into the bottom of his pants! Stepping into his blind to look like "one of the boys," I cautioned him to constrain his actions and not let the cat out of the bag about a conservation officer being so close to the rest of the brethren. I asked how many birds he had killed, and he stuttered, "Three."

Sitting down on the sandy floor of the driftwood blind, I said, "Son, there is no need to lie to me. I saw you shoot six with one shot."

From the look on his face, I thought he was going to vomit. He just looked at me like one would look after emptying his six shooter at John Wesly Hardin and not seeing him fall. Digging in the sand at his feet and uncovering the bodies of several brant, I looked up at my latest customer. Under that revelation and a cold stare, he broke like an egg. "Mister, I really didn't mean to kill six with one shot, but it just happened. Please don't write me a ticket. I am a senior wildlife student at Humboldt [the excellent state wildlife college in nearby Arcata], and if you do, I will never be able to get a job in the field of wildlife management."

Having graduated from the same college, I knew exactly what he was talking about. Getting a job was tough enough in the wildlife field. Getting one with a knowing wildlife violation hanging from your carcass, especially one dealing with an illegal take or possession, was tougher, if not impossible. I said, "If you had stopped hunting after your screwup, you might have escaped a real hammering from justice. However, you continued to hunt, and you of all people should realize these brant populations aren't inexhaustible. I suspect you took your waterfowl management instruction from Dr. Stan Harris, and if you did, he more than made you aware of the brant's plight. That is one sharp 'quack doctor,' and he never lets any of his students out of that class without one of the best waterfowl educations going in the U.S. today. And that outstanding dose of instruction includes instilling a healthy respect for the critters."

The kid looked at me as if I had just read copy from the deepest recesses of his soul. It was pretty obvious that he had slept through the part of Dr. Harris's lecture that concerned the brant. Without any further discussion, I stood up and told him to finish digging up the brant and meet me at his car. I strode out of the blind carrying his shotgun and three brant like I was his hunting partner helping him pack up. Glancing at my two shooters to the south who had taken the large over-limit of brant earlier, I satisfied myself that they were holding tight for the moment and took my cite book from my hunting jacket. Using the wildlife student's open car door as a shield, I sat down in his front seat and commenced to write out the information for later issuance of a citation. That way I could record the information in privacy and still watch my two remaining suspicious shooters through the front windshield. When the college shooter arrived with the remaining three brant, I took the physical information from his driver's license for the citation and gave him a seizure tag for his birds. I could see that he was almost physically ill. I guess he figured his career, for all intents and purposes, was gone. Since he hadn't taken any more birds then those first killed and only followed his instincts in trying to get all the birds back to the car, I figured I would give him a break. After all, he wasn't a bad outlaw, just a stupid one. Taking a business card from my wallet, I handed it to him.

"Son," I said, "if you ever need a reference regarding what happened today for an individual interviewing you for a position, have that person call me. I will try to square it with that interviewer. What got you hung on this one was you made a mistake and then compounded that mistake by continuing to hunt after you exceeded the daily bag limit. I would suggest a little more care in the world of wildlife in all future endeavors."

Taking the card like it was a frail lifeline to his future, he mumbled a scared, "Thank you," and then loaded his empty shotgun and wet hunting gear into the car. I sent him on his way with an admonition not to alert any other hunters to my presence. I don't think that poor kid stopped until he got to a toilet where he could clean out his shorts. (I learned later that that college fellow went on to become a high school teacher in life sciences.)

Sitting down on a half-buried redwood log next to where his car had been parked, I lit up a cigar like any other good Italian in that part of the country and casually dug a hole in the sand with my feet. I nonchalantly slid my latest seizures into the hole and covered them. With them safely out of sight, I was ready to ruin someone else's Christmas.

Readjusting my wet tail end on the redwood log, I turned so I could see the last two shooters, who now had my undivided attention. They were still in their driftwood blind looking as if they were going to stay a while. Getting up, I casually walked over to a pile of driftwood close enough to intercept them if they tried to leave the beach. Digging in like any other hunter, I continued my surveillance.

For the first time that morning, I became aware of the intense shooting taking place in South Humboldt Bay. Having spent a lot of years in the area, I realized the scull boaters and stilt-blind hunters must be having a heyday killing brant if the frequency of their shooting was any key.

A scull boat is a small, shallow-draft, narrow-beamed, camouflaged boat that rides mostly beneath the water's surface. They were originally made out of strips of cedar, but many today are composed of fiberglass or some sort of composite fibers. Because they ride very low in the water, they present a small, narrow silhouette to an unwary duck, brant, or goose. Depending on the scull boat's size, one or two hunters lie on their backs in the bottom and, with the sternmost hunter using a single sculling oar, scull with a lateral movement back and forth into resting or loafing waterfowl. There is a small eyehole on a raised portion of the gunwale of the boat for the sculler to look through, so the resting waterfowl see only the partially submerged bow coming their way. I have seen ducks that were previously resting on the water swim over to the scull boat as it approached, lift themselves out of the water onto the bow of the boat, and preen as it slowly moved toward its unsuspecting kinfolk. Once in shotgun range, the sculler rises to a sitting position and collects the fruits of his labors with a few well-placed shots. It's a very successful way of hunting, especially in waters where waterfowl have seen little of such a device. They are deadly in the right hands—legal but deadly. That day it sounded as if the scull boaters were killing brant in the bay like there was no tomorrow. For many of the four or five hundred brant I had seen flying over the spit and into the bay that morning, there wasn't.

The stilt blind, on the other hand, is a wooden waterfowl blind built up on heavy wooden stilts over shallow bay waters. The stilts position the shooting platform high enough to allow the shooters to remain high and dry during tidal fluctuations. At that time there were approximately six stilt blinds in South Humboldt Bay built on public land (the state of California owned some land under South Bay) and maybe another ten built on private lands. Hunters building a stilt blind would wait until a low tide came along in the summer months, find an eelgrass-covered mud flat next to a channel, and haul out sacks of concrete and other supplies in a boat to pour footings for the blind. Over a period of several low tides, stilts would be positioned and fastened over these concrete footings. Then a platform floor would be built onto the stilts and four low walls erected. Sometimes I would see wooden stilts driven deeply into the mud of the bay by a pile driver, with the platform built on this configuration. Either way, you eventually had a wooden box built on four to eight stout wooden stilts, sitting four to six feet above the high-tide mark in the bay. Boats from shore would take the hunters to the stilt blinds, and once everyone was inside, one of the group would use the boat to set out hundreds of floating, anchored decoys. Then the boat operator would either move some distance away and anchor, tie the boat under the blind and join his buddies, or go back to land and watch as his companions hunted waterfowl from this unique hunting contraption. Cut into the sides of the walls of the blind were slots so crouching gunners could remain unseen yet observe birds moving into their decoy area and shotgun range. The birds would not see danger until the shooters stood and began firing over the walls of the blind as they landed in and around the strings of decoys. In South Humboldt Bay, the stilt blinds were used primarily for the taking of brant, which were notorious for coming into decoys, sometimes inexplicably several times in a row after being shot at over the same set just moments before. I have observed such redecoying occurring several times until every bird in the flock was killed. Brant are a very gregarious animal, and to be without their flying partners is tantamount to disaster in their world.

The stilt-blind occupants that pursued this level of the sport, like scull boaters, had to be watched very carefully. They seemingly had a very hard time when it came to counting what they had killed, especially if it was the fragile, almost helpless black brant. As in any walk of life, there are the good, the bad, and the ugly. Killing of brant by scull boaters and those in stilt blinds could get ugly very quickly if the shooters had the right conditions and the wrong intentions. This combination often occurred in South Humboldt Bay. Based on the frequency of shooting that morning, I made a mental note that I should get into South Humboldt Bay with my canoe to see if I could put a crimp in the style of the folks in the scull boats and stilt blinds.

Bringing my thoughts back from the South Bay crowd to the South Spit, I saw my two shooters starting to move their belongings from the driftwood blind to their rusted-out hunting vehicle. I started walking slowly their way like a hunter seeking the right place to be under the next flock of brant. As I got closer, I heard one of the shooters say, "Oh, crap!" Looking closely at the man for the first time, I recognized him as one I had cited for a commercial fishing violation when I had been a Fish and Game warden in Eureka years earlier. Knowing the jig was up, I picked up my pace and strode straight to their blind without further ado. There was much frantic digging going on as I approached, and I arrived just in time to see the last brant from an over-limit go into a deep, sandy hole.

"Morning, Roger, still breaking the law I see."

"Screw you, asshole," was his quick, heartfelt greeting.

"I love you too," was my smart-assed reply as I walked over to the spot in the blind where the brant were stashed. "You want me to dig them up, or do you want to do the honors?" I asked. Met with silence from both men, I knelt in the sand and commenced to dig up nine brant, all the while keeping a careful eye on my violators. Including the six birds they had kept by their feet, that would put them nine over collectively, or looking at $500 each in a federal court of law, I computed. Couldn't happen to two nicer fellows, I thought as I identified myself with my badge and asked for their driver's and hunting licenses. Roger stared hard at me as if contemplating throwing a punch, and I said, "Don't even think it, Roger; it will get you five years' jail time."

Roger's partner, another commercial fisherman I recognized, said, "Back off, Roger. This bastard's big enough to eat hay and pull our fishing boat up into any dry dock of his choosing." Even though the moment was pretty damn dicey because of Roger's reputation as a hothead and street fighter, I had to chuckle inside at his partner's words.

Roger hung tough for a few more surly seconds with his ugly, "I would love to kick your butt" stare before he thought better of it and did as I had asked. It didn't take long to record the deed, and with the seizure of the brant, we went our separate ways. On the way out, I noticed Roger stopping his pickup and telling other hunters of my presence on the beach, even going so far as to walk out to their blinds and point me out. That's OK, Roger, I thought; that little move will cost you dearly. In fact, it cost Roger a mandatory appearance in Sacramento and loss of his hunting privileges for one year once the federal magistrate heard my story of his violation and Paul Revere–like attitude. Normally the violator would have been allowed to simply forfeit bail through the mails. However, in this instance my boss, Jack Downs, thought it would be best for all concerned if Roger got to drive the several hundred miles from Eureka to Sacramento to tell the magistrate personally about his decision to point me out on the beach.

Walking back to my pickup with their seized birds, I had time to muse over the incident that had led me to catch Roger the first time in a commercial fishing violation. But before I got far into my memory of Roger and his several boxes of illegal short crabs, the constant rolling thunder of guns in South Bay brought me back to the moment. I thought, Damn, I had better get over to the east side of the bay and launch my Grumman Sport Boat (like a small freighter canoe with excellent handling characteristics) as I made haste to my truck. Opening the large cargo box in the back, I deposited my latest acquisitions and then visited my two sandy hiding places to retrieve those illegal birds. Once they were deposited in the cargo box and secured, I took another look around South Spit. The brant had pretty much stopped flying, and most of my lads were walking off the beach with a bird or so each. As it turned out, the six I had cited had been the only ones lucky enough to get in deadly gun range of the morning's flights and do some real damage. My satisfaction at knowing I had caught the only over-limit violators that morning was tempered by the constant thundering guns in the area of the scull boaters and stilt blinds. Placing my 10-gauge shotgun in its scabbard after wiping it down with an oily rag coated with STP Oil Treatment (great in a saltwater environment), I fired up my three-quarter-ton Dodge and eased it down South Spit Road en route to a public launch site on the east side of the bay.

By the time I arrived, the tide was again getting ready to change, and the brant hunting was about over for the day. Pausing near the landing where the Coast Guard cutter was tied, I glassed the stilt blinds with my binoculars. There was a lot of activity, but none of it was of the shooting nature, as the shooters were loading their hunting gear, dead birds, and decoys into their boats for the trip home. It was too late for any real action, so I made a mental note of my plan for the next day's adventures, lit a Toscanni cigar, and headed for North Humboldt Bay to see what devilment I could stir up.

I didn't want to check the brant hunters from South Bay as they came in for two reasons. First, they would have the limits all accounted for, and I would find no violations. Second, I didn't want this group of folks to know a federal agent was in the area and interested in their hunting activities. So I turned my attention elsewhere and let these folks and their activity, legal or illegal, age for another day.

Good old North Bay, scene of many of my adventures as a college kid and later as a state Fish and Game warden, soon hove into view. It didn't take long to kindle a situation, one that always brings a grin as well as makes me feel a little sheepish to this day. I had no more than hit one of the main levees and started to walk along it with my dog Shadow than I found a ringer not a hundred yards away. I had just checked a couple of unsuccessful brant hunters, and as I left them, here came another hunter from a little feeder dike that angled off into North Bay.

"Warden," he yelled excitedly, having seen me checking the two previous hunters and guessed my profession, "I got my first goose today; come see."

I walked over to the sport as my gut feeling that something bad was about to happen began working overtime. Sure as hell, the happy chap was in fact holding out, for me and the whole world to see, one huge, stinking old cormorant! Oh no, I thought; illegal as hell, being protected by state and federal laws. So much for this happy chap's first goose. This was just not my day. Getting my arsh whipped by those in the stilt blinds in South Bay and now having to ruin the day of this delighted fellow with his "first goose."

"Let me see that goose, partner," I said. He handed that damn cormorant to me like it was the catch of the day. I guess it was if you were a first-time hunter. The goddamned thing was huge and crawling with feather lice! Quickly handing it back to him and wiping off the dozens of feather lice crawling up my hand, I noticed that he had lice by the hundreds crawling all the way up the right arm of his hunting coat, no doubt soon to be in his hair. I just couldn't do it! I decided I wasn't going to cite this poor bastard, ruining his day in the process, and then carry that lousy cormorant the mile or so back to my truck as evidence. About that time the damn devil got under my hide and into my devious thinking compartment. That sucker could hook me sometimes from a mile or so away! "Well, partner, you have a good one here" (I didn't lie—he had the biggest damn cormorant I had seen in a long while).

"How do you cook it?" he asked, bright eyed and cheerful.

Now, when a man asks another in the know how to cook wild game, one has to respond professionally, and I did. "Sir," I responded, "here is how I would do it if I *had* to cook something like that." (Again, I didn't lie. ...) "Here is how I would fix it if I were you. I would pick the bird because there is a lot of flavor in the fat of the skin [it's true—the *real taste* in such a bird is in the fat of the skin]. Then I would soak it overnight in strong saltwater to get the blood and wild taste out of the meat. Then I would rub it with a lot of garlic salt and pepper, fill its cavity with slices of apple, carrots, onion, and celery, then pop it in an oven and bake it for two hours at 350 degrees. After it's cooked, you can throw away the stuffing, and there you have it."

From the way the chap looked at me, I could tell he was committing my words to memory. Obviously a conservation officer couldn't be wrong, especially one as large as the man standing in front of him. I could just see the wheels turning in this novice's head. It was obvious the officer had to be an eager eater based on his size, and if so, he had to be a good cook as well. Trying hard not to laugh, I again congratulated him on the size of his bird (I didn't lie!) and moved out of earshot so I could have a hearty laugh and wonder what the outcome of that experience would be. I felt pretty safe because I never identified myself to that fellow or showed him my badge. He assumed I was a state game warden, and after the devil got hold of me, I decided I had best let sleeping giants lie in the possible form of a subsequent congressional letter raising hell about my behavior. I knew he would identify the culprit who had given him the cooking instructions as a state Fish and Game warden. If the local warden captain got an angry letter by mistake from a sportsman who had had his tail twisted and thought he had been done in by a local game warden, all the better. The Coast Fish and Game squad captain was Duncan Snell, an old friend and classmate from the Fish and Game academy, class of 1966. Snell had gone on to great things within the Fish and Game Department, so I'm sure he handled the complaint very professionally if he received one. We are both retired now, and remain friends to this day. If he is reading these lines, he will finally figure out which of "his" wardens twisted the tail on the fellow with the cooked cormorant. ...

Cormorants are fish eaters, and not too picky about what they consume. I don't think even a bear would eat one, and I have seen hungry coyotes pass dead cormorants without a second glance. Consider that, if you will. A coyote will eat a stinking sheep, but not a cormorant. Even Shadow, after taking one sniff, moved off a short distance and rolled in the grass as a dog will do when sprayed in the face by a skunk. As I walked away from my "goose" hunter, it was hard to suppress a grin that was so wide, it was beginning to crack my face.

O'dark-thirty the next day found my Grumman launched and riding easily alongside the Coast Guard cutter in South Bay. As daylight arrived, I was sitting in a big chair on the bridge of the cutter (being a federal officer does have some perks), drinking a large mug of hot cocoa from the galley and watching South Bay sportsmen with my spotting scope. Sweeping the bay, I saw six scull boaters quietly anchored on the pilings of an old deserted stilt blind, waiting for the arrival of the flights of brant from the ocean. They appeared to be visiting, but I noticed that every one of them was keeping a wary eye skyward over South Spit. Soon they spotted a flock of brant flying over the spit and landing in the bay. Marking the spot, several sculled over to ambush the feeding birds. This was a deadly business, especially if the brant were new birds and not used to the danger a scull boat represented. As the season progressed and the birds got used to the scull boats, it got tougher to get close to the feeding birds for a shot. In any event, it was always a good calm-water way to get a brant meal if one was patient and good at one's avocation. However, if the water was rough, the bouncing outline of the scull boat was a dead giveaway, flushing birds many times far outside shotgun range.

A sweep of the stilt blinds with the scope showed that most of them were occupied with expectant hunters, as evidenced by the spreads of decoys and the masses of heads ringing the tops of the blinds. It wasn't long before the hunters on South Spit announced by the popping sounds of their shotguns that the brant were starting their daily flight into the bay. Swinging my spotting scope in that direction, I saw several flocks of brant fly over the spit and quickly drop into the bay. Some landed out in the vast open-water areas and began feeding on loosened eelgrass floating on the changing tide. Others circled the bay looking for exposed eelgrass beds.

The scull boaters started to converge on the little unsuspecting flocks with the same purpose as the U-boat commanders of old when they sighted a convoy of ships. Other flocks decoyed to the stilt blinds, and a dozen or more fell each time to the accurate volleys of shots from the blind occupants. In fact, sometimes so many would be killed that I couldn't get an accurate drop count. I would attempt to get a count when the birds were picked out of the water by the boatman, but that was also difficult because of the heat-wave distortion in the scope, the distance from the activity, and sometimes the way the boat was positioned when the birds were retrieved. I didn't want to show my hand until I knew I had a case, and those factors made it all the more difficult. If I couldn't get an accurate count, it was almost impossible to know when to drop the hammer on the multitude of shooters. I began to realize that this detail was not going to be a nice little walk in the park.

Ignoring the activity of the scull boaters, in essence saving them for another day, I spent my time watching the chaps in the stilt blinds, where most of the killing appeared to be occurring. They were doing well right from the get-go; in fact, at least six of the stilt blinds had to have limits already, and in two cases over-limits. I thought so not because we had so many birds in the area but because it seemed as if every time a flock of brant decoyed into the stilt blinds, none would leave. All were falling to the lethal barrages! With a bag limit of only three birds per person, it didn't take any kind of a shot at those ranges to quickly limit out.

Figuring it was time, I bade the Coast Guardsmen good-day, loaded Shadow into the bow of the Grumman for balance, and started the half mile or so across the bay toward the nearest stilt blind that I suspected had an over-limit. Once the shooters in that blind realized I was coming their way, I saw a handy-talky antenna go up, and shortly thereafter, the boat responsible for watching that stilt blind approached at a high rate of speed carrying four new shooters. Tying their boat to the stilts, the new arrivals scurried up the ladder into the blind. Then three different shooters emerged from the blind with two partially filled gunnysacks. Throwing them into the boats, they jumped in and sped off to an anchorage among some farms half a mile to the south. In one well-planned swoop, they had essentially stopped me from apprehending the seven shooters I felt had shot over-limits of brant. Obviously the over-limits of birds had been dumped into the boat in gunnysacks and removed from the scene as I approached. Since all I had on my Grumman was a nine-and-a-half-horsepower outboard, there was no hope in hell I could catch my bird-running culprits with their forty-horsepower motor. To make matters worse, I was sure the remaining shooters in the blind now had few enough birds to appear to be under their limits. Since I had been watching at least six blinds during the shooting, it had been impossible to keep accurate counts of birds killed, blind by blind because of the distance between me and them. As a consequence, I couldn't really testify that the three men in the boat had or hadn't shot the birds, or even that they had over-limits in their possession, so I was legally stuck. I also noticed that several of the shooters were changing some of their outerwear so as to appear to be different folks. These fellows were not only clever but damn streetwise, I thought as I sat bobbing in the bay watching all that activity unfold through my binoculars. I could see very little as to which shooter shot what because they were partly hidden behind the walls of the blind, so unless I caught them with over-limits in their possession, they had me. As if to make matters worse, I could see antenna pop up in other blinds as my current blind apparently alerted all the others as to a suspicious boat in the area.

Shortly after the antenna party, other boats came out to the other stilt blinds, and I saw the process repeated as new hunters went into blinds and birds were offloaded or tossed into boats passing underneath the blinds, which then headed to the ranches at the south end of the bay at a high rate of speed. I suspected that the birds were quickly offloaded into the hands of relatives or friends on shore. No matter how I looked at it, because of the distance I had to travel over open water or through the channels during extreme low tide, these killing bastards had the upper hand. Little did they realize that to play this kind of game was to get the dander up in a rather large, German sort of fellow, and that was not good. It was a bit like messing with Mother Nature. ...

Not wanting to waste my morning being met by arrogant, grinning faces knowing they had beaten me, I slid in behind some unknowing scull boaters and managed to scratch several of them for using unplugged shotguns or using their small electric trolling motors instead of sculling to illegally take brant. They quietly took their medicine, but I could see them memorizing my face and the boat I rode in on so they wouldn't be caught again with their pants down. The whole time I was taking information on the pink slips for subsequent citations, they would grouse about the stilt-blind shooters wrecking the hunting by taking excessive over-limits.

Historically, there was no love lost between the stilt-blind hunters and the scull boaters, and I knew the stilt-blind shooters would say the same thing about the chaps in the scull boats. Many a fight had occurred between the two factions over the years, and scull boaters had even been shot at when they got too close to a stilt-blind spread (located in many of the best feeding areas) or if they tried to steal a cripple from the stilt blind before the pickup boat arrived. In return, several stilt blinds were burned each year, and the stilt-blind hunters blamed the scull boaters. I just listened to the litany of complaints from my scull boaters, saying nothing. That didn't mean my mind wasn't working. Oh, no—it was in gear! From the frequency of the stilt-blind shooting going on to the south, the boaters were probably right on regarding the numbers of brant being illegally taken.

For the next few shoot days, I tried several times to catch the folks hunting out of the stilt blinds. I hid in a dangerous abandoned stilt blind that was about to fall over, even pulling my canoe up into the blind with me. No luck. By the time I got my canoe back in the water and under way after lowering it from the blind, they had their portable radios going, and I was whipped at every turn. Then I tried hiding on the land side of South Bay and catching the shooters as they came out to drop off their over-limits at the ranches. Again, no luck. The south end of the bay was riddled with many deep channels. If I wasn't in the right channel, by the time I got over to the channel occupied by the boat I was pursuing, the shooters were gone or the illegal birds had been handed over to willing hands on land. If I tried to openly launch my canoe in the canals on the land side and trap them as they came in, the portable radios on the ranches would get going and warn the shooters in the blinds. Then they would send their boats full of dead brant down a different channel, or have family members meet them at a different part of the bay and make the exchange. It was apparent that these folks had been here before.

I even tried to sneak into an area by one of the ranch houses early in the morning along a canal used by what I considered as one of the worst poaching families in the area. After I dug into the soft, muddy ground within running distance of their usual drop-off site and covered myself with a tarp, the hole I was lying in commenced to fill up with water because of the high water table. Not to be beaten by a foot of cold water, I placed my gun and wallet on the bank to keep them dry and stuck it out. About an hour later, three ranch dogs out hunting gophers found me shivering like a dog passing peach pits in my bed of cold water and set up such a racket that a family member came out to investigate. I got up to leave, embarrassed and frustrated at being discovered, not to mention wet, cold, and muddy as all get-out. I had never been so unsuccessful. Every way I turned, I hit a brick wall, and the brant continued to die in large numbers. The only good thing to come out of these fiascoes was that my determination was hardening like the cement in Hoover Dam!

As I walked across the field by one of the family homes, muddy and wet as a muskrat, I suffered further indignity by being shot at by two five- or six-year-old kids with BB guns. As if that were not enough, boat after boat of shooters came down the canal I was walking along, holding up their three birds each and asking if I would like to check them. Believe you me, that did nothing but set the hair on my last part over the fence to the depth of about two feet! *It isn't nice to mess with Mother Nature and her minions,* I grimly thought.

In order to let me in particular and the arena in general cool off, I went to North Bay to see what I could stir up on the next shoot day. I wasn't going there to really work brant hunters because there were so few brant in the area owing to the lack of eelgrass. However, I was hoping the time away would let me thoughtfully plow through my "possibles" bag. I soon got more than I had bargained for from another quarter. The first brant hunter I chanced to meet was none other than my "first goose" hunter who had taken the louse-ridden cormorant home to cook. Boy, was he pissed! He let me know in no uncertain terms that he had cooked the "goose" and his own goose as well, as he told it: "It like to ruint my house, not to mention my marriage." He went on, as I tried hard not to laugh, to say that the bird had stunk up his house something awful! His wife had thrown the bird, cooking pan, and him out for the night and told him that if he wanted to stay married, he should take the game he killed elsewhere. I tried to cover my tracks with other cooking suggestions as a smoke-screen to avoid an ass chewing that I figured was justified, but he could tell he had me by the hind end and hung on like a pit bull.

I didn't tell him what he had shot, and I bet that damn fish-eating cormorant really did stink up his wife's kitchen. I also didn't tell him it would have been a $250 fine if I had gone the other way. I would have bet that he would have taken the fine or even jail time to avoid the hind-end chewing he got from his wife. I would also bet that for quite a while, every time that woman fired up that oven, she was greeted with the residual essence of cormorant. I imagine that every time that occurred, another fresh hind-end chewing accompanied the aroma of "eau de cormorant." Oh well. Sometimes you eat the bear, and sometimes he eats you. ...

I walked away with less than all of my tailfeathers as a result of my pissed-off goose shooter but with a damned big "it was worth it" grin. During the "woodshedding," the devil had gotten under my hide again, with a truly great idea this time. Not about the poor "goose" shooter—I had had all of him I could take. It was about the stilt-blinders in South Bay. Damn, why hadn't I thought of this idea before? After all, it was not only great but historical. I had seen my devilish idea in a movie about an American prisoner of war who had blown up a German ammunition train. He had seen that the munitions trains were loaded with straw so they would ride more easily and not accidentally explode. When the prisoner was unobserved for a moment, he placed a lit cigarette over the heads of the matches in a matchbook, with the burning tip extending about half an inch past the match heads, and folded the cover over the cigarette to hold it into place. Then he threw the matchbook affair into a boxcar carrying munitions and straw. When the cigarette burned down to the match heads, it set them on fire, and that in turn set the straw in the boxcar afire. Needless to say, the ammunition train lost its "head of steam" and "hind end" of ammunition cars in the resultant fire. And of course our hero, being out of the area because of the delayed "fuse," was not caught.

With that devious thought firmly planted in my mind, the devil and I were off to a hardware store thirty miles up the coast in Trinidad to purchase a few items. I drove thirty miles so no one could put two and two together if I were suspected later. If anyone discovered the items because my plan hadn't worked, I didn't want that person to go to the local hardware store and have the clerk tell the questioner, "Yeah, the big game warden just purchased these items a day or two ago." I had worked in that area for a year and a half as a state game warden, so many people still knew me.

Daylight the next morning found me back on the Coast Guard cutter trying to keep track of the brant killed blind by blind. Most of the blinds took over-limits that day, one with six shooters taking thirteen brant over the limit. All made liberal use of the shuttle method of rotating in new hunters every time a flock of birds was killed because they knew the "fed" was in the area. This way they could almost shoot all day long and remain untouchable by the long arm of the law. Or so they thought! That crap of killing my little brant until one tired of the blood sport was about to stop, I thought as I sat in a deck chair smoking a cigar. These killing sons of bitches were about to meet the devil and the game management agent, and you could bet your bottom dollar it wouldn't be pretty.

About four in the afternoon, I announced to the Coast Guard crew that I was off to check some scull boaters at several of the landings in North Humboldt Bay. I said in a voice loud enough for many on the bridge to hear that this particular group of scull boaters, although less numerous than those in South Bay, hadn't been checked in a long time, and now was as good a time to surprise them as any. I further loaded the deck by saying I planned to use the Grumman. With that, Grumman Sport Boat, dog, German, and the devil went to war. North Bay is a fair distance from South Bay, and that was just the seed I wanted to plant with the Coast Guard. I was sure the information would be shared with the outlaw stilt-blinders in South Bay as soon as I was out of sight. I discovered later from a petty officer that I hadn't even started my truck in the parking lot when one of the Coasties got the word out on my plans via land line to some of the worst brant-killing outlaws in South Bay.

Dark, under the faint sheen of city lights, found me quietly tying the Grumman to one of the stilts of a blind on the public land portion of the bay. When the shooting was tremendous, that blind would be full of chaps, first come, first served. If the shooting was normal, the other stilt blinds farther to the south and west would rake in the birds, and hunting from this particular blind would be a waste of time. With that in mind, and because it was illegally placed on state land, it became my first target. ... The devil had gotten a piece of my soul, and in return I was to get several pieces of hind end from the brant-shooting, over-the-limit, sons of bitches in South Bay.

I had motored my Grumman from the old blimp hangar landing on the North Spit via the main channel all the way to South Bay and was now ready for action. Crawling into the blind, I found the floor covered with spent shotgun shells and the remains of several partly eaten lunches, along with six dead brant forgotten under some tarps. Dog happily ate the lunches as I tossed them down into the canoe, the spoiled brant were pitched into the bay for the seals and gulls to eat, and the game management agent and his newfound friend the devil attended to their nefarious duties.

Taking a gallon of kerosene, I liberally sprinkled most of the contents around the floor and walls of the blind. I placed a pile of rags against the west wall corner (the wind was strongest from the west, hopefully creating a hotter flame once the fire got going), sprinkled it with the remaining kerosene, and lit a Toscanni cigar. After making sure the cigar was really going, I took a booklet of paper matches from my pocket and opened it. Taking a roll of tape from my pocket, I placed my cigar over the top of the matches with the "cherry" just outside the match heads. Then I closed and taped the flap down over the cigar to hold it firmly in place. Again making sure the lit portion of the cigar was far enough from the match heads, I gave it another puff and, satisfied it was a go, laid the whole package down next to a small hole in the wall (to let in the wind, which helped keep the cigar hot) and the kerosene-soaked rags. Down the ladder I scurried, damn near falling in when a rung broke, and headed the dog, Grumman, and me away from the blind and back toward the old blimp hangar on North Spit. It was dark enough that I figured no one would see me or the Grumman riding low in the water as we made our escape, and I was right, damn near getting rammed by a returning fishing boat as I crossed the main channel!

As I boated across the wake created by that vessel, I figured the cigar would take about four minutes to burn down and ignite the match heads. Then it would be a few more minutes before the kerosene-soaked rags really got going and a few more before the blind was really blazing. With that time edge, I would be out of the area and, I hoped, throw any hounds of suspicion off my trail.

Once north of the blimp hangar in the main channel, I swung back southwest so any fishermen on the landing would see me coming from the North Bay side. I wanted to be sure no one would suspect that I had been anywhere near the South Bay stilt blind. I would be sure to visit with the fishermen, letting them know I had been in North Bay all afternoon looking for scull boaters taking brant and had just gotten back. That should establish my story in case anyone got lucky at guessing what was *really* going on. I couldn't help but develop a big grin on my rather salty puss at my own ingenuity. Well, I had a little help. ...

Pulling up to the landing, I anchored the Grumman and scurried up to my pickup. In passing, I spoke to several bottom-fish fishermen at the dock's edge. Backing my pickup down the boat launch, I loaded my Grumman, and tied it down on the truck. Moving the truck up out of the way, I walked back down to visit with the fishermen, all the while keeping an eye directed toward my stilt blind in South Bay.

For a long time nothing happened, and I suspected my cigar may have gone out. To pass the time and make sure the fishermen remembered me, I started checking fishing licenses. I memorized four of the chaps' names as I did and, when I got a free moment, put them down in my field diary. That way, if I needed a witness to throw the stilt-blind crowd off my track, I would have the ammunition. Then, way off in a distance, there it was! A small glow began to manifest itself to the south. As it got going, what a blaze it made with those dry redwood timbers. Finally some of the fishermen noticed the blaze, and I made a show of going back to the truck for my binoculars. Soon we all got a look at the "mysterious" blaze in South Bay.

Timing was everything. I had planned it so the fire would take off at low tide. No one could easily get out there to put it out even if they wanted to. It was great sitting there surrounded by "friends," entertained by a blaze in the bay, a soft breeze out of the west, a great cigar firmly clenched between my teeth, and thoughts whirling around in my head as to who was next.

The following day when I went into South Bay to work the scull boaters, all I could see of my previous night's work was smoldering pilings and a dump the dog took in the front of my boat to get rid of

Four federal and state conservation officers in Louisiana with a large over-limit of ducks. Note the white boxes containing additional breasted-out duck meat.

First day's seizure from the U.S. Fish and Wildlife Service (USFWS) covert operation in Colorado/Montana of endangered cat skins, velvet antlers, bighorn sheep horns, and eagles (in plastic bags).

Undercover photo of cactus thieves in action in Arizona.

Electrocuted golden eagles at the bottom of a transmission pole in Utah. (photo by Special Agent Schroeder)

Coral smuggled into the port of Los Angeles from Asia. Seized by USFWS Wildlife Inspectors. (photo by Wildlife Inspector Rich Grosz)

Interstate game check in Wyoming. Over-limit of deer and pronghorn antelope being seized by Wyoming and USFWS officers (LE and Refuges Divisions). The author is mid photo with his back turned (white lettering on jacket). (State of Wyoming photo)

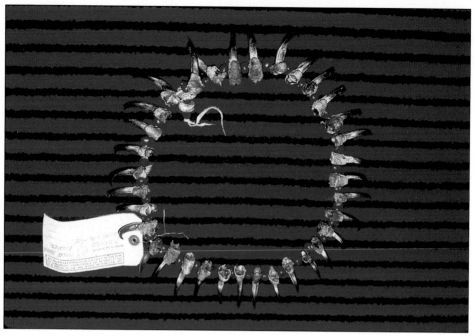

Eagle talon necklace sold to USFWS covert officers in South Dakota by Lakota Indian. There are thirty-four talons—more than four eagles' worth.

Illegally gill-netted walleye seized from Native Americans on Lake Oahe in South Dakota by state and USFWS officers. (photo by Agent John Cooper)

Part of an 11,000-pound seizure of illegal walrus ivory taken by Alaskan Natives. Refuge officers assist in seizure and documentation.

Female paddlefish being opened up to extract the roe. Part of a USFWS covert operation into the illegal take and sale of paddlefish. (photo by Agent Larry Keck)

Two buckets of paddlefish roe taken during USFWS covert operation. (photo by Agent Larry Keck)

Line of dead eagles illegally taken by Lakota Indians in South Dakota for sale and export. (photo by Agent Jim Klett)

Illegal brown bear taken in Katmai National Park, Alaska, with use and aid of an aircraft. USFWS undercover agent John Cooper poses with the kill. (photo by unknown outlaw guide)

Illegal elk kill by a hunting group from Louisiana in the Rand area of Colorado. Two truck-loads of illegal elk had already been removed. (photo by Deputy Chief Dave Croonquist)

the salami sandwiches she had eaten from that stilt blind the night before. There wasn't anything left except a memory when I slowly passed its remains. One for the brant, I thought. However, the devil and I weren't through.

Talk on the bay was that someone had left a burning cigarette in the blind, so concern about the existence of a fire danger in their midst rode at low ebb. Well, I was about to pop that theory and fire up some concerns regarding the mystery of fires at "sea." The next evening, I visited another stilt blind that had been erected illegally on public lands, whose usual occupants were known for killing over-limits of brant, and set up the same little "treats" I had used the night before. This time I knocked a board off the west face of the blind so the wind could whistle across the cigar and keep it glowing for all it was worth. I also used less kerosene so the fire would take longer to get going, giving me even more time to get out of the area. That way I would be more than clear, enjoying another cigar with my fishing "buddies" on the North Spit while another stilt blind burned. It worked perfectly, especially with the brisk westerly breeze we had that evening. Again we all stood there musing about what was happening once the blind commenced to burn and light up the area. Everyone got excited as the blind lit up the night sky, and everyone standing there, fishing forgotten, had a theory about what was happening out there in the bay. That was, everyone except the devil and yours truly. ...

Since both of the burned stilt blinds had been built illegally on public lands, and as is typical in government, no one had done anything about them, no law was broken. (I had asked one of my old, close-mouthed police department buddies to check with the county attorney before my little escapade. He had informed me that there would be no laws broken by "removing" those illegal blinds unless someone inside was injured in the process.) With two stilt blinds burned to the waterline, the accidental-cigarette-fire theory was out the door — and so were the South Bay stilt-blind hornets.

What happened next was pure gold. The stilt-blind shooters blamed the burnings on the scull boaters! And the scull boaters, with their big mouths, helped the assumption along by razzing the remaining shooters in the stilt blinds that they would be "next." In fact, at one of the landings, several hotheaded chaps recently left without a stilt blind threw a scull boater into the bay and punched a hole in the bottom of his boat, thinking he was the culprit. In times past, that particular fellow had burned several stilt blinds on private ground because their occupants had given him crap over a wounded brant. He had not been able to keep his mouth shut in a local bar after his escapades, forever "endearing" himself to the stilt-blind fraternity. Now those loose lips ended up getting his scull boat "holed." Jesus, the war between the two factions was on, and what a pretty sight it made!

Over the next three nights, South Bay burned. One of the remaining stilt blinds was torched to the waterline, two more scull boaters had holes chopped in their boats, and so it went. I continued to wreak havoc among all concerned over waterfowl violations as they warred among themselves, forgetting the "fed" was still among them like a maggot. God, it was great, and the catchin' was good. However, some of the culprits started sleeping in the remaining blinds so no one could burn them out, and eventually the burnings, including mine, stopped.

I noticed something else. The rampant killing of brant by those in the remaining stilt blinds slackened by about 90 percent. It seemed they had become aware that their killing excesses might in part be responsible for the demise of their beloved stilt blinds. Locked doors to the blinds were the order of the day for those remaining few, and when a limit was killed, those folks left the blind for the day. A lesson had been learned, the stilt blinds mysteriously stopped burning, and the migrating brant got a breather.

It was Sunday, the last weekend of the season, and the north coast had a strong blow. The hunters from two stilt blinds on public lands who were still taking more than their share slept in their own beds that evening instead of in their stilt blinds, feeling that the scull boaters would not go out into the bay in their little boats without great peril on that particular night. However, there was a dark set of blue eyes watching their game-hog behavior, and there was no smile on that face. Apparently the lessons had already been forgotten by a few as the season neared its end. As it turned out, those few had had it their way for years in killing over-limits of brant and were reluctant to change their ways. Well, I thought, change is inevitable, even for a concrete-reinforced redwood stilt blind with a set of locked doors. ...

Dark for the last time, in two-foot-high seas, found a very wet and stupid-for-being-out-in-that-kind-of-weather game agent, Grumman canoe, and dog. Even the devil didn't go out that evening! Heading into the waves at steerage speed allowed me to get to my two targeted stilt blinds. Once on the bay there was no turning back. I took on a lot of water and was glad that God was my copilot. ...

Dispensing with the match-cover trick since it was two in the morning and blowing like there was no tomorrow, I busted the locks off the doors with a hammer. Soaking everything down with kerosene, I set it off. Running out of kerosene partway through on the second stilt blind and, exhausted from bailing and controlling the canoe in buffeting heavy rains, I lit the fuel, cut my canoe loose, and let her drift with the wind. Going with a fifteen-knot wind was a hell of a lot easier then what I had been through getting to the blinds, and I welcomed the relative calm. Drifting and motoring through the large swells in the channel, I looked back through salty wet eyes at my work. Both blinds burned merrily and would be of no use to anyone without a lot of work and expense to repair them. Most of the blinds had been built in the heyday of the brant populations. Now, with the brant being greatly reduced in numbers, I doubted anyone would go to the trouble and considerable expense of rebuilding the destroyed blinds. I felt a warmth go through me that overrode the wet and cold. Maybe I couldn't catch these gunners breaking the wildlife laws, but now they wouldn't give me any reason to bother, or the brant to worry, and again a wet, salty grin began to form on my now truly weathered "Robert Redford" face. The grin didn't do much for my wet ass still bouncing around on the seat of the boat, though! It was so rough that the dog just lay the whole time in the bow of the canoe, occasionally looking back at me as if to ask, "What the hell are we doing out here?"

Then Shadow stood up and turned her head to look intently into the inky dark and wind toward two stilt blinds located on land I assumed was owned by the Trionne family. The blinds in that corner of the bay were in my mind the real killers. They were located on some of the best eelgrass beds and seemed to have the best gunners in South Bay. Many times I would see twenty brant swing into one or the other of these blinds and none coming out! I wanted to visit these blinds with my cigar but thought better of it after thinking over the state arson laws. Squinting through the flying salt spray to find what Shadow was looking at, I was rewarded with nothing but the inky black of night. I could faintly hear what sounded like a chainsaw, but knowing there was no logging in the area, especially at that time of the morning, I dismissed the noise as a trick being played by the winds. Pulling my float coat higher around my neck to prevent spray from the entire South Bay running down my back, we continued on our way to the landing.

The next morning, after a hearty breakfast at the Samoa Cook House (an old-style lumbermen's cook house with an all-you-can-eat menu), I drove over to the Coast Guard dock and parked my Dodge so I could overlook the bay. Sitting there, ready to leave the Humboldt Bay area for another year and whatever adventures life would bring, I leaned back and surveyed my domain. It was Monday, the day after the brant hunting season had closed. I had spent two hard weeks trying to bring conservation laws to the land of the redwoods and had been partially successful. I had apprehended about sixty chaps breaking the law under the Migratory Bird Treaty Act, had removed several of the facilities encouraging the violations (with a little help from the scull boaters), and had had time to grow a little in the process. The stilt blinds would be back next year (with any luck not as many), as would the scull boaters—and maybe I would too. Time would tell, but for now the little brant were out of harm's way. Looking over the bay one last time with my binoculars, I found many brant feeding quietly around burned-out pilings that used to represent supports holding up killing platforms. Again, the Robert Redford grin managed to creep onto a weathered and tired face.

Then I saw it! Two of the stilt blinds in the far end of South Bay were nowhere to be seen! Taken aback, I grabbed my spotting scope from the seat and fastened it to my window. Soon the area was in focus, and sure as God made little green apples, *they were gone!* It was low tide, and I could just barely make out their supports on the concrete footings. No smoke came from any of the supports, leading me to believe they had been cut off at their footings sometime during low tide. Then it dawned on me: the noise of chainsaws over the wind last night. That was what Shadow had heard and stood up to look at. Some damn crazy fool (even crazier than me) had gone out in the night on those seas with a boat and chainsaw to put an end to two infamous stilt blinds known for killing many hundreds of brant. They must have motored in from the South Spit side; that would have been the shortest way, and safest. Sitting slowly back in my seat, a grin of thanks formed over my face, and I celebrated my good luck with another strong Toscanni cigar. My guess was that some scull boaters or other stilt-blind shooters whose blinds had been destroyed had blamed those folks in the extreme end of the bay and taken their revenge. ... Conservation sure has some strange turns in its sack of "possibles," I thought.

The Pacific black brant have probably been even more severely reduced in numbers by the time I write these lines. As I said earlier, when I went to college in the 1960s, there were about fifty thousand in Humboldt Bay. It truly was a sight to behold those little guys storming over the spit and sailing into the bay in such glorious numbers. It was especially neat to see them gather in the bay in numbers resembling a long black feathered oil slick after the hunting season closed. Those sights, plus the brant's unique call, have left me with memories I will never forget.

There is one light at the end of the tunnel. The Fish and Wildlife Service, with sportsman duck stamp monies, has purchased a large portion of South Bay and made it into a national wildlife refuge, primarily for waterfowl and shorebirds. That includes my little friends the Pacific black brant. Finally they will have a breather in their quest for life. Today brant are probably counted in the low thousands in Humboldt Bay, but the hunting continues outside the refuge boundaries because of the usual politics of hunter opportunity, I suppose. They are overshot in great numbers (some reports of one hundred per day per gunner) in Mexico by wealthy American shooters. (Note that I don't call them sportsmen.) And they continue to be shot at and killed all along the West Coast as they struggle to migrate north to perpetuate the species. Another mortality factor is the number of deaths attributed to oiling from passing ships illegally pumping their bilges. Once oiled, the brant is a spent unit, if you get my drift. No one has a handle on those mortality figures, but they can't be small when you consider the number of ships using the shipping lanes, the same areas many brant use to rest. When they arrive in the high arctic, a good high tide and offshore wind could easily wipe out most of that year's eggs and nests. Because of the nature of the species and the arctic environment, there is no renesting for the brant, and the little guys must migrate all the way back to Mexico and wait another year, again under constant gunning by Americans who get their thrills by killing many hundreds of waterfowl just so they can brag about it when they return home.

After about two good shots in the bill on the nesting ground, coupled with current hunting pressures and offshore pollution, and it is possible that the brant will start that long skid toward the black hole of extinction. Another part of our American heritage destroyed and a lesson in natural history unlearned. It makes one wonder what will be left for those yet to come and, even worse, if anyone really cares. ...

seven

It's a Very Small World

LOOKING AT MY WATCH, I saw that it was five-fifty-nine P.M.
Damn! I thought. I had told Donna, my long-suffering wife, that I
would be home for dinner no later than six. It had been a month since
I had had dinner with my family because of the monstrous workload
associated with the Sacramento Valley's waterfowl hunting season.
Tired of my frequent absences, Donna had finally asked if I could be
home on time for at least one dinner per month for the kids' sake.
That very morning I had promised over a fantastic lumberjack breakfast of fried side pork, spuds, six scrambled eggs, and homemade
bread, with a fresh-out-of-the-oven pie for which she was regionally
famous. After wolfing down such a great load of grits, designed to
keep my furnaces going all day no matter what the challenge, I gave
her a quick kiss and headed back out into the California waterfowl
season with all its warts.

Quickly forgetting my dinner promise, I noted the time on the citation I was writing to the first of my five violators. As luck would have
it, I *had* been heading home to keep my dinner appointment, only to
get tangled up with these now-in-tow late shooters. Dinnertime was
usually when folks inclined toward shooting late would be busting the
flocks of waterfowl coming into the rice fields to feed. For a conservation officer, eating dinner at the normal hour was to miss the opportunity to catch those late-shooting boneheads. And when one is
young and foolhardy as I was, catching those violators meant more
than missing a few dinners. Missed moments I now regret some
thirty-five years later. ...

In those days when patrolling, I ran with all my windows down,
winter, summer, rain, or shine so that if something occurred within

earshot—such as shooting—I would hear it and often end up with an "illegal" or two as my reward. As I hurriedly drove south that evening through Terrill Sartain's properties after turning off the Colusa-Gridley Highway onto Putnam Road, it was as if the devil had intentionally littered my homeward route with late shooters. Rattling and splashing my way over the pothole-strewn road, I overheard shooters in a field to the west who, from the sounds of it, were having the time of their lives. It didn't seem to matter much to those with the itchy trigger fingers that they were shooting thirty minutes after legal hours.

Throwing the cutoff switches that turned off my taillights and brake lights, I slammed on my brakes and slid to a stop in the middle of the road behind a clump of willows. *Boom-boom—boom* went three shots from what sounded like two shooters. Quietly pulling the truck out of the middle of the road onto a muddy, weed-lined berm, I bailed out and walked around the willows for a better look. In the middle of a harvested rice field were five hunters walking toward a parked Suburban a hundred or so yards away. The air was jug-full of ducks and geese coming off the Butte Sink marsh to the east, all looking for a meal in the many recently harvested rice fields.

These shooters had probably quit hunting at the end of legal hours but then, walking back to their vehicle under wave after wave of low-flying waterfowl, couldn't believe their eyes. Many shooters presented with such low-flying temptation let the itch of their trigger fingers override their common sense. *Boom-boom-boom-boom-boom* went four of the shooters' shotguns. Watching through my binoculars, I could see flame from the ends of their barrels pointed skyward as they shot at an especially low flock of ducks. Three ducks dropped dead not far from the shooters, and as two fellows ran to retrieve those ducks, the others stopped walking to wait for their partners. Hordes of ducks and geese continued to sail thirty-five yards above their heads in the dusk, and this sight, coupled with the sheer living energy presented by the spectacle, made those waiting loose another barrage of shots. This time four mallards dropped, and that was all it took for the man behind the binoculars. I had now seen all five men shooting after legal hours, and it was time to put an end to this foolishness.

I figured I probably had five city hunters leasing a small piece of rice ground at a premium to hunt waterfowl who probably hadn't killed a thimbleful of birds all season. That evening, as the gods would have it, the heavens had opened up with aerial bounty as far as the eye could see. Overwhelmed by that spectacle, my eager shooters had found constraint and the promise of a duck in every pot too much temptation. Hammering away with visions of plump rice-fed ducks for the bag, they soon gathered unto themselves one plump, *unfed* enforcement minion of Mother Nature.

It doesn't take a duck or goose long to figure out where it is safe to reside. They quickly memorize when shooting hours begin and end and, except in unusual conditions such as fog, strong winds, baited areas, or heavy rains, don't venture far from their sanctuaries until these parameters have been safely eclipsed. Then, pressed by an overriding hunger, they come from those sanctuaries with an urgency not to be denied. When that occurs, if there is still light enough to shoot, the devil gets his due with the American sportsman—as does the conservation officer if he is out and about.

Churning across the muddy rice fields toward the shooters as fast as my tired legs allowed, I soon had them rounded up. Normally I would have let my errant shooters hang themselves with all the late-shooting "rope" they desired. However, I had promised my bride I would be home for dinner, and figured I had better make tracks or I might get a well-deserved knot on the head! As I had expected, my lads were docile and contrite, having let the devil overcome their common sense. Finishing my last citation amidst the smell of brimstone that was obvious only to my nose, I asked the shooters if they had any questions and, hearing none, thanked them for being good sports about the citations. With that, I hurriedly walked back to my truck with seven evidence birds, a handful of citations, and a smile for the end of a great day. Hurriedly drawing the birds so they wouldn't spoil, I washed my hands in a mud puddle and headed home for what I knew would be an even greater dinner and get-together. However, not before rolling up all my windows. ...

Arriving home thirty-three minutes late, I slipped off my hip boots and washed the worst of the mud off my face and hands in the outside sink in the garage. Opening the back door, which led directly into the kitchen, I was met with the warmth of a living home in exchange for the damp, cold air prevalent in the winter rice fields of Colusa County. Then it hit me! The heavenly smell of fried chicken, mashed potatoes, gravy, and green beans, the sight of two rough-and-tumble boys happy to see their dad, and the delicate smell of a lemon cake soon to be. There were few things better than a great home-cooked meal, my kids, a warm house, and a wife with the world's most beautiful blue eyes.

I noticed Donna watching me with a wry smile. "Glad you are home, even if it is thirty-five minutes late," she said. That shot across the bow was quickly followed by a knowing and understanding smile. Damn, I thought, no one could put me in my place quicker than that woman, and she did so when it was needed—or many times just for practice. ... It was probably for the best, though, because otherwise I could never have gotten my swelled head in and out of the cab of the patrol truck.

I didn't try to explain my lateness, just lamely asked, "Is soup on?"

"Just as soon as you and the boys get washed up and sat down," she said with a smile that betrayed the fact that she was thankful I was home safely once again. "Do any good?" she quietly asked.

"Got four with large over-limits of geese on Butte Creek, three folks without federal duck stamps, and five late shooters on Sartain's," I replied.

"Good," she said, still smiling. "If you are going to be late for my special dinner, I want it to be for good reason." There, she had done it again! *Damn!* Walking over, I gathered up her small frame in my arms and held her until she smacked me with a wooden spoon and informed me that the gravy needed stirring. Letting her go, I got my two errant puppies cleaned up and seated, then followed suit. Donna served dinner, and after a prayer of thanks for our family's many blessings, we all fell to with gusto on a delicious dinner prepared by one of the best cooks in the country.

I had just taken a bite of spuds smothered with delicious homemade chicken gravy spiced heavily with garlic and a bite of Donna's out-of-this-world crispy fried chicken when, as if on cue, the phone rang. Damn, I thought, what timing. Putting the chicken down and wiping my hands on a napkin, I hurriedly swallowed my mouthful of food. Donna, used to frequent interruptions at every meal and all times of the day or night, grinned knowingly as she shook her head. The boys, involved in wolfing down their grits, didn't even hear the phone ring. Hell, a bomb could have gone off and those two wouldn't have noticed unless the blast knocked the food off their plates. Those two are going to be healthy boys someday, I thought with a proud grin (today one at six foot seven inches is strong as a bull, and the other at six foot with twenty-six-inch biceps *is* a bull).

Picking up the phone, I said, "Good evening; may I help you?"

For a long moment there was no sound, and then a voice quietly asked, "Terry, is that you?"

"Yes, it is," I replied. "Who is this?"

"I don't want to say over the phone, but I need to talk to you, and *now!*"

"Well, OK," I said slowly, puzzling over the voice's identity. It was familiar in a far-off sort of way, but damned if I could place it. "Can we get together in about thirty minutes? I just sat down to my first hot meal with my family in over a month and would like the chance to finish it."

There was another long pause, and then the voice said, "I don't know if I have the guts to wait that long for you. In fact, I should probably just hang up right now and not get involved."

"Not get involved with *what?*" I fired back, scenting something illegal and not wanting my informant to go limp-kneed and hang up on me.

There was an even longer pause, in fact so long I thought the caller might have hung up. Then the voice continued, "Would you meet me on the back side of Jess Cave's duck club by his boat dock between the two shooting areas—alone? Then we can talk face to face, and I'll feel a whole lot better than discussing this issue over the phone. I will wait for thirty minutes, and if you aren't here by then, all bets are off. Also, if you bring anyone I'll know, and I won't be there." Those words were followed with a loud *click*, signifying that the conversation had ended. Holding the phone to my ear for a long moment as if more were sure to come, I was rewarded with silence.

Because of the mystery of the call and my suspicious nature, many thoughts began whirling around in the back of my mind, most of them black. Turning, I could see my bride's blue eyes looking clear through me for some sort of explanation. "I know," she said, "you have to go." She got up from the table, ignoring my two chow-hound boys grousing about who was going to get a chicken leg from a plateful of fried chicken, and hurried to the kitchen counter to make me a sandwich.

Walking into the reloading room (a room set aside for me to reload ammunition and store firearms), I unlocked the pistol drawer under my gun cabinet. Taking out my Smith and Wesson .44 magnum, I opened the cylinder, stuffing six sausage-sized, 240-grain soft-point cartridges into it. Then I put on my shoulder holster, designed for a man my size and a weapon that size, closed the cylinder carefully (unlike the way they do it on TV!), holstered the pistol, and put two speed loaders full of magnum cartridges in my left vest pocket. Then I took the Colt .45 ACP from my right hip and checked the magazine to make sure it was fully loaded (I had a nasty habit of shooting skunks and feral house cats and sometimes forgetting to reload). It was fully loaded, so I placed two extra magazines of 230-grain cartridges in a magazine holder on my belt.

Turning, I saw my bride quietly standing in the doorway watching me. She knew exactly what I was doing, and why. She is a crack shot herself with a handgun and rifle and was able to put two and two together, especially when I was loading up with ammunition for two weapons. "Your sandwich is ready," she said without an ounce of emotion in her voice, her knowing, beautiful blue eyes never leaving mine.

Walking over to her, I gave her a big, gentle bear hug, but her body was not as relaxed in my arms as it had been earlier in the kitchen. "Thank you for the sandwich, honey," I mumbled. I added, "I love you," trying to make the words sound casual.

"Call me through the sheriff's office radio when you are done, will you?" she said. With that, she went back to the kitchen as the battle for the chicken leg grew serious if volume of verbal combat meant anything. It is a damn good thing chickens have two legs, I thought as I headed back into the garage for my hip boots.

For the life of me I couldn't place the voice on the phone. It had sure sounded familiar, but I just couldn't put my finger on it. The place picked for the meeting was accessible only by foot. It would be at least a two-hundred-yard walk through a closed gate and some damn isolated terrain; hence the magnum now riding comfortably in the shoulder holster. I had been set up and shot once before, and once was enough. But I wanted to meet this mysterious caller to see what he had on his mind, even if it was on his terms and choice of ground. Who knows? I thought. It might be someone with good information, and with a little luck maybe I could apprehend some *real* outlaws before this was over. With that incentive, I loaded my dog Shadow into the back of the truck (she could see, hear, and smell a person more quickly than I, especially in the dark) and headed out on another adventure.

Driving across town to the Colusa County sheriff's office, I met Deputy Sheriff Del Garrison coming out the front door. "Just the man I wanted to see," I said. Del was a bear of a man with a heart to match, a great friend and one who understood the meaning of serious law enforcement. "Del," I said, "got a minute?"

"For you, my little friend, anytime," came his familiar soft voice. However, you never wanted to let that quiet voice fool you. Del was as big as a mountain, strong as a bear, yet gentle as any man you would ever meet. However, if anyone needed to be handled or squared away for stepping out of line, you could bet a month's pay Del would be the one who would walk out of the arena eating the lunch the other guy had brought for the occasion!

I told Del about the phone call and explained my plan to meet the man behind the voice. Knowing that the meeting spot was very isolated, I asked Del to slink into the area and sit off to one side of Lurline Road just in case the shooting started. If it did, and I was unable to finish it, I was hoping he would. Grabbing me by one shoulder with his bear paw–like hand, he said, "Count on it, little buddy, and be careful." Off he went to get the rest of his gear loaded into the county patrol car for his regular night shift. One might think it was a casual send-off, but Del's eyes told it all.

Leaving the sheriff's office, I headed my truck north through town and then west out Lurline Road. Minutes later I was next to the gate leading into the back side of Jess Cave's Duck Club, having driven the last mile without headlights. It took only a few moments to hide my truck in a stand of willow trees on the south side of Lurline. Killing the engine, I stepped outside, listening and looking. All I could hear was the wind rustling through a few dead leaves in the trees and the plaintive calls of some wigeon flying overhead. My eyes observed nothing but the inky black of a Colusa County winter night. Quietly I commanded Shadow out of the truck and removed her noisy chain collar. She was midnight black and very well trained, so when I took off her collar no one ever knew she was there until she was ordered forward to "greet" an assailant. She knew that when I took off her collar, it was a business situation, and all 110 pounds of her reacted accordingly.

Grabbing my Starlight scope from the seat, we quickly crossed Lurline Road and headed into the dark of the duck club on a muddy access road. Turning on the scope the minute I crossed through the gate onto the Cave property, I scanned the area. Finding nothing out of the ordinary, I continued walking down the road bordering the club on the east boundary. Arriving minutes later at the intersection of a road running west toward the boat dock where I was supposed to meet my caller, I heard the soft crunching sound of car tires moving slowly down the graveled Lurline Road. I couldn't see any vehicle, so I aimed the scope at the noise and spotted Del Garrison in his patrol car quietly slipping into position on the southeast side of the duck club. Good old Del, I thought. Barely hearing the sound tires make on a gravel road once again, only this time from the southwest, I turned and with the Starlight scope saw another darkened patrol car slipping in from the San Jose Road side of the duck club. That vehicle quietly moved out of sight among some parked rice harvesters. Who the hell was that officer? I thought. I had shared my secret only with Del. I later discovered that it was Peter Grevie, another deputy who was getting to be a close friend. Pete was fairly new to the job but, as I soon discovered, was a damn good man to have at your side in a pinch. Pete wasn't as big as Del but was built like a brick outhouse and had no fear when it came to getting the job done. It was ironic that Pete came from a Colusa County duck-hunting family with an alleged historical tradition of market hunting. As the stories went—no proof, mind you— Pete had once been involved in that tradition himself. But now here he was, protecting a conservation officer, the very breed not readily welcomed around his farmhouse in the days of old. Well, his being there was fine with me, as I knew Del would only bring the right kind of cavalry, so Shadow and I turned back to the business at hand.

Shadow always walked on my right side with her head and neck just inches from my leg. If she noticed anything unusual, she would place her massive head on my right leg and leave it there without tripping me until I acknowledged her discovery by reaching down and petting her. Then, as if on cue, she would move forward a few feet, stop, and look in the direction of whatever had caught her interest. She would examine the item for a moment and then look back at me as if to say, "Do you see it, boss?" Never a sound, just a revealing action.

I would pet her upon locating whatever she was examining, and she would move back to my right leg as we recommenced walking. This trait, along with many others just as unusual, made her one of the most unique dogs I have ever known. It was obvious that she was made for me and no one else. Donna had selected and named her, knowing she herself would never be able to accompany me in my adventures, but Shadow could. I miss that dog to this day, even after her death from cancer in 1975. In honor of her greatness and our times together, I have never owned another dog that I called my own.

Scanning the road and row of trees leading to the boat dock through the Starlight scope, I was surprised to see the fuzzy green figure of a man standing motionless! I was also aware of Shadow's head now resting on my right leg. Assuring her that everything was all right, I raised the scope once more and watched the figure for a few moments for anything out of the ordinary. Sensing that he was alone, I continued walking toward him, still some hundred yards away. I stopped every twenty yards or so to examine the brushy, treed areas on both sides of the road in case someone was waiting in ambush. That had happened once before in 1967 (see my first book, *Wildlife Wars*, Chapter 12), and I was not going to let it happen again; hence the extreme caution. I was also comforted by the fact that Shadow hadn't indicated that there was anyone else in the area. Seeing nothing but my man on the boat dock, I continued the stalking procedure until I was within thirty yards of where he stood, nervously checking his watch. I took one more long look around 360 degrees with the Starlight scope. Seeing no other company, I told Shadow to sit by quietly pushing her hind end down. I knew that if anyone jumped up and tried to surprise me from behind, he would get the surprise of his life in the form of a large mouthful of slashing teeth.

The grass-covered center of the road was damp, and I used every technique my dad had taught me for stalking someone, including walking on the outer sides of my feet as the Indians used to do, quietly rolling my feet inward at the last moment of each step. I continued this manner of movement until I was no more than ten feet from the person on the boat dock. Ever so quietly, I slowly dropped to one knee in the road, unzipped my vest, took the .44 magnum out of the shoulder holster, and laid it on top of my right knee. I put the scope back on my man, whom I now recognized, for one last look, then laid it off to one side.

Hoping not to badly spook him, I quietly said, "Good evening." As soon as the words came out of my mouth, I quickly and quietly moved several feet to the left, clutching the magnum tightly in case this meeting was not all it was cracked up to be. If someone was prepared to shoot at the sound of my voice in the dark, they would get the surprise of their life as well as "July come early" from the "fireworks" a .44 magnum would bring to the dance.

"*Holy crap!* Terry, is that you?" came his surprised, emotion-laced voice. Now I was able to confirm the voice on the telephone. It was Craig Hoover, the gamekeeper from the Black Mallard Duck Club on San Jose Road (of course, I'm using pseudonyms for both the man and the club).

"Yes it is, Craig," I answered quietly, moving noiselessly back toward the center of the road.

"*Jesus Christ! You scared the hell out of me!* I never even heard you walk up. *Jesus,* you scared me!"

"What do you want to see me about, Craig?" I asked as I moved once again, picking up the Starlight scope in the process.

"Jesus, I need to let my heart start beating again," he squeaked. Realizing Craig was not a life threat based on my previous contacts with him, I holstered the .44 and walked up to him. "Damn, Terry, you scared the hell out of me," he repeated once more as he tried to settle down from his scare. "Can I sit down on the boat dock until I get my legs back?"

"Go ahead," I said, raising the Starlight scope and sweeping the area once more for any other folks lying in the bushes. I figured that if someone wanted to shoot me, he would do it when Craig was out of the line of fire.

"What are you doing?" Craig asked, hearing the faint hum of the scope as I swept the area.

"Just checking to make sure you're alone," I said.

"Jesus, Terry, if my boss or any of the other duck clubs knew I was here talking with you, I'd be fired in a heartbeat."

"Why am I here, Craig?" I asked.

"Terry, there's bait a foot deep on the Jess Cave Duck Club, and it's going to be shot over Saturday."

Those were the magic words needed to get my attention over the tenseness of the moment. If true, it was exceptional news because Jess had been a thorn in my side for years. Upon my arrival in 1967, there were abundant stories about over-limits and the extensive use of bait on the Jess Cave Duck Club, especially on the portion of the club Jess kept for special guests and himself. However, old Jess was a clever one and broke the law only when he knew he would get the brass ring and not a handful of citations. Suffice to say, the many hours spent chasing him in my capacity as a state game warden and a federal agent for over five years had all been for naught. Now that I finally had some inside information, someone would find that Christmas was coming early in the form of the local "fed," whether or not I fit into their stockings hung by the chimney with care. ...

"Where?" I asked, trying not to sound overeager.

"Just listen," Craig replied. "Listen to that area on the club to the south."

Now that I took the time to tune in to my surroundings instead of concentrating on the man by the dock, I could hear that the area to the south contained many ducks, by the sounds of it all busy getting their dinner. That feeding behavior was not out of the ordinary at this time of year in the Sacramento Valley, home to many thousands of species of waterfowl. But on a deep-water duck club with nothing but tules lining the shore of a muddy pond, grits were in scarce supply on the bottom unless the pot had been sweetened. I had been so focused on meeting my mystery man that I hadn't even listened to Nature's clues around me. Sure as hell, Jess had one heck of a pile of ducks on his club, and they appeared to have found something to eat in a normally rather sterile deep-water environment.

"Do you know if the pond was baited by Jess or his gamekeeper?" I asked.

"Don't ask, Terry. I can't tell you that. But it is baited, and I'm prepared to show you where the bait is if you're interested. Not only that, but I heard Jess tell one of his friends he was going to put out some more 'candy' for the ducks just as soon as they clean out this batch."

"You bet I would like to know where the bait is located. That way I won't have to stumble around in the dark trying to find it. When can we get together for a look?" I asked.

"How about right now?" he responded.

"That's OK with me," I said, "but I'll have to drag my sport canoe across Lurline Road, and about another hundred yards, in order to get to this pond so we can get out on the water."

"No need," he said. "I have the keys to the locks on the boats on this dock, and we can use one of Jess's own boats to wring his damn drunken neck."

"Great," I said, "but I'll have to walk back to my truck to get a bait scoop so I can gather up some evidence."

"How long will that take?" Craig asked.

"Why?" I asked. "Do you have a date, or a time you have to be somewhere?"

"No, but the longer I'm gone, the more someone at the clubhouse is apt to ask awkward questions."

"Good point," I said. "Let me take off right now, and I'll be back shortly with the bait scoop." Hearing no argument, I took off at a ground-eating trot with Shadow hot on my heels.

A bait scoop is nothing more than a small rectangular steel-framed contraption, eighteen to twenty inches long, sixteen inches wide, and about four inches deep, with a fine mesh screen on all sides except one. The open side has a one-inch-wide steel lip welded along the bottom on one side of the opening and bent downward to aid in scooping up bait. After being dragged over the bottom of a pond by a rope attached to a handle on the open end, the scoop is retrieved and then dunked repeatedly over the side of the boat so as not to lose any of the contents out the open end. This dunking motion filters out the mud and water and captures all the larger chunks, including the bait or food source left as evidence.

Back at my truck, I retrieved my bait scoop from the locked back box and placed my Starlight scope therein, leaving Shadow in the truck bed for safekeeping. Then I got on the radio and called the sheriff's office, asking that they get hold of Del Garrison and the officer assisting him to inform them that everything was all right, with thanks for the backup. I also asked that they call Donna and tell her all was well. With that, I trotted back to Craig, who by that time had a boat in the pond in question. Within moments we were in the decoy area of the target blind on the southern portion of the Jess Cave Duck Club. As we arrived, about five hundred mallards and pintail rose off the water in unison, quickly fleeing the scene with a racket to match the activity level. Memorizing the spot from which they had lifted off, we quickly paddled to the area, which was muddy as hell from the feeding and covered with feathers. Stopping the forward motion of the boat with the oars, I threw out the bait scoop attached to a twenty-foot nylon rope. We made one drag across the bottom, and upon retrieval I found that the scoop was full of mud and lots of fresh, hard barley (hard barley connotes a recent application; soft, soaked barley connotes an old application of the bait). Turning off my flashlight, which I had shone between my fingers to provide as diffused a light as possible, I told Craig I had all I needed, and we'd best get the hell out of there before we were discovered.

When we reached the boat dock, Craig was shaking like a dog passing peach pits and I had a wide grin scarcely concealed by the darkness. Seeing the effect this work was having on him, I told him to head for home, and I would handle the rest.

"Terry," he said, "don't tell anyone about this, will you, because if you do I'll lose my job."

"Have no fear, Craig, no one will ever know. Even if I have to forfeit the case, I don't identify the names of folks willing to get involved. However, if I get to the baited area tomorrow and discover that anyone let the cat out of the bag, I'll probably have some words with you in front of your boss about this evening's meeting. Do we have an understanding?"

"Don't worry, Terry, that bait is hurting my club through reduced kills with the birds going into Jess's club, especially the mallards. So anything you do would be a help to us, and we'll call it even." Craig paused for a moment and then slowly added, "There's one other thing. The people you find hunting there tomorrow are game hogs from up north. They've been killing ducks out of season, over bait and in large numbers, including market hunting, since they were old enough to carry a shotgun. And it's not just them but the whole of their clan. A few of their old-timers even went to jail for selling ducks years ago when the 'Peanut Farmer' was in the country." The "Peanut Farmer" was a local nickname for none other than an early Fish and Wildlife Service undercover agent named Tony Stephano who had bought and sold ducks up and down the Sacramento and San Joaquin Valley towns in the early 1950s. As a result of his work in the commercial-market-hunting underworld, a fair number of the locals who were captured buying and selling ducks went to jail or the penitentiary because selling sport-shot waterfowl is a felony. Craig continued, "Jess is friends with these people and lets them hunt on his club occasionally to pay off old debts. However, it seems that every time they hunt on Cave's club, they have him sweeten the pot, and shooting on all the other duck clubs along the San Jose Road goes to hell. So the quicker you get rid of them and close the area to hunting, the faster our hunting will improve. It's that simple, Terry—but watch yourself. These guys are killers, and I'm not so sure that behavior wouldn't extend to game wardens trying to catch them if they get half a chance."

"Who are they, Craig?" I asked.

"You'll find out soon enough. I have to run now, or my boss is going to ask me questions that I won't be able to answer."

I thanked him, and he disappeared along a small, weedy levee between several duck clubs.

I put some of the mud and barley from my bait sample into a plastic bag, zipped the bag shut, and stuck it in my pocket. After washing the mud off my hands and bait scoop, I took out a small notebook and rough-sketched the duck pond with the decoys, blind, and location of the baited area. Finishing that while everything was fresh in my mind, I headed for home with a smile on my face and a realization that I might still get in on some chicken and that wonderful lemon cake Donna had made for my dinner, if my young sons hadn't eaten it all. Fortunately, Donna had seen to it that they didn't.

Saturday morning, a shoot day for the duck clubs, found me in my Grumman Sport Canoe hidden in the tules at the far edge of the baited pond. Shadow and I had been hiding in those tules since about three in the morning and, needless to say, were half frozen by shooting time. However, once the first shots were fired by the duck clubs in the area, my blood heated back up to normal, and except for shaking like a dog passing razor blades as cold blood from the extremities rushed to the vital organs, life was good. There were a lot of birds moving in the air during the first few moments of shooting, and it appeared from the number of shots fired that I had at least three guns shooting over the baited area.

The Migratory Bird Treaty Act (MBTA), passed in 1918, does not prohibit the feeding of migratory game birds under most conditions.

However, you can't take or attempt to take them going to, from, or over a baited area with the use and aid of a shotgun where *placed* feed is present. That particular regulation was passed in the 1930s because of the slaughter of migratory game birds over baited areas, a common gunning practice in those days. A baited area is one holding some sort of placed feed desired by waterfowl (corn, wheat, barley, etc.). For over sixty years, those regulations prohibiting the taking of migratory game birds over a baited area worked well to keep that kind of unethical slaughter in check. During that period, the state and federal courts upheld those regulations many times (clear to the Supreme Court in some cases), providing excellent case law that was subsequently used against unscrupulous killers, even those with high political influence, and run-of-the-mill game hogs gunning over bait.

However, in the late 1990s, the powerful directors of several state Fish and Game agencies, associated organizations, and their less-than-ethical clientele, not satisfied with killing more than the generous limits allowed, began squalling to certain congressional types about federal baiting regulations. The complainers thought the regulations too restrictive and unfair, and provided many outrageous examples, some *outright lies,* of the baiting regulation enforcement inequities. Those lobbying included many of note who were being apprehended hunting over bait and flat resented being caught and treated like the common man.

Those less-than-educated-on-the-baiting-issue members of Congress, led by Don Young from Alaska, chairman of the powerful Resources Committee and supported by John Dingle of Michigan (normally a friend of the environment) and others, along with several state Fish and Game organizations, forced their political wills and greed on a weak Service leadership. Those leaders, headed by then Director Jamie Clarke, Deputy Director John Rogers, and their staffs, all generally unschooled in the real world of wildlife law enforcement and related issues of hunting waterfowl over baited areas, folded like a bunch of pigeons hit with a load of number 4 shot! To this officer's way of thinking, the Service leaders prostituted themselves by cooperating with the congressional "gangs" and their barracudalike minions in the gutting of a decades-old and working conservation law. The result of this congressional bullying as they fed on the remains of the Service carcass was to force weakened waterfowl regulations applying to hunting migratory waterfowl over baited areas down the protection community's throat. In essence, this new set of regulations increased the burden of proof on the officers to the point that enforcement of baiting regulations could barely occur. Attorneys and judges reviewing the new, politically weakened regulations were concerned and confused by the language contained therein. Basically, they felt the new regulations, because of the increased burden of proof, were largely unenforceable except in extreme, unlikely situations. Much of the previous case law generated over decades now barely applied, if at all! Sadly, it turned out that there wasn't a bucket of guts among the Service leaders or their staffs regarding this issue. Today, as a result of those greedy, shortsighted, and destructive politics, waterfowl are paying the price of reduced survivability and the American People are paying the price of lost heritage.

I was told by Service law enforcement personnel at the time of this writing that the number of baiting cases, because of the new weakened regulations, has declined sharply because no one knows how to enforce the laws except in flagrant situations. When they do enforce them, the cases' travels and success through the court system are iffy at best. As a result, many officers spend their time in the field working different types of cases, leaving most of the now legally confused baiting issues to God. I have also been told by state Fish and Game wardens from several states that when they now check people hunting waterfowl, especially in parts of Illinois, California, Maryland, Texas, and Louisiana, they are finding amazing quantities of corn and other bait around the blinds, and even stuck to the mud on their boots when they return to their vehicles. They just sadly shake their heads because there is nothing they can do. It's just another example of humankind's lack of awareness of history and failure to give a damn about its consequences.

Well, my shooters were certainly not paying attention to the then "workable" baiting laws as they killed their fifth mallard, who was winging into the decoys as if he had been there before—and he probably had. I carefully listened to the number of guns shooting and documented the times shots were fired, along with the times and numbers of birds killed, and it didn't take long to develop a case against my shooters. When they had killed fifteen birds, I began to paddle my canoe into the area along a route that would cut off any attempts at escape because they had arrived by boat as well. I continued counting and documenting what they were doing.

As I silently paddled around the lower end of their pond, whistling wings overhead told me more ducks were decoying into the baited area. Stopping behind a thin veil of tules, I watched seven pintail pass overhead. They quickly dropped into the decoys by the baited area, only to rapidly rise again to the firing of three shotguns. Only two birds managed to escape the fusillade, the others remaining on the water as concentric circles moved away from where they had fallen. Picking up my notebook from the canoe seat, I recorded three gunners shooting fifteen shots, killing five pintail! The fact that fifteen shots had been fired told me that the shooters were using unplugged shotguns, or shotguns capable of firing more than three shots at a time (a violation of state and federal law). Putting down the notebook, I paddled out into the open area of the small duck pond to put an end to the killing, heading directly for the decoy set and the three gunners in the blind.

Moments later the shooters in the blind saw me coming, picking up their dead ducks as I moved through the water. One stood up in the blind to have a better "look-see" at their surprise visitor. Satisfied that I was a game warden or the like, he quickly sat back down out of sight, and a hushed buzz of talk began in the blind. They were probably trying to put the plugs back into their shotguns, I thought as I sped up the paddling to get to the blind before they succeeded. Even if they successfully managed to replug their shotguns, I would have written the lot of them for using unplugged guns because I had seen all three stand up and shoot at the incoming pintails just moments before. Conservation officers learn to count very quickly, especially when the action is fast and furious. It's no different than flying an airplane, or anything else that takes practice—you get more proficient the more you do it. After a time, you get very good, and I was. Bottom line, if a shooter fires more than three times in a given moment, he is in violation. The courts take judicial notice of testimony given by the officer, and with few exceptions, that testimony is weighted over that of the accused unless the testimony given by the accused, for some reason, is overwhelming. Ducks weren't the only thing these fellows were going to get that morning!

Paddling the few remaining feet to the blind, I heard a *sproing* and, looking up, saw the magazine spring, magazine cap, and plug to a shotgun sail over my head and go *ploink* into the pond. Well, I thought with a grin, that will make one unplugged-shotgun case fairly simple to prove. One of my hunters had tried to replace his plug (a small wooden dowel that fits inside the tubular magazine of a shotgun and is of sufficient length to limit the magazine capacity to just two shells), but with the spring in the magazine under tension, his cold fingers had slipped as he tried to shove the wooden plug back down into the magazine. The magazine spring, along with the rest of the components, shot out over the edge of the blind and into the pond to a watery grave. It couldn't have happened to a nicer guy, I thought.

"Good morning, gentlemen, federal agent. I would like to check some shotguns for plugs if I may, along with your hunting licenses, duck stamps, and birds." With those words, the brushy side door to the duck blind opened, and inside the blind sat three glowering middle-aged men whom I recognized as members of old Sacramento Valley families with, let us say, rich and colorful histories of breaking the wildlife laws of the land.

Holding up my badge and credentials for all to see, I instructed them to unload their shotguns and pass them one at a time to me, butt first, barrel pointing away from them or their partners, so I could inspect them for plugs. Amidst some grumbling, this was done, and I found all three shotguns to be unplugged. My arrival had been so sudden and surprising that none of the three had had time to replug their guns before I was at their door. Sure as shooting, one of the shotguns didn't have a magazine spring, magazine cap, or plug. With just a little humor in my voice, I pointed out to the would-be hunter where his parts had gone in the pond in case he wanted to go looking for them in four feet of muddy water. My humor was met with a pained, steely silence. Carefully laying all three Browning AL-5 shotguns down in the bottom of my canoe, I again asked for and this time received all three men's sets of driver's and hunting licenses along with their duck stamps. So far they had been relatively quiet. Grinning inside, I thought, That will change once I inform them of my knowledge of the bait they were shooting over.

Examination of their licenses showed that I was dealing with one rather large chap named Michael Donovan from Butte City; his younger brother Billy, who wasn't much smaller, from Princeton; and Orrin Olson, a rather tall drink of water without much meat on his frame, cousin to the Donovans, also from the Butte City area. I recognized two of them as workers at the Butte City dryer and the other as a worker on several farms in the area just north of Princeton. All had reputations as big game and waterfowl hogs, but this was the first time I had personally run across them as they practiced their questionable outdoor avocation.

"Gentlemen, may I have your ducks, please?" I asked. The men handed me fifteen assorted ducks from the blind. I had picked up five pintail as I paddled my way through their decoys, making twenty in total. I continued, "Gentlemen, all three of you were shooting shotguns capable of holding more than three shells. That is a violation of state and federal hunting regulations, and a citation will be issued accordingly. Additionally, all of you will lose your ducks because they were taken illegally with unplugged shotguns, and as such will be forfeited to the U.S. government." Still hardly a sound from my shooters, only pained looks at being apprehended by what I am sure they considered just a dumb-ass game warden. "Additionally, gentlemen, all three of you will be issued a citation for taking migratory game birds over a baited area." That brought them back to life!

"*What?*" Michael bellowed. "Baited area my ass. You don't know what the hell you're talking about!"

"Would you like me to show you what I'm talking about?" I asked softly.

"If you think you can, cracker ass, have at it," Michael answered arrogantly, knowing the bait was invisible under four feet of water. Billy and Orrin chimed right in, backing Michael's outrage. I always made it a point to show the bait to any shooters cited for shooting over a baited area, and these folks would be treated no differently. I had just asked for the hell of it, to see what kind of reaction I would get.

Paddling the canoe over to the spot where I had discovered the bait the night before, I dropped my bait scoop over the side with the rope attached.

"What the hell was that?" Billy asked.

"It's a bait scoop I use to dredge up bait in deep water," I responded. After a short drag, I brought the bait scoop to the surface, fully loaded with mud and fresh barley from top to bottom. Paddling the few feet back to my chaps, I handed them the bait scoop with its barley seed shining beautifully against the mud backdrop.

Michael, looking rather sick and now with a quieter voice and a big, weak grin said, "Well, you can't blame us for trying, can you?"

"No," I replied, "but don't do it in my district, because if you do, it's just a matter of time before I'll be on your trail."

"Well, you have us fair and square," said Orrin. "Have at it so we can get back to the business of duck hunting."

Ignoring his arrogant tone, I issued each chap a citation for unplugged shotguns ($50 offense in those days) and for shooting migratory game birds over a baited area ($250). Tagging their birds with evidence tags, I told the men their waterfowl hunting was over for the day unless they wanted to plug their shotguns, hunt elsewhere, and only kill four ducks between the three of them since they had already killed twenty ducks (the limit was eight per hunter per day). They decided they had had enough for the day and would go home to face the music with their wives. Returning their driver's and hunting licenses, I asked if they had any other questions. They all looked at each other, and finally Orrin said, "Terry, I am not trying to be a hardass, but how did you find out about the bait?"

"Simple," I said, "no one saw you put the bait out [a ruse to throw them off the track of my informant in case they had suspicions]. But I watch the degree of killing that goes on in each of my duck clubs, and if the kill all of a sudden gets larger than expected on a particular club, then something is usually wrong. I also watch the flying and feeding behavior of the birds using the area. If they fly right to an area instead of cautiously circling, land, and then dive immediately for food, that tells me I have a baited area. Also, if an area loads up with coots or the pond area is muddy and full of feathers, I again think, 'Baited area.' These clues will give it away every time."

My three violators just shook their heads and then began to discuss the notion that maybe, on second thought, they ought to keep this secret from their wives. Billy even went so far as to remind the others that his wife, who was from Colusa, was a blabbermouth, so in just a few days news of their apprehension would be all over Butte and Colusa Counties. The other two agreed with knowing nods that meshed perfectly with their sour faces. I grinned at their discomfort as I returned their shotguns after recording the information on the citations, then bade the fellows good-day. Before I left, I told them that this hunting area could not be shot over again until all the lure and attractant was gone, and an additional ten-day period after that. There was some grumbling, but they knew they had screwed up and were willing to pay the price. As I left, I heard Orrin say he knew several other places they could still hunt, most of which had never seen a damned game warden. No doubt about it, these three were killing fools who were long overdue for being caught.

On the way out I stopped and let Jess Cave know that all duck hunting was on hold on the baited area until ten days after the lure and attractant was eliminated. Because the pond was isolated from the other duck blinds on the club and the flight pattern of the ducks in the area, that was the only area I decided to close. As was to be expected, Jess, after another night celebrating something in his life with one hell of a party at the clubhouse, was not in the mood to have a lowly federal agent tell him what he could and couldn't do on his club. He bellowed at me in his drunken voice all the way in and all the way out. I love you too, Jess, I thought as I left the clubhouse with a smile on my face and $900 worth of citations in my pocket. Drunken ass chewing aside, life was pretty damn good, I thought as I headed into the marshes and rice fields of Colusa County to see what else I could scare up in the way of waterfowl violations. Yep, life was *real* good! And just think, this whole mess started with my bride wanting me to come home for dinner. God really does move in mysterious ways. ...

In September 1974, I was promoted and transferred to Bismarck, North Dakota, as the senior resident agent for North and South Dakota. Packing up my distraught wife (leaving her friends, family, sorority sisters, teaching position in Williams, and first-ever beautiful new home), two sons, and dogs, I left the Sacramento Valley for what adventures the new assignment would bring. After arriving in Bismarck, it was only days before I was immersed in the wildlife wars of that region: wars involving the protection of wetlands from illegal drainage by farmers; protecting over one hundred national wildlife refuges; regulating wildlife passing through the ports of entry from Canada; checking waterfowl hunters in both states; teaching at the National Academy in Georgia; apprehending those using aircraft to take fur bearers (fox, coyotes, bobcat, and lynx) for the then rich profits of the fur trade; assisting state Fish and Game officers; and trying to regulate the illegal take of and commerce in eagles by Native Americans. Suffice to say, I was on a dead run, as were all of my officers trying to hold the "thin green line."

As supervisor, I was responsible for information disseminated to the public about regional law enforcement issues regarding the illegal take and commercialization of wildlife. Because of aggressive enforcement programs in the Dakotas and numerous successes, especially by agents such as John Cooper, Dave Fischer, and Joel Scrafford, I found myself talking to national and international groups about illegal onslaughts in the world of wildlife. On one of those occasions in October 1975, I was invited to speak to a conservation group in Toronto one day and then to *The Fifth Estate*, a Canadian TV news program, the next. I got the appropriate clearances for foreign travel and kissed my bride and family (which now included a Vietnamese baby girl named Kimberlee whom Donna and I had adopted in April, just as Vietnam fell) good-bye.

Taking an aisle seat on the plane, I busied myself in the speeches and slides to be used during my presentations. The plane continued to fill, but I hardly noticed as I studied the reams of information I had gathered. Soon, because of seat movement, I became aware that the row in front of me was occupied.

"God, that was some duck hunt at Dad's farm, wasn't it?" came a voice from the seat in front of me.

"I never saw so many ducks in my life in and around the decoys, not even when I hunted in the Sacramento Valley," exclaimed another voice.

Boy, those statements instantly turned on my built-in radar, especially with the use of the words *Sacramento Valley*, my old stomping grounds.

"How many birds did we get altogether?" a third voice asked.

"Over a hundred the first day, and I lost count after that!" the voice from the window seat quietly responded. Looking up from the papers and slides scattered across my lap and the vacant middle seat, I examined the backs of the three passengers' heads. From that limited look and their voices, it was no one I recognized. Then one of them turned slightly to speak to his partner in the aisle seat, and I damned near fell out of my seat! It was Orrin Olson from the Butte City area—one of the fellows I had apprehended in 1973 shooting over a baited area on the Jess Cave Duck Club! Quickly grabbing a plastic sheet holding thirty slides from the middle seat, I held it before my face as if I were viewing the slides. A few moments later, peeking from behind my sheet of slides, I recognized the profiles of the Donovan brothers, who had accompanied Orrin that day on Cave's duck club. "Dad thought he could give away all those ducks we got to his neighbors around Medina so that when we return from our big game hunt in Canada in ten days, we can start the next day and kill a fresh batch to take back with us to California," added Orrin.

Man, I thought, *this can't be. This is just too good to be true!* Here I am in North Dakota and these guys from my past in the Sacramento Valley are talking about a violation in my new backyard. And for good measure, they were fellows I had previously tagged for some serious wildlife violations! *Talk about a very small world!* So small, in fact, that the thought *this is just too good to be true* kept whirling through my mind. When they were looking forward, reducing my chance of discovery, I put down my sheet of slides and grabbed a discarded newspaper from the pocket of the seat in front of me. I opened it up and kept my head behind it as if I were reading, all the while listening in on the happy conversation before me. I just sat there shaking my head in disbelief at the turn of events and my possible good fortune to come. My grin was so big, my face was beginning to develop cracks.

Then I got the real surprise of the day from Billy Donovan. "Are you sure we won't get caught if your dad puts that barley around the duck blinds and in the decoys like he did on this last shoot? It just seemed to be awfully close to our blinds. If a game warden comes by, he is sure to see it," he said in a concerned tone.

Damn! I thought. Not only are we talking about gross over-limits but now shooting over a baited area as well!

Michael said, "Billy has a point, Orrin. We got lucky on that first shoot, but I'm concerned that if your dad gives all those ducks away, someone might put the game warden on to us."

I couldn't get over my surprise and excitement at what I was hearing! God, I thought, I have got to catch these guys shooting over bait again, only this time in my new state. What a coup that would be—plus what a stir it would create among the folks in the Sacramento Valley if they ever found out!

"Don't worry about it, you guys. That wetland we are shooting in Section 16 is leased to the Wildlife [a name given to the Service by

local farmers], but it's so isolated hardly anyone can hear the shooting from the nearest section line or prairie trail. So relax. You had a
shoot of a lifetime the first time, and now that Dad has more time to
put out the barley, think of what will be waiting for us when we get
back. Dad knows what he's doing. He has done this in the past for the
hunting benefit of his banker and others and never got caught. We will
be all right," exclaimed Orrin.

The two Donovan boys relaxed and got excited about the upcoming duck hunt. After another few minutes of discussion, the talk
turned to the big game hunt (moose) in Canada, and I lost interest in
those apparently legal plans. If they had been intent on doing in the
moose illegally, I would have called some of my provincial warden
friends and we would have done these lads up right nicely on the
Canadian side. But since that hunt appeared to be on the up and up,
I just tried to stay out of sight and hoped I wouldn't be discovered.

That was the longest trip to Toronto I had ever taken. I had to go
to the bathroom so badly that everything I saw was yellow, and out
of fear of discovery, I just stayed put hoping I wouldn't bust a gut in
the process. Then I had the problem of holding up a newspaper for
what seemed eleven million hours. It was a good thing I had arms like
Popeye, or I would have been discovered as my three outlaws got up
and went to the bathroom several times. We finally landed, and I
waited until the entire plane offloaded before I dared leave. Man, the
first place I headed was the men's restroom, and then I carefully left
the airport. Luck was with me, but I sure didn't rest until I was in my
hotel and out of sight.

My trip back to Bismarck was uneventful, except that the plane
couldn't fly fast enough for me to get home and start looking for the
Olson farm somewhere in the Medina area of North Dakota, and for
the mysterious Section 16.

Pulling into Dave Goeke's wetland office parking lot in Valley City,
I leaped out of my patrol car, entered the building, and trotted toward
his office.

"Hi, Terry, what brings you here?" came Dave's voice from the map
room as I slid to a stop in the hallway.

"You're just the man I'm looking for," I said. "Dave, I know this is
like looking for a Mr. Smith in this neck of the woods, but do we have
anyone under easement [under contract to the Service not to burn,

drain, fill, or level certain wetland properties on their farm] in the
Medina area with a last name of Olson, with an 'o'?"

Dave just looked at me and laughed. "Terry, this is North Dakota.
I have a million Olsons in my district."

"I know," I said. "But will you look in the Medina area and see if
we have any under easement contract, say within a thirty-mile radius
of the town?"

Dave looked at me and, realizing I was hot on a trail, got excited
and without any questions began plowing through his wetland easement records. After what seemed hours, he had located three Olsons
within my thirty-mile radius under wetland easement contract to the
Fish and Wildlife Service. One contract holder was a young man in his
thirties who had recently purchased the farm from his mother. A check
of the original easement contract and files showed that the father, the
original contract holder, had died ten years earlier. One down, I
thought. The second easement contract holder was a woman who was
so old that she no longer farmed the land, which was leased in the
name of a middle-aged Russian couple. Two down, I thought, on my
long-shot hunch. Hell, the Olson I was looking for could have been
one who had never done any business with the Service, I began to
think. If that was the case, I was looking at walking my fingers
through all the Olsons in the phone book in the Medina area, one at
a time, until I was able to locate the farm through the county's
landowner records. If that ended up being the case, I wasn't quite sure
how to approach those folks without tipping them off but figured I
would worry about it when the time came. Then Dave said, "How
about this last case file? I have an Orrin Olson Sr. who owns six sections of land just north and west of us in Stutsman County."

When Dave mentioned that name, my heart actually skipped a beat.
Not believing what I had just heard, I slowly asked Dave if any of
those lands under Service contract was Section 16.

"I don't know," Dave said. "Let me take a look." After a few moments examining the maps Dave said, "Nope, every other section in
the book is leased to us, but no wetlands are covered under Section 16
in this contract."

Damn, I thought. Now the detective work begins all over again.
Orrin Jr. had spoken about Section 16 being leased to the "Wildlife,"
and being an old farmboy, I was convinced he knew what he was

talking about. If he didn't, or had gotten his sections crosswise, I would be looking at wetlands on those sections on his dad's farm until I was blue in the face, trying to isolate the one they were going to shoot over. And I didn't have much time, as they were due home shortly. "Thanks, Dave," I said. "I'm off to Medina to see what I can dig up in the county records. In the meantime, would you run off copies of the map of Orrin Olson Sr.'s lands, and I will start from there on shank's mare if I run out of ideas in Medina."

With the maps and a handshake, I was out the door heading for my vehicle. God, I knew it was too much to hope that the Olson I needed would be under contract to the Service and would have some paper to lead me to the section in question. That kind of luck was apparently not to be. Entering my sedan, I started to drive out of the parking lot on my way to Medina. Then I heard Dave whistle at me from the door. "Terry," he said, "take a look at this."

Stopping my car, I got out, met him halfway across the parking lot, and took a look at the paperwork he was holding. "I have a Smelski who sublet 640 acres to Orrin Olson Sr. right next to the Olson farm, and there is a Section 16 in that land under wetland easement contract, if that would help."

Damn, if Dave hadn't been so ugly I would have kissed him right then and there. "Dave," I said, "this may be it! Would you make copies of that map and easement document and let me take them with me as well?"

"Sure," said Dave, and off he went to copy the requested materials. North Dakota wind–burned face or not, I now had an ear-to-ear grin and a look in my eyes that said the "hunt" was on. ...

Several hours later found me talking to Dale, a friend who could keep his mouth shut and owned a J-3 Cub single-engine aircraft. Twenty minutes later we were in the air, heading for the Smelski property. After we found the property, we flew over it fairly high so as not to arouse any suspicion in folks on the ground. From the maps on my lap, I was soon able to locate Section 16. In the middle of that property, a good-sized meandering wetland, probably thirty acres in size, was located as pretty as you please. It was horseshoe shaped with a long finger of land protruding into the center of the wetland. Even from the air, I could see that the area was covered with resting waterfowl. What made it even more suspicious was that all the surrounding wetlands within a mile were almost bare of waterfowl. Tapping Dale on the shoulder, I asked him to go down and make a single pass along that finger of land, then, using the hills for cover and hugging the ground, get the hell out of there. As we got closer, I could see that the wetland, especially the area on both sides of the finger of land, was muddy as hell. Great! I thought. That was a sure sign of feeding waterfowl. Then, there they were! Two sunken duck blinds on the tip of the finger of land. As Dale started his close-in pass, I could see what appeared to be tractor tire marks in the tall prairie grasses the full length of the finger of land leading to the blinds. As the ducks rose into the air in clouds at the sound of the airplane, there appeared to be small streaks of yellow along each side of the finger of land near the sunken pits. There was also a third streak of yellow in front of the duck blinds, looking suspiciously as if someone had dumped some kind of bait out there for the ducks as well. No two ways about it: what was on the land and in the water was of extreme interest to the hordes of ducks. Quickly imprinting on my mind what I was seeing from the air, I told Dale to head for home. Dale, taking to heart my request to ground-hug the hell out of there, stopped my heart as he nearly hit a golden eagle feeding on a duck on a hilltop. The duck was probably a cripple from my suspicious wetland, I thought once my heart started beating again. When we landed, I paid Dale $5 for the gasoline (gas was cheaper then) and split for the area to see what was behind the wetland full of ducks and yellow streaks.

Ten o'clock that evening found me at the edge of Section 16 where the tractor tire marks left the gravel road, passed through a gated fence, and disappeared toward the wetland. When I looked back toward where I had parked my car a quarter of a mile down the road (leaving a note on the dash that I was out of gas but would be right back), the way appeared clear. Crawling over the fence, I bypassed the locked gate, and started walking out into the quiet of the prairie.

Once out of sight of the main road, I used my flashlight and jogged along the tracks through the tall prairie grasses to the finger of land that jutted into the wetland. What a look it turned out to be! On either side of the tractor tracks at land's edge was a stream of fresh barley, easily ten inches deep, that stretched almost thirty yards up to the two sunken duck blinds. In front of the duck blinds, in the water where one would place the decoys, was another several hundred pounds of barley. In the sunken-pit blinds were a zillion recently fired shotgun shells (as I could tell by smelling the fresh burned powder) and about one hundred floating-type duck decoys. I just shook my head. This was an excellent setup, isolated behind fences, down in a natural bowl out of sight and sound, all equating in my mind to a waterfowl killing ground.

Standing there, I thought, You almost certainly have the place your California lads and the North Dakota dirt farmer are going to shoot. With that, I collected bait samples from the water in front of the blind and on both sides of the finger of land. Next I took flash pictures of what I had collected and the spots it had been located. Then I diagrammed the entire area in my notebook, noting where everything of interest to a court of law (blinds, bait) was located. That work finished, I headed back out to the road, my car, and some sleep back in the town of Medina. Aside from almost stepping on "Nature's tank," a badger hunting for his supper in the dark on the prairie trail, I had an uneventful trip back.

Daylight found me driving around Section 16 trying to familiarize myself with every road and trail into the area and places where I might hide my patrol car. My three errant shooters on the plane had been right: the wetland was impossible to see from the road, and parking a strange car out there in the middle of nowhere would certainly draw unwanted attention. Yet I needed to be in a position where I could watch the area over the next few days to ascertain whether new bait was being placed and who was doing the placing. That meant that, strange or not, the vehicle would have to be parked in the open because I couldn't find any abandoned barns or machine sheds in which to hide it. I would have to depend on one of "Grosz's Rules" for salvation: *If they are not looking for you, they won't see you.* I had successfully applied that rule many times elsewhere, and it was about to be tested on the windswept prairies of North Dakota.

I knew that definitive detective work and documentation would be extremely necessary because I had a federal judge in Bismarck who didn't like wildlife cases in his court. Even though I had one of the best assistant U.S. attorneys in the country in David Peterson, the judge, in an earlier investigation of illegal trapping and selling of migratory waterfowl, had found the mallard duck to be nonmigratory (contrary to the Migratory Bird Treaty Act) and dismissed the case.

I couldn't believe what the judge had done, and neither could Dave. The judge had asked me on the stand whether I had observed the mallard ducks in question (my evidence) migrate north in the spring. I answered, "No" (how in the hell was I supposed to be able to observe twenty-three particular mallard ducks migrating north in the spring?). Then he asked me if I had seen the ducks in question migrating south in the fall. Brother, I had no idea where he was going with that line of questioning, but I said I had not. "Then I declare the mallard duck nonmigratory and dismiss the matter before me," he said. Then he abruptly left the courtroom as Dave and I sat there stunned! With that at the top of the federal bench in Bismarck, and not wanting another goofy damn dismissal, I needed an airtight wildlife case—and by damn, I was going to have one.

Five days before the return of my three outlaws from Canada, I parked an undercover pickup about half a mile from the gate leading into my baited area. Crawling under the truck, I let down the exhaust system from the manifold so anyone coming down the road would see that the pickup was crippled. Then I firmly affixed a note to the inside dash where any passerby could read it. I had printed in big, bold letters that I had broken down and would be back soon to repair the truck. That way, even if it sat there for a week, everything would probably be all right. I wasn't worried about vandalism because in that part of the country, people were still good and honest. That was, except for the chaps involved in my baited duck marsh! Grabbing a sleeping bag, spotting scope, cold-weather gear, raingear, water, toilet paper, and some old military C-rations, I headed across the prairie to a large rock pile overlooking the baited wetland.

Once my gear was hidden, I took some rocks and built a walled, natural-looking observation position into the rock pile where I could sit or lie unobserved and watch any proceedings in my wetland. I constructed it so I had a line-of-sight advantage, could use my spotting scope or binoculars, and would never be seen unless someone walked up to the rock pile looking for me. There was a small draw loaded with prickly pear cactus that would offer cover when I left the rock pile to travel down to the prairie trail and shooting area. Building a chair with a stone back, I set my sleeping bag in it for comfort. I pulled a camouflage parachute over the top of the observation post to hold off the sun's rays, anchoring it with large, flat rocks from the pile and armloads of weeds taken from the corner of the field. Dug in like a wood tick and hidden like a sniper, I settled in to wait.

On Monday all was quiet, and nothing out of the ordinary happened. The same prairie quiet that drove many homesteaders to the edge of their mental limits was my only companion on Tuesday, other than a few curious field mice. Wednesday I saw nothing but the normal activities of nature until two o'clock in the afternoon. I was dozing in my observation chair when deep in the recesses of my mind, I heard the *putt-putt-putt* of a John Deere tractor. Quickly bringing myself back to the world, I saw a tractor heading down the prairie trail toward the duck blinds. Ducks, disturbed by the tractor's arrival, poured into the air by the hundreds. They flew around in ever larger circles, and it was obvious that they wanted back into their little wetland. That sure spoke to the quality of chow they had been consuming, I thought.

The tractor was pulling a small trailer, and with the spotting scope I could see at least ten bags of what appeared to be grain of some sort, stacked two high. The driver was an older man, and as he pulled the tractor first along one side and then along the other of the spit, he stopped several times to empty out sacks of what appeared to be wheat or barley in long rows at the land's edge and into the water. Saving two sacks for the tip of the spit, he drove to the blinds and, after putting on hip boots, waded out into the water and dumped the sacks of grain in the area I supposed would be the eventual location of the decoys. The farmer walked back to land and surveyed his work, circled by hungry ducks on the wing.

Satisfied, he walked back to the tractor and, taking out a pair of binoculars, did a complete 360-degree sweep of all the hills surrounding the wetland basin, apparently looking to see whether anyone had observed his actions. I just grinned from my place of concealment. Anyone that careful would be a fine catch, I thought as I recorded his every move in the diary at my side. Along with those observations went a detailed physical description of the man who had placed the bait. He would be an easy one, I thought, with his shiny bald head, potbelly, and large, dirty-yellow walrus mustache. His dark plastic-rimmed glasses rounded out my recorded description of a man approximately sixty-plus years of age. He drove the tractor back up the prairie trail several hundred yards, stopped, and placed the grain bags in a small coulee. I figured they would be used later to haul ducks if the lads had a great shoot. Also, with the sacks hidden so far from the shooting area, a game warden not on his toes might miss the baiting issue altogether. Then my fellow stood up on the tractor seat for a better view and watched the fruits of his labors being attended to by many hundreds of ducks happily paddling around the newly placed grain buffet.

About four o'clock my farmer left the area, and I waited until dark to make sure he wasn't coming back. Then I moved into the freshly baited area. The driver had again used barley, and I used my small point-and-shoot camera to photograph the bait clearly spread out on the land and at the water's edge. I photographed the tractor tracks leading up to each grain dump and took pictures of the bait in the shallow water at the tip of the land spit. I also took fresh samples of barley from the area and photographed those, using my badge as a reference. Walking up the prairie trail, I photographed the hidden barley sacks and then retreated to my rock pile for another night's sleep under the stars, with the spirits of yesteryear making their soft night sounds around me and in my dreams. On each of the next two days, my yellow-mustached friend came out in the afternoon around three and checked the wetland. He would stand and observe the area for about thirty minutes from afar, as if not wanting to frighten the ducks, and then departed after a trademark 360-degree look around with his binoculars. Figuring that by Saturday my three California outlaws would be back from Canada to shoot the baited area, I took my rather strong-smelling carcass home for a much-needed bath and home-cooked meal after a short stint under my pickup hooking the muffler system back into place.

On the way home, I had to grin. This fellow placing the bait was a wise one, putting it out late in the afternoon, when most officers might be resting in front of a TV (or so most thought), and in the middle of the week. This timing allowed the ducks to almost feed out the entire baited area by the shoot day. The ducks' urge to return to the area would still be strong, but any game warden checking the area during the shoot would find little or nothing in the way of bait to make him suspicious. Pretty damn clever—but not clever enough. He had three loose-lipped fellows coming into the area to hunt who couldn't keep their mouths shut. Especially when the law was in the back seat. ...

Saturday at three in the morning, I parked my yellow Ford sedan (a different vehicle than I had used earlier) about a mile away from the baited area on another gravel road and, after leaving a note on the inside dash about a fuel-line problem, trotted over to my rock pile and stood there drinking in the softness of the morning, the faraway hoot of a great horned owl, and the smells of the prairie when they were the most pronounced. It was easy to appreciate my many blessings. Many of my kinfolk had settled and worked the Dakotas at the turn of the century. They had cut the prairie for the first time with their steel plows and oxen, using the sod to build their homes and lives. Hopeful in their dreams, yet tempered by the harsh crucible of the prairie, most died not much richer than the day they started. But they had helped build America, and I was proud of that. Knowing all this, I couldn't help but identify with some of the voices of the past borne on the wind. They were tough and determined people, my family, and only four are left alive as this story is written. One of those four, a much-beloved uncle, is close to crossing over the Great Divide as I think back over the wonderful times and lessons he provided a young man (me) lacking a father.

My thoughts continued to drift with the gentle breeze, back to my mother, who had been born in a sod house, endured hard times growing up, and left North Dakota as soon as she could. She was a tiny woman and used to tell me about being blown around by the "darned old wind" and "always being cold clear through when the winter storms arrived." She was one tough lady who raised a family by herself after going through a divorce in the 1940s, and who lived into her early eighties before her struggling heart said, "No more." No matter how you looked at it, the hard prairie existence took the best years of their lives, just as it took the wheat and corn during the droughts. The prairie didn't have any favorites after European settlers killed off the bison and Plains Indians, wiped out the prairie chickens, and let the topsoil blow clear to Kansas.

Working alone on a baited-area investigation with all its inherent problems was counter to everything I had learned. Anytime anyone worked a baited area, they had better take more officers than they figured they needed. But for the effect and a bit of ego (the root of many evils), I wanted to catch my three California shooters doing the same thing I had caught them doing 1,500 miles away, two years earlier.

I felt that if I could pull this off, the effect on these folks' souls might be just what the doctor ordered to stop or at least slow down this kind of behavior. Yes, I thought, it was time to open the "prairie school" and teach a few things associated not with "book-learnin'" but more directly with life's experiences.

Around five in the morning, I noticed a set of headlights wildly swinging from side to side as the vehicle bounced along the heavily rutted prairie trail leading to the duck blinds. At the first sign of the headlights swinging across the wetland, I could hear several thousand ducks lifting up, heading for safer places to roost. The car continued down the spit of land to the sunken blinds and then stopped. Its headlights remained on, but the driver shut off the motor (I could tell because of the dimming of the headlights). In a few moments it was plain that the shooters were using the lights to put out their decoy sets. I could see tiny figures through my binoculars removing the decoys from the sunken pits and placing them in a "J" pattern on the water, the most conducive set for a good duck shoot based on the prevailing winds. While three of the men placed decoys, one moved the shotguns and other gear from the car to the two sunken pit blinds. After the decoys were set, one man moved the car from the shooting area, parking it out of sight where the barley bags had been placed in the coulee along the road. I could see the driver getting out of the car, picking up the bags, and stuffing them into the trunk. Slamming the trunk with a thump clearly audible even at my distant observation point, he walked back to the duck blinds in the semidarkness, seen only by the man near the rock pile with his binoculars, the field mice scurrying away from his shuffling feet—and the Old Boy above whose creatures they were about to kill. ...

Dawn came that morning in North Dakota as it had for centuries. First a false dawn of deep reds illuminated black remnant cloud formations to the northwest, followed by lighter purples replacing the reds as the sun hove into view. Along with the colors served up in the sunrise came the first traces of the ever-present breeze from the northwest, ushering in another great day on the prairie. Waving armies of prairie grasses showed the paths of the winds and brought fresh smells of curing grasses to herald the new day. All I needed was a herd or two of bison, elk, and deer, with a "pinch" of colorful Lakota on a distant ridge, to make the morning even more memorable. Thanking God for

His many blessings, I turned to the business at hand, and it wasn't long in coming.

The first hungry flock returning to the barley buffet was met with flying lead, and for many the morning's early colors turned to a stinging red, followed by the soft black of eternity. Soon the shooting was fast and furious as surprised ducks sailing back into a place that earlier had been a quiet buffet of barley returned to an unwelcome hail of lead from four well-placed gunners. Soon I had twenty-nine marks in my notebook connoting ducks killed in the hail of lead over the baited area. From my distance, it was impossible to correctly identify all the species of birds other than drake mallards and pintail. Because of that and a totally protected redhead population that year, I decided to stop the slaughter early. The quickness of the killing caught me by surprise, and during the few minutes it took me to make up my mind to get going, the figures of death rose to thirty-eight! My shooters had exceeded their limits of ducks not thirty minutes into the shoot and showed no sign of slowing down or leaving, and neither did the winged flocks! What a perfect place for a modern-day duck slaughter, I thought. It was in the middle of a 640-acre piece of prairie, and because of the wetland basin's depression, with the wind blowing at cross angles, the shooting could hardly be heard even by anyone who was listening. However, they may have had a fortress around them in land isolation, but they had forgotten to put a roof on it ... and unwanted eyes were looking in.

Grabbing my enforcement gear, I crawled out of my hiding place, being rewarded with cactus needles in the hands and knees. Once out of sight of the shooters in the wetland below, I trotted down the prairie trail, using the protective cover it offered. I soon arrived at my subjects' automobile. Stopping, I took the time to write the license plate number down on my left index finger and in my notebook with the date. That way, if my intrusion caused someone to do something stupid and I didn't make it out, the chances were that someone would find the incriminating license number on my person or in my notebook, providing a starting place to look for the culprits in case I went the way of the ducks now cooling on the water. I had also left information with my wife regarding whom I would be contacting and what township, range, section, and wetland description I would be rattling around in. *Just in case. ...*

Glancing down the road with my binoculars from a kneeling position behind the cover of the prairie grasses, I could see that my shooters were still hammering the birds and not retrieving them. It was an old market gunner's trick whereby they could kill more in a short period of time and not disturb the flight frequency or patterns by walking around in the decoys. Good, I thought. As long as they continue to do that and not look back, I should be able to stalk right up to them and hang a grand surprise on them before they realize what is spooking the ducks: namely, me making my approach from the rear. The wind was picking up in velocity as I picked up my pace, dog-trotting right down the prairie trail leading to the two sunken pit blinds. The birds were pouring into the decoys, figuring that was a safe place to land, and many of them made it their last. The killing was going as hot and heavy as any I had seen, so I doubled my pace until I was only ten yards from the two blinds and directly behind them. Neither set of gunners had seen me because of their killing frenzy, so I stopped in plain view behind them and stood there getting my breath.

About half of the arriving ducks, seeing me standing there in front of God and everybody, decided they needed to go elsewhere and began to flare off from the decoys. The other half, greedy and drawn to the bait like magnets, roared in, ending their days with a faceful of shot. After about two minutes of this behavior, I heard Orrin Sr. say, "What the hell is the matter with the birds?"

"I don't know," said Orrin Jr., turning from his sunken pit blind to respond. For just an instant his eyes looked right at and then past me as he spoke. Then he did a double-take as he stared right at me, finally uttering, *"Holy Christ! Not you!"* I just stood there, smiled, and gave him a little high sign with my right hand.

Orrin Jr. just stood in his pit blind in disbelief, and then the other hunters turned around and stared as well. I heard Billy softly say to his brother, "Is that who I think it is?" Then more loudly, "Michael, what is that son of a bitch doing here?" As if his brother had the answer. ...

"Morning, gentlemen," I said as I walked the remaining few feet to their blinds. "Federal agent. Would everyone please empty their shotguns and hand them to me with the barrels pointing in a safe direction?" With that request, and just in case someone tried to do something foolish, I slid my hand down to my Colt .45. If it is going to happen, I thought, it will in the next few seconds. Best be prepared or, as Low Dog from the Lakota said on the day he battled Custer, "Today is a good day to die." Then I initiated my always faithful Plan B. Taking a big chance, I slightly turned and waved my arm back at the rock pile as if I were waving to someone still on stakeout. Turning back to the still awestruck shooters closely watching me, I said, "Those are the other two officers, one at the rock pile and the other at the hill by the gate. They are waiting for the signal to come in and pick up the birds and help me haul them or you folks out of here if need be. If not, they will work another case they have going. The guns, gentlemen," I said as I boldly walked toward them.

My four lads still stood in their pit blinds, not moving. I am sure three of them were thinking this couldn't be happening to them. The last time they had seen me was several years ago, some 1,500 miles away. Now their worst nightmare was in their backyard! Orrin Sr. finally jacked the shells out of his Remington 870 and handed me the empty weapon, which I quickly checked and laid at my feet with an open action. Then Michael Donovan did the same, and Orrin Jr. and Billy followed suit. With the four shotguns comfortably in my custody, I instructed my shocked and silent shooters to pick up the ducks, bring them to me, and pile them alongside the guns. "And," I said, "the first person I observe stomping ducks in the mud to avoid the issue of over-limits will go to jail in irons. Is that clearly understood?" There were nods from all the men.

It is a common trick for outlaws to stomp the less desirable ducks such as shovelers, wigeon, and the like into the mud, keeping only the big, better-eating ducks such as the mallards and pintail. This allows them to kill until they tire of the blood sport and then bring out only a legal limit, as if to say, "Look at me, the good sportsman." Because fines in the federal system for possession of an over-limit in those days were predicated on the total number of birds killed, you can understand my warning to the shooters to make sure all the birds were retrieved. In addition, the idea of wasting something that took Mother Nature several years to make is not only legally but morally wrong. ...

Slowly at first, and then with resignation, the three men wearing hip boots began to walk among the decoys, reeds, and tules retrieving the dead and dying ducks. Twenty minutes later, sixty-one mallards, pintail, wigeon, gadwall, and redheads lay at my feet. Separating the redheads, a totally protected species, I laid twelve off to one side.

"Gentlemen," I said, "this species is totally protected." The looks I got in return showed that they had no idea what a redhead was or, even worse, how to tell them from other ducks in the air before they pulled the triggers. "I will need hunting licenses, duck stamps, and driver's licenses from each of you, please." I kept a sharp eye out for any trouble, but it seemed that my shooters, especially in light of my two "partners" to the rear, were going to roll over like cocker spaniels.

With the documents in hand, I sat down on a large rock some ten feet from the nearest chap and instructed them to sit down and take a load off their feet because the paperwork was going to take a while. This they did while the air charged again with ducks whistling to nature's call, dropping into the decoys and along the spit of land looking for the easy grits to which they had become accustomed. All that in plain view of five humans in the open not twenty yards away. I just shook my head. Any damn fool who advocates liberalizing the baiting regulations is no different than the poacher, I thought, or at best is one of the dumbest people alive. All you had to do was see the narcotic effect on the game birds of a baited area to be sickened by the potential for destruction.

"Well, gentlemen," I began, "your shotguns are plugged in conformance with state and federal regulations, and all your licenses are in order. You adhered to legal shooting hours, and not one of you fired even a minute early, and for that I thank you. However, I have at my feet a rather large over-limit of ducks in total and a smaller but just as important pile of totally protected species of which none may be taken." I looked into their eyes for any reaction. None was forthcoming. They all acted as if I held all the cards and they were waiting for the other shoe to drop. Well, they were right on both counts, I thought. "Gentlemen, what I propose to do, since none of us can determine who killed what, is to charge all of you with the joint taking of over-limits and joint taking of a protected species, namely the redheads. Additionally, all of you will be charged for taking migratory game birds over a baited area." You could have heard a pin drop even in that prairie wind. I think they were hoping I hadn't noticed the bait. "As all of you can see, there is evidence of a baited area everywhere, including on the land within six feet of your blinds. Any normally prudent man could see the bait, and all of you are responsible for reading and understanding the hunting regulations that prohibit the use of a lure or attractant when hunting migratory game birds. Additionally, I personally observed Mr. Olson Sr. putting out ten bags of barley on Wednesday of this week in the shooting area, and I overheard you, Billy, Michael, and Orrin Jr., talking about the bait you were going to shoot over during this hunt. But I won't disclose how I was able to do that except in a court of law. Lastly, you three Californians know about the baiting regulations, seeing that our paths crossed over this very issue on Jess Cave's duck club a few years back. It will be pretty clear to any federal judge that you knowingly conspired to shoot over bait and take over-limits of migratory waterfowl. How am I doing so far, Michael?"

Michael said, "Terry, you and I have been here before, and I was wrong then and am wrong now. I won't lie to you; we all knew what we were doing—but *God o'Friday,* who would have thought we would be found way out here on this godforsaken prairie, in the damn middle of nowhere? And that brings up another matter. Where the hell did you come from? The last I heard you were transferred back East somewhere, and now I find your ugly puss standing in the middle of one of the best duck shoots I ever had."

"Well, Michael, the good Lord works in mysterious ways, and this just happens to be one of His finer moments."

He just looked at me and disgustedly threw down a stem of grass he had been chewing on.

"Gentlemen, I am going to issue each of you three citations: one for taking a joint gross over-limit of ducks; one for taking a closed-season species; and lastly, one for taking migratory waterfowl over a baited area. Any questions? Not hearing any, I will start with Mr. Olson Sr. The rest of you can draw the ducks while you are waiting for your turn at the paperwork so I don't lose them to spoilage."

With that, I worked through the four shooters with the citations and got all the ducks cleaned in the process. I and Mr. Olson Sr., who seemed embarrassed beyond all get-out, walked back to the car after I gave the wave-off to my "partners" at the end of the citation session. Without a word, we got in and brought the vehicle back to the blinds. I loaded the ducks into one of the grain sacks from the trunk of the car. Turning to my three California gunners, I informed them that they might as well put the decoys into the remaining sacks because this area, with evidence of the bait still in abundance, could not be hunted again that year. Winter was only a few weeks away, along with freeze-up, and migration out of the area would take care of any further shooting opportunities. In short, for all intents and purposes and given the ten-day rule, shooting over this wetland was finished for the year. Then I loaded my evidence ducks into the trunk of Mr. Olson's car, along with all their shotguns, and had him drive me back to where my patrol car was parked.

Mr. Olson broke his silence at the end of that ride saying, "Officer, I am physically sick over what we did here today and two weeks ago. I swear to you, as God is my creator, I will never break the wildlife laws again." The old man had tears in his eyes as he reached out to shake my hand as if that simple act would put a stamp of validity on what he had just said. I was so moved by the man's simple act of contrition, coupled with his emotion, that I couldn't say anything but just nodded my head in approval. I never saw that man hunt again. Of course, North Dakota is a big place, and I was only one set of eyes. Removing my hand from his, I transferred all the ducks and shotguns into the trunk of my car and then followed him back to the hunting spot.

Seeing that the lads were ready to go, I got out of the patrol car and walked over to them. I didn't need to say anything to Old Man Olson. I could tell he was so embarrassed and ashamed that he hurt. I thought his kid had probably put him up to the bait and subsequent over-limits, and that would have to be worked out later between the two of them, as I bet it was. ... This little act of greed was going to sting the whole crew. Each hunter eventually paid the maximum, $500 per charge, or $1,500 each, and in those days that was a lot of coin. Looking over my group of downcast shooters, I said, "Michael, when are you going to get this urge to kill outside the law, out of your system? This is twice you have been tapped for the same thing, and it has got to be getting expensive."

"Screw you and the horse you rode in on!" was his curt reply. "My grandfather and father shot the ducks until they died, and I will too. If you don't like it, asshole, then try and catch me again. It will be a cold day in hell before you do, and that I can guarantee. Now, if you don't have anything else to do with us, and unless we are under arrest, are we free to go?"

"Yes, you are free to go," I said, "but you may find hunting a little difficult in the future."

"Why is that, asshole? Because you have my shotgun? Don't sweat that; I have access to more."

"No," I replied, "that will be returned to you just as soon as you settle up with the clerk of the court on these citations."

"Well, what then?"

"You just might find that when the federal judge reviews these citations, he may get a little disgusted with your shooting habits, and when he discovers your priors, he may go through the roof regarding your sentence. If I have any input, it will fall on the side of the critters."

Every bit of color drained from Michael's face, and he blurted out, "You mean I might lose my hunting privileges because of this here duck shoot today out in the goddamned middle of nowhere?"

"That may be the case, and if it isn't, your 'positive' statements today relative to your future illegal hunting plans should push it over the top with the judge," I answered coldly. Michael just looked at me with a blanched face. It was obvious to me that to lose his hunting privileges was almost akin to losing his life blood, especially living in the Sacramento Valley, the wildlife horn of plenty. "And if that happens, Michael, I will see to it that my counterparts in California are aware of your adjudicated nonhunting status." Turning to Billy, I said, "What about you, Billy?"

"I will do what my brother does," he said firmly, but I could tell from his tone that he wasn't sure he believed what he had said.

Turning to my last California chap, I said, "Orrin, what about you?"

"I don't have any comment," he said with a hard, cold stare. Seeing that I was going nowhere with these three lads, I thanked the men for their cooperation, shook their hands before they realized what I was doing, and departed.

As I drove away from that wetland, I felt no excitement about the apprehensions I had just made. Their catching was needed, but it was also plain that the lads would continue to kill until they got it out of their systems, ran out of critters, or died. Earlier, in the plane at Bismarck, I had felt excitement over the prospect of once again catching several old hometown fellows. Now I just felt drawn and tired as I thought over the notion that maybe I wasn't winning this war for the world of wildlife after all. Maybe all of us manning the "thin green line" were no different than George Custer or a dinosaur, the only difference being the separation of time and place. ...

Billy, Michael, Orrin Jr., and Orrin Sr. lost their hunting privileges in the United States for the next three years in addition to their fines. I guess my federal judge wasn't so bad after all, or maybe I had a better case this time. As a sequel, over the years I have tried to stay in touch with the good people of the Sacramento Valley. A call to a friend in Butte City at the time of this writing brought bad news. I learned that Michael had died of bone cancer four years after this incident, leaving a family behind. Billy discovered he had Type II diabetes, didn't take care of himself, especially with his wild bouts of drinking, and went blind. Orrin lost a hand and forearm in an accident with a piece of farm machinery and is unable to shoulder a firearm anymore. Checking with a friend in the Medina area brought me the not surprising news that Orrin Sr. has been dead for years.

Somehow, I wonder if God was listening to their angry outbreaks that day when I asked about their future hunting intentions. After all, those were His critters falling illegally to their guns that fine prairie morning. The subsequent history of those folks caught shooting over bait in North Dakota in 1975 surely validates the beliefs held by many of us who defend the natural world. That being the case, maybe He did listen to my voice from the wilderness—and held court of a different kind.

eight

Uncle John's Cows

IN THE WINTER OF 1975 I received a telephone call from Jim
Matthews, refuge manager at Arrow Wood National Wildlife Refuge
in eastern North Dakota. We exchanged pleasantries for a few minutes, but I could hear a strain in his voice. Sure as hell, it wasn't long
before Jim shifted gears and said, "Terry, we have a major cattle trespass problem on one of our Waterfowl Production Areas." Waterfowl
Production Areas, or WPAs, are small parcels of land purchased in fee
title by the Service because of their national wildlife refuge–like qual-
ities. They are too small to be deemed national wildlife refuges and
hence are covered by one of the Service's many small wetlands programs with the Waterfowl Production Area designation. WPAs are
protected by many of the provisions of the National Wildlife Refuge
Administrations Act. In short, they are mini national wildlife refuges.
Jim continued, "The fellow responsible for the cattle trespass problem is downright nasty and politically influential. He has illegally
grazed his cattle on our refuge lands periodically now for the last five
years. For whatever reason, we just can't seem to get his attention so
he will stop these destructive practices." He was talking now as if he
had something big to get off his chest that had been there for a while.
"This person also allows his cattle to illegally graze on all his neighbors' lands, even grazing off their winter haystacks. As if that isn't
enough, he cuts down our WPA fences and runs his cattle into those
areas to graze off our lands too. If caught in the act, he tells the
landowner, us included, to send him a bill for the feed his animals ate
and hangs up. He is an arrogant son of a bitch and cares little for anyone else's feelings, their lands, their winter hay supply, or the laws."

I said, "That's no problem—we will take this chap off at the knees if that's what it takes to get compliance with the law. I guarantee *that* will get his attention. He may get away with grazing on his neighbors' property by browbeating them, but as long as I am the senior resident agent, he will not graze on government lands without a permit. To do otherwise will land his arrogant hind end in a court of law or jail. Who is this guy anyway?"

There was a long pause, and then Jim slowly and in carefully measured tones said, "Well, Terry, I think he is one of your relatives!"

Surprised at that revelation (most of my family from both sides are from the Dakotas), I laughed and told Jim that would be no problem. Whoever he was, he was no different than any other violator as far as I was concerned and would be treated accordingly. I said, "If he chooses to graze his cows on *my* national wildlife refuge lands, then his cows will just have to become government cows, won't they? Which one of my kin is it anyway?"

After another nervous pause, Jim replied, "It is John Grosz from Melville."

I shook my head, not in disbelief but in amazement. Because of a divorce in my family in 1946, I had never had a chance to get to know my grandparents on my dad's side until the summer of 1964, when I drove from my place of work in Wyoming to Mott to meet and get to know them. I had met John twice during that brief visit. He was a different sort of fellow, to say the least. He was not a tall man but bore himself like a nobleman, monocle and all. I soon discovered that he was an arrogant, imperious bastard to whom I took an instant dislike. In Grandma's great-smelling kitchen one morning I asked her who he was and where he fit into the family tree. At first she did not want to talk about John and tried to change the subject. She seemed to be ashamed that he was even in the family because he had done something wrong to her way of thinking. However, after more questions from her newly discovered grandson, she opened up—not a whole lot, mind you, but enough for me to get a picture of the man I was destined to meet again over crossed swords. According to her, Grandpa's family had migrated long ago from Germany to the Grim in southern Russia, lured by the promise of land; freedom from conscription; and a chance to worship as they chose, speak their own language, and maintain their culture. However, sometime around the turn of the century, Russia changed the rules for the worse, and Grandpa emigrated to the United States to make his new life. He stepped off the train in Mott, North Dakota, in 1905 with only a nickel in his pocket and proceeded to make a new life. John, my grandfather's oldest brother, returned to the family roots in Germany and disappeared. He resurfaced at the end of World War II under mysterious circumstances. There was no doubt in my mind that John was the black sheep in the family, and that notion was reinforced by my grandmother's reluctance to speak of him further. In fact, she advised me in her thick German accent to forget our entire discussion and cautioned me with a wagging finger not to mention any of my newfound knowledge in front of my grandfather, *ever.*

I noticed after that session that my grandfather was no more than civil to John and that was that—strange behavior for brothers, but I am sure it was based on some strong historical reason. Old-country Germans are hardheaded son of a guns who never forget a wrong or slight. They are wonderful, strong-hearted, patriotic people, but don't piss them off because if you do, it is for life.

John was a hard-bitten old son of a gun, but he didn't come off as a dunce. He was bright and articulate and to me seemed like the stereotypical picture of a senior Prussian military officer. However, he sensed my dislike and kept his distance in our two short meetings, as I was sure he considered me an upstart, shirt-tail kin who was unappreciative of his position.

I came back from my recollections to the present and said, "Well, that still doesn't make any difference, Jim. If John wants to play the illegal grazing game on our WPAs, I am just the lad to bring that kind of behavior to a screeching halt."

We both chuckled, Jim out of relief that I would treat my own like anyone else and I because this problem would open a whole new chapter in my book of life experiences. Boy, if I had only known what a chapter it would turn out to be before all was said and done. ...

I told Jim I would meet him the following morning at seven at a Melville gas station. He could show me which WPA had been trespassed upon, and I would initiate a criminal investigation and take the appropriate action. After hanging up, I stood there for a few moments and ran the conversation through my mind. It was illegal to graze cattle on federally controlled and protected grasslands, and many WPAs had been fenced at great expense to the American taxpayer just to preclude this practice by unscrupulous dirt farmers trying to save a few dollars. The culprit in this instance had to be my grandfather's brother, my great-uncle John. Damn, I thought, my uncle had all the trappings of a crusty, hard-bitten, bullheaded German dirt farmer in the finest tradition of the North Dakota sodbusters. In short, he was a man even God didn't mess with without carefully thinking it over first!

John was older than the glacial dirt he plowed, and my birth dad had once quietly rumored, in answer to my constant questioning in 1964, that John had sinister Old World connections. Supposedly, he and several other high-ranking officials had stepped ashore in Argentina from a German submarine just three days before the end of World War II. Afterward John had legally emigrated to North Dakota with help from the German embassy in Buenos Aires. With money of mysterious origin, he purchased three large cattle-farming operations in the north and central parts of the state. It was easy to see why my grandfather, out of embarrassment, patriotism for America, and disdain, barely acknowledged John's existence. They were still brothers, but the connection seemed to end there. I could see that this case was not going to be a walk in the park once we tangled horns over who had a right to graze what and where. A lot of ground would be torn up beneath the feet of an old German and a new one once this battle commenced. ...

Getting up at three the next morning, and while my bride was fixing me a hearty breakfast, I stepped outside to sense the weather. What greeted me was a typical North Dakota overcast winter morning: 30 degrees below zero (just a little colder than the Fourth of July in North Dakota) and no wind, with more cold and snow in the offing if the mare's tails from the northwest were on the money. It was late November, so the ground was covered with about a foot of snow and everything was frozen hard as a brick. Walking down the steps to my driveway, I unplugged the engine heater from the electrical source and started my patrol car so it would be warmed up before I left for the field. At 30 below, that took some doing, especially with the cheap, small-engine vehicles the government purchased for us in those days. The government even purchased vehicles for law enforcement with no AM/FM radios because the purchasing officials believed we would sit around all day listening to ball games. That was a really stupid decision because when the weather folks in the northern extremes predicted blizzards, they used radio broadcasts alerting the traveling public to such dangers.

My kind of day, I thought with a smile as my wife called out the front door that breakfast was ready. Sitting down to fresh-out-of-the-oven homemade sweet rolls, loaded with brown sugar, butter, and cracked walnuts, I couldn't help thinking that this had to be a spot of heaven. Before I could launch into that treat, my wife placed a huge plate of bacon, spuds, and eggs in front of me and, with a quick kiss, went back to her duties in the kitchen. Watching her walk away, I marveled. Christ wasn't even up at this ungodly hour, yet here she was preparing me a feast, knowing it might be all I got to eat that entire bone-chilling day. She was seldom wrong, and I was glad she had loaded me up with good heat-producing supplies, because they would be needed long before that day was done. In fact, I didn't get anything else to eat until eighteen hours later!

Leaving the house shortly after breakfast, I picked up Special Agent Joel Scrafford, and drove to Melville to meet Jim Matthews at the CENEX gas station. Jim had parked his vehicle at the station so he could leave it plugged in because of the intense cold. (Warmer-clime readers may not know that cars at that latitude and season need a heater built into their engine block if they are to function. That handy device is routinely plugged in to an electrical source to keep the engine warm. Otherwise, the oil cools to thick sludge, and seldom will an engine start before the battery runs down.) Jim climbed in, and off we went to look over the WPA that my great-uncle had illegally grazed as he moved his cows from his northern ranch to his Melville ranch.

The chain of events was readily apparent. Trailing cattle from the northern ranch to the southern ranch, John Grosz's cowboys had run out of daylight. Because it was unsafe to continue in the dangerous low temperatures, and the WPA was convenient, they cut the fence and dumped the stock on the WPA. Then they headed for the home ranch in Melville before they froze to death. They probably intended to retrieve the cows the next day, before we became aware of their destructive and illegal presence. Unfortunately for them, Jim happened to pass that way en route to a meeting with a farmer over an illegal drainage issue on other Service-administered lands, and he spotted the cattle and cut fences.

I soon learned from Jim and his raft of files that John had been trespassing in this manner for at least the past five years. Jim explained
that John trailed his cattle north in the spring to his ranch in Heaton,
letting the cattle feed off the WPAs en route. Then, come late fall, he
reversed the process and fed his cattle off the public land as he trailed
them south to the home ranch in Melville. Jim and his staff had been
unable to catch John in the act because there were hundreds of WPAs
in the refuge district. Knowing that, John grazed at will and counted
on not being caught. Because of the refuge's limited manpower, John
was likely to continue his practices. That arrogant behavior burned
me up, to say the least. Here was John, cutting the fences placed
around the WPAs to protect the vegetative cover for the spring migrants, ignoring our signs against trespassing, and dumping his cattle
as if it were his God-given right. Damn his arrogant German hide, I
thought. It is time this behavior comes to a screeching halt!

Walking into the WPA, I counted 258 head of cattle contentedly
feeding on the only grass for miles around (and the farmers wondered
why their topsoil blew clear to Kansas every spring). These small
islands of vegetation were almost all the migrants would find in their
spring return because the farmed lands around them were stripped
bare; hence their high value for wildlife. Retrieving my fencing tools
from my patrol vehicle, Joel and I mended the cut portions of the
fence, making John's cows officially government stock. I retrieved my
camera from the car and took a series of evidence pictures while Joel
fastened evidence tags on the fence so that when John or his cowboys
returned, they would see that the cows had been seized as government
evidence. The numerous evidence tags happily flapping on the various strands of barbed wire in the cold wind sweeping across the plains
from Canada made it very clear to all that anyone tampering with the
livestock on that WPA would court prosecution for evidence tampering and theft of government property. Clear in any language, I would
say—or so I thought!

Regulations governing cattle trespass and subsequent seizures gave
the rightful owner five days to reimburse the government for all expenses associated with the process (for example, salary, travel, per diem,
equipment rental costs) before the livestock would be sold at public
auction. After the sale, the government deducted its costs and turned
over the remaining money to the previous owner of the livestock. This

harsh treatment was intended to get the attention of livestock owners who chose to gamble with their herds on protected Service lands for a few blades of grass. It also showed the importance the Service placed on those small vegetative islands because of their value to all forms of wildlife, migrant or resident.

In many areas, especially in eastern North Dakota, the WPAs were lands whose wetlands had not been drained and the vegetation completely removed by the farming community's destructive land management practices. The farmers, in order to have the snow blow clear to Kansas during the winter, would plow their lands bare in the fall and burn everything left standing, leaving nothing for any heartbeat that happened across that landscape, be it man or mouse. When the winter storms arrived with the winds out of Canada, there was nothing to hold the snow on the farmers' lands, or "moonscape." Then, come spring, they could start working their lands earlier, avoiding the wet soils caused by lingering snow cover.

Destruction of the land's vegetative cover in the fall sure didn't help the migrating waterfowl and other birds in their nesting attempts the following spring. Without some kind of water and cover, nesting was out of the question, and many of the birds would be forced to move farther north, looking for nesting essentials. In that extended migration, the birds would use up most of their essential nutrients and arrive exhausted, in poor condition, and unable to nest. Hence the purchase of lands for national wildlife refuges and their smaller waterfowl production areas throughout the prairie wetlands forming the "duck factories," as they are sometimes called. Without those little islands of life, most migratory birds would have few places to call home. So it was important to keep the farmers at bay and the WPAs green (or brown, as the season dictated) if the birds were to survive and propagate.

Joel and I finished our evidentiary work at the WPA and returned Jim to his vehicle in Melville. On the way, we laid out a plan for how we were going to seize and transport John's cattle the following day. Seizure was not the way we would have done business if the animals had accidentally strayed or been forced onto the WPA during a blizzard or by some other natural force. The government was a neighbor like everyone else in that community, and we tried to act that way. However, because the violators had committed a deliberate act in cutting a four-strand barbed-wire fence to let the cattle in, and because of John's documented history of disregard for the laws, all bets were off as far as neighborly treatment went.

Leaving Jim to gather his refuge officers and the equipment needed to support our operation the next day, Joel and I headed for the Carrington Livestock Yard in the small town of Carrington. When we arrived, I got my shirt-tail cousin Dave Butts, who worked in the stockyard, to arrange for five stock trucks and trailers to transport the cattle, a portable corral to assist with the loading, several horse-mounted cowboys, and a veterinarian. I also arranged a secure corral in their stockyard where I could place the seized cows and agreed on fees for their detainment until sale. If the process got to that point, I was now prepared for any eventuality. Keep in mind that the government was allowed to sell the stock after five days to recover expenses associated with this operation unless the trespasser paid all associated expenses incurred up to the moment of seizure. I didn't know what John would elect to do, so it was necessary to make all the arrangements in advance in case he balked and went to war. I made sure Butts had it all together and would be at the WPA at five the next morning. It took a lot of guts to go out and help the government seize your neighbor's cattle, but Dave was a good businessman and trusted me. We were good to go.

With those details squared away, Joel and I hurriedly left Carrington to make one last check at the WPA. The sun had dropped lower in the sky, and the temperature had dropped as well. Damn, it was really getting cold, and poor old Joel was starting to freeze, even in the car with the heater on full blast. I had told him the night before to dress warmly because he was fairly new to the North Dakota type of cold, but he had growled that he knew how to prepare for winter weather after his stint as an agent in Nebraska. I let it drop after that retort, but looking across the seat at him, cold as he was, I wondered if one could derive any body warmth from eating crow. ... Not that I had ever noticed any temperature change in my body the many times I had had to eat crow, but maybe it would work for someone thinner, like Joel. Of course, Joel had never ridden with a chap who always kept the window down, no matter what the temperature was—with me being the boss and him being Texas stubborn, I am sure he didn't want to show any weakness. Well, Joel was tough, but not that tough, and I chuckled to myself as we hammered down the darkening, deserted dirt roads in the full blast of winter.

By now it was dusk and easily 40 degrees below zero as we drove back to our seizure site to bed down our charges and make sure all was well. As we drove across that bleak, forbidding winter landscape, my thoughts drifted to my mother and her days as a pioneer in North Dakota. She was born in a sod house and raised on a hardscrabble farm; the family never had any money; she lost her father to cancer at an early age and left home when she was eighteen with $10 in her shoe, a piece of chicken, and an orange in a napkin, hope and head high as she sought a better place to live. She headed for the state of Washington, where her oldest sister lived, and a life she knew just had to be better than the one she left on the wind-blown prairie.

My constantly sweeping eyes and history-drifting memory were rudely shaken back to reality when we rounded the hill overlooking our WPA and discovered that the cattle were gone! I looked at the empty WPA in shock, and Joel was speechless. We, the government, had been robbed—rustled! Closer examination revealed cut fences, trampled evidence tags, and tracks heading southeast across the barren, frozen, rolling hills. Damn, I was furious! Never in my entire career had I lost so much government evidence, and I wasn't going to start now! I told Joel to get his tail end back into the car; we were going after those cattle-rustling sons of bitches! I turned my piss-ant yellow 1975, one-wheel-drive, gutless Ford sedan and wheeled it out across the frozen prairie, since no road followed the cattle tracks. In those days the Service would not purchase four-wheel-drive vehicles for prairie agents because they figured we didn't need them, and sedans were $1,000 cheaper. ... The land was frozen harder than a bullet, so traction wasn't a problem, but I bet Ford never planned on this car being used like this. Out across the prairie we flew, with poor Joel doing some of his own flying around inside the car when I found the inevitable rough spots at thirty miles per hour. After about five miles of this cross-country quest, following the tracks left by the rustled herd and rapidly freezing, steaming cow flops, we drove over a hill, and there they were!

Strung out before me were my 258 evidence cows being pushed down an old prairie road with two cowboys at the end of the herd, wrapped up in a dark gray winter evening on the prairie. Over the hill a yellow Ford sedan (my mechanical horse) came roaring down on them, driven by a guy the size of a horse, with his trusty companion bouncing around inside with eyes by now the size of a horse's eyes! Pulling up in a cloud of frozen dust, I slid to a stop. Still pissed over my loss of evidence, I sailed out of the vehicle, identified myself through rapidly blurring eyes in the searing cold, and ordered the first cowboy off his horse, informing him that he was under arrest for theft of government property. He just sat there and blankly looked at me as if I were nothing more than a fresh cow flop! His eyes were almost frozen shut, tears had long since frozen on the sides of his face, and his mustache was covered with frozen snot, all highlighted by the ugliest set of purple lips and eyelids you ever saw. I told him again to get his butt off that horse or I would drag him off! That time the message got through to his half-frozen brain. He blinked and slowly said, "Mister, I would love to get off this horse, but I'm so cold I can't move." A quick look revealed that the poor son of a gun *was* almost frozen in the saddle. Helping him off the horse, I saw Joel doing the same for the other cowboy, and we assisted them, stumbling and shuffling, into the backseat of my vehicle.

As they warmed up, they came back to life a little. Seeing that they were more alive than dead now, I began to interview them about the day's events. I asked the oldest-looking fellow if he had seen the evidence tags hanging on the WPA fence.

He said, "I sure did."

"Didn't you read what the tags said?" I asked.

"Sure did," he said in matter-of-fact tone.

I said in disbelief, "Didn't the tags tell you that the cows were government property, and to fool with them would get you into trouble?"

Without any emotion, he answered, "That's what they said."

"Well, then, why did you cut the fence and take the cows?"

He replied, "John said to cut the fence and take them because they were his cows."

"What did you just say?" I said in surprise.

He repeated, "John Grosz said to cut the fence, take the cows home, and piss on his badge-carrying nephew. He is the boss, so we did what we was told, mister."

I could see that these two lads were not-too-bright North Dakota farmhands and decided I would not accomplish anything by throwing them in jail for theft of government property. Shaking my head, I asked for their driver's licenses so I could record the information for the investigation and possible later testimony against John in a court of law. When the first driver's license was handed to me, I saw that the fellow in the back seat, who looked eighty, was only twenty-six years old. Thinking something was wrong there, I asked him for his date of birth. The date he gave was the same as the one on his driver's license. Seeing my consternation, he volunteered the information that he had a rare aging disease. After a little more explanation, I bought his story. Man, the crosses some people have to bear, I thought, and I fired off a quick thank-you to my guardian angels for my blessings, cold or no cold. I asked the lads where they were taking the cattle, which by now were cold, hungry, and bellowing like there was no tomorrow. They looked at each other, and the "old" one said, "Over the hill to one of John Grosz's pastures."

Realizing that night would soon be upon us and that I didn't have any other choice, I told the cowboys, now they were warmed up a bit, to get back on their horses and drive the cattle over the hill to John's pasture. Once there, I would retag the area with evidence tags and would pay John for one night's pasture for holding the cows on his land. The two lads in the backseat looked foolishly at each other again, and then the "old" one said, "Mister, we was lying. John doesn't have a pasture over the hill. We was taking them cattle to another WPA for the night." Damn, I could hardly believe what I was hearing. Talk about arrogance—Uncle John sure had a corner on the market for that trait, I thought. Well, it wasn't getting any earlier in the day, and the cattle were still telling us to get with it, so I told the cowboys to remount their horses and we would follow them to the WPA and leave the cattle there for the night. Out they went to their horses and quickly moved the cattle just over the next hill to another WPA. At the gated fence of that WPA, I discovered that John had already dumped 158 head of cattle in there as well! He had to be the thickest-headed one in the whole damn family! I thought. Oh well—in went my herd of 258 cattle, and then both bunches became the property of the U.S. Government. On went the seizure tags once again, along with the chains and locks on the gates. I instructed the two rapidly freezing cowboys to head for home, saying Joel and I would personally inform John of the day's events.

It didn't take the cowboys long to get the hell out of there, and Joel and I headed south to Melville. Joel was driving, and I again became lost in my thoughts, remembering Uncle John's alleged landing in Argentina by submarine. I don't recall what branch of the military he was in, probably the Gestapo, but I do remember that he was what they called a colonel-general. Each time I had seen him, he had had two young, German-speaking bodyguards constantly at his side. I thought back to our last meeting at my grandfather's house in Mott, when John and I had gotten into a "hoorah." He said something about America that I didn't like, and I told him he could go back to Nazi Germany any time he liked. That led to him calling me a "dumb schitz" (in German—a term I understood), and I told him that some people would probably love to see him back in Germany to atone for his past behavior. Before I knew it, Grandma had to break it up. John left that morning after calling me a "schitzkopf," and I told him to take his goons, go home, and cool off. You can probably tell we weren't really that close. ...

Reality returned as I saw John's farm appear in the headlights. As Joel turned into the long driveway that led to his farm, I noticed a lot of lights near one of his barns, so we drove over to that area and saw John and his two bodyguards working on a tractor with a broken front-end loader. By now it was about eight o'clock and colder than "billy hell." I stepped out of the vehicle and started to walk over to John to inform him, as the law required, about his recently seized cattle. The two bodyguards stopped their work and stepped in front of me. John waved them off, and they let me pass.

What a tough old man he was—it was way below zero, he was more than ninety years old, and was working on the loader bucket without a coat or hat. Shaking my head in disbelief, I said, "John, I just seized the cattle you had grazing on our two WPAs north of here, and unless you are prepared to redeem them by paying for all government expenses associated with that seizure, they will be auctioned off within five days." John continued with his work as if I hadn't said anything or didn't even exist. I waited for a few moments and then said, "Did you hear what I said?"

Finishing work on the bucket, he turned to me and said, "Vat you say?"

I slowly replied, "John, I just seized over four hundred head of your cattle grazing on two of our fenced WPAs. That's illegal, and you know it." He just looked at me with his trademark hard, cold stare. I continued, "The way the law works in matters like this is that you can pay all the Fish and Wildlife Service's expenses related to this seizure, or the cattle will be auctioned off."

"Terrrry," he said in his thick German accent, "I vant my cows back."

"John, they aren't your cows anymore; they are government cows," I said.

He gave me a steely look and said with even more determination, "Terrrry, I vant my cows back!"

"They aren't your cows anymore, John. They belong to the U.S. Government, and until you redeem them, they will remain in our control."

John looked at me long and hard and said, "Screw the government. I vill call Link" (Art Link, then governor of North Dakota).

I said, "I don't care if you call Link or not. John, you broke the law. You have been illegally grazing WPAs for years, and it's time this lawlessness came to a halt. You have five days to redeem your cattle or I will have them sold. Do you understand?"

He gave me one of the coldest looks I had received from any man since I had been in the business of law enforcement and then quietly said, "Terrrry, if dis vas forty years ago, dis vouldn't haf happened. I vould haf shipped your ass off."

I said, "John, you can have my hind end anytime you want; there is plenty to go around. Bottom line, you are out some cows. Square it away or they become hamburger."

I turned, brushing by the two bodyguards, and walked back to my vehicle. Joel, who was by now frozen solid, and I turned our car toward Bismarck, heading home for some warmth and dinner since we hadn't eaten since four o'clock that morning. Arriving in Bismarck at nine-thirty, I dropped Joel off at his house, advising him to dress more warmly the next day because it promised to be bone-chilling at best. With a grumble and a wave of the hand, he went inside. I hoped he had listened because it takes some time to load over four hundred head of cattle in the dead of winter at thirty below. .... Home I went to get some rest and something to eat—or so I thought.

As I turned into my driveway, I noticed how hungry and bone tired, not to mention cold to the very core, I was. Intense cold has a way of wearing you out, especially when you are working outside.

Plugging my car in, I gathered up my gear, and started up the steps to the front door. My wife opened the door and met me with a kiss. Man, with treatment like that, it was no wonder I loved her so much. She waited until I got inside and out of my cold-weather gear and then said, "You really did it this time."

Surprised, I said, "What do you mean?"

She said, "The governor wants you to call him just as soon as you get home."

My dander went up like there was no tomorrow. Boiling over at the apparent political interference, I said, "To hell with him. This is a federal matter, and I'm not having some piss-anty state governor telling me what to do on a federal matter."

Donna looked at me with those beautiful blue eyes of hers and said, "I may have gotten you into a little bit of trouble also."

"What?"

She continued, "Well, I was cleaning the house, and the phone rang, so I answered it. The caller identified himself as Governor Art Link and said he wanted to talk to Terry Grosz. Thinking it was a prank call, I told the caller, 'Yes, and this is Maid Marion from Robin Hood's merry band' and hung up on him. He called right back and finally convinced me he *really* was the governor, and I think you had better call him as soon as you can."

Tired, cold, and pissed as I was, I couldn't help but laugh at the toughness my wife showed when the occasion required. What a sweetheart!

I went into the kitchen to make a phone call to the assistant U.S. attorney and damn, did the kitchen ever smell great. I forgot the pressing need for my phone call. That bride of mine had fixed me an outstanding snapping-turtle stew. No two ways about it, when it met my mouth, it was pure heaven. With this treat came homemade biscuits and a fresh homemade cherry pie with one of the world's flakiest crusts. Boy, did that take me away from my bowed neck, cold bones, cracked lips, and windburned face.

Finishing my meal, I remembered that I had better touch base with Dave Peterson, my local assistant U.S. attorney. I got him on the phone, and after a few pleasantries, he grilled me on the elements of the case and then said there would be no problem prosecuting this investigation in federal court. He did think it was funny that the defendant

was my uncle and had several laughs at my expense. I also informed
Dave about the phone call my wife had received from Governor Link
and asked him to call the governor since this was a federal matter.
Dave agreed, and I hung up and returned to a second piece of homemade pie, thinking I had that bull by the horns.

A few moments into that second piece of pie, the phone rang. Picking up the phone, I recognized Dave's familiar voice as he outlined the
discussion that had occurred between the governor and himself. The
governor still wanted to discuss the issue with me, and Dave suggested that I call him. Now, notwithstanding my excellent dinner,
I was really pissed! I told Dave I didn't want to discuss this matter
with the governor; it was none of his business, and this was after all a
federal matter. Dave calmly replied that I should be less thickheaded
and more understanding and return his call. Damn! He was right, but
still being thickheaded, I told him, "You tell that son of a buck to call
me; I'm not calling him."

Dave chuckled and said, "OK, I will have him call you. Just remember, when you discuss this matter with him, lay it out just like
you would with me." With that Dave hung up, leaving me to fume at
what I considered unwarranted interference by a lesser mortal! Kind
of raises the question if Uncle John was the only arrogant one in the
family?

A few moments later my phone rang again, and I picked it up. The
voice on the other end of the line identified itself as Governor Art
Link, and I unprofessionally responded, "Hi, Art; what can I do for
you?"

Behaving a lot more professionally than I was, Link continued,
"Mr. Grosz, John Grosz, a close friend of mine, just telephoned to tell
me you seized over four hundred head of his cattle. Would you fill me
in on the details, please?"

Shamed by his courteous manner, I settled down and laid out the
case in a professional fashion as I would for a U.S. attorney. I explained that it wasn't the first time John had trespassed but at least the
sixth time that he had illegally grazed federal lands. The government
had taken action only three times, and that action had been nothing
more than sending John a bill for the lost forage, while the Service had
fixed the cut fences on the WPAs at government expense. I continued,
"This time we are going to take action. He cut the fences on two

WPAs and had over four hundred head of cattle feeding at government expense. He can redeem his cattle, or the government will auction them off to recover our expenses as the law prescribes."

It was quiet on the phone for a few moments and then Link responded in a surprising manner. He said, "Terry, here is what you are to do. Release the cattle back to John and send him the bill for forage lost on those WPAs. Other than that, I want you to call it even."

I was shocked! I said, "What?"

He repeated what he had said, and I came unglued! I said, "Governor, this is a federal matter, not a state matter, and it will be adjudicated in federal court and not some governor's office!"

He responded in a threatening voice, "Terry, if you folks in the Service ever want me to sign off on your future land acquisitions involving WPAs, I suggest you do as I say." In those days, the governor had to approve such sales with his signature.

Damn, did I go ballistic! I told Governor Link that he could go back and tell the six hundred thousand hardheaded German, Russian, and Bohemian farmers in his state that if they ever again grazed their cattle on government WPAs without official permission, they could expect the same treatment. "Those WPAs belong to all the American people and have been set aside for wildlife, not for a bunch of goddamned German dirt farmers to go forth and illegally do as they pleased. You can also tell them that if I catch them intentionally grazing these areas, their cows are going to be government cows, and it's just that simple." I hung up the phone at about "force 5" to find my wife intently watching me eat the hind end clear off the governor of the state of North Dakota. Without batting an eye or raising her voice, she asked what Kansas or Oklahoma were like as duty stations, full well realizing that was where I was heading once the director of my agency found out how I had handled a sitting governor. Damn, that woman sure had the ability to put things into perspective. ...

Before I had the time to dwell on this "hoorah," the phone rang again. It was my trusty sidekick Joel, who started off by telling me that the cattle transport trucks we had ordered for the next day weren't coming.

I said, "What?"

Joel said, "Your uncle figured out who might be hauling his cattle, called Dave Butts, and told him if he brought his trucks to carry his cattle off, he would kill the drivers! I just got a call from Dave Butts, and boy, is he nervous about the shooting threat."

I said, "God o-Friday, John can't do that—that's illegal!"

"I know, but he did. Now what?"

"I will call Dave Peterson and let him know what the hell is going on, while you call Dave Butts back and let him know that he will have all the protection he needs and to be there with his trucks regardless."

I called Peterson again and told him what John had done. Dave said, "He can't do that!"

I said, "I know, but he is old-country German and used to taking the law into his own hands."

It was late, and Dave just wanted to get back to sleep so he said, "You figure out what needs to be done and I will support your decision, but keep me in the loop."

Sitting down at the kitchen table with an old typewriter, I began to type out the terms and conditions of a contract so John could redeem his cattle on the spot the next day if he chose to do so. I hadn't been typing for more than ten minutes when the phone rang again. Damn, it's after midnight, I thought. Doesn't anyone in this state sleep when the sun goes down? Answering the phone, I found Dave on the other end. "Terry," he said, "the governor just called and wants to talk to you again but is afraid to call you. I don't know what you said to him, but you sure got his attention. He said you are the hardest-headed German he ever ran across and that he might have made you really mad. Is that true?" Before I could respond, Dave quickly said, "Don't answer that," and chuckled. He continued, "The governor wants to call you; is that all right?"

I said, "Sure, Dave, whatever." My hackles were still up, but Dave was not only a fine attorney but a damn good man as well. Because of the respect I had for him, I would do as he suggested.

A few moments later the phone rang. I responded and Governor Art Link's voice came through with an urgent request: "Please don't hang up, Mr. Grosz."

Under a little better self-control, I said, "What can I do for you, Governor?"

Link requested that I call John and try to resolve the cattle trespass issue. I told the governor that the issue would be settled in federal court and that if John wanted to talk to me, he was family, knew my phone number, and could call. Link said he would call John and pass that information on and, after thanking me, hung up. At one in the morning the phone rang again, and this time it was John Grosz on the other end. I said, "What do you need, John?"

He said, "Terry, I vant my cows back."

I said, "John, listen. They aren't your cows anymore; they belong to the U.S. government until this issue is settled to a legal satisfaction. That means you must pay all the government's expenses plus go to federal court in Fargo to settle up on the criminal cattle trespass charges I am about to file. Do you understand?"

"Ya," he said, "but I vant my cows back."

That did it! This knothead wasn't going to understand anything but another German speaking to him as he needed to be spoken to, so I gave him both barrels! I said, "John, did you threaten Dave Butts?"

"Ya," he said.

I said, "John, that's a goddamned felony; do you understand that?"

"Ya," he said, "but I vant my cows back."

"John, listen to me closely. Those are government cows, and you will not get them back unless you redeem them for those expenses associated with the government seizure. If you choose not to do that, then I will have them sold at public auction, and they will be gone." Remembering John's threat to Butts, I added, "John, tomorrow I will have an officer with me who will be armed with an AR-15 semiautomatic rifle. If you so much as step out of your truck with anything in your hands, I will have him kill you. Do you understand?" Not waiting for a response, I said, "Now, when I said anything in your hands, that is exactly what I meant. A rifle, thermos bottle, turkey sandwich, crescent wrench—anything, and you will be shot clear full of holes. Do you understand what I am trying to say?"

There was quiet at the other end of the line, and finally he said, "Ya, I understand goot."

I said, "Good. I will see you tomorrow at daylight at the WPA. Good morning, John," and hung up.

At two-thirty in the morning I finished the contract work needed to redeem the cattle and finally got to bed. The alarm went off at four A.M., way too early for my tired and still cold-to-the-bone body, but that was the way it was. As I crawled out of bed, the first thing I noticed was the smell of breakfast cooking. Damn, that wife of mine had gotten up without waking me, knowing I had a hard day ahead, and was helping me meet that day. And what a day it turned out to be—42 below zero, heavy overcast skies, and no wind. Shoveling in my breakfast of bacon, eggs, homemade toasted bread, and spuds, followed by some strong, hot tea, seemed to get my tired body into gear. Two pieces of yesterday's homemade cherry pie set me straight and ready to do battle.

As I passed out the door into the intense North Dakota winter cold, I patted Donna on the last part over the fence and told her to stay away from Robin Hood. Her special smile told me Robin wasn't even in the running. ... With a warm heart from that exchange, I went out to meet the cold winter morning on the North Dakota prairie and whatever it would bring.

I picked up Joel, who was better dressed than the day before, and we drove the one hundred–odd miles to the WPA over totally empty, wintry backcountry roads. We rode in tired silence. Between us lay an AR-15 with a full thirty-round magazine. Joel was a crack shot and knew how to use the weapon if needed. Joel also had great common sense, and I knew he would only use it as a last resort. But he would use it, and well, if necessary ... well enough to take a limb off the family tree at three hundred yards. ...

It was a bone-chilling, gray winter dawn in the rolling hills of east-central North Dakota. In the valley below, dotted all over the fenced WPA, were 416 head of seized cattle. Outlined against the skyline on a ridge road of rolling hills to the north were five cattle trucks, several smaller trucks carrying portable corrals, and pickups filled with cowboys and hauling horse trailers waiting (out of rifle range) for the command to come down and load John Grosz's cattle. To the east, on another ridge on a north-south prairie trail (also out of rifle range), patiently sat several refuge vehicles and refuge staff members ready to help load cattle. Off to the south on a wide spot on the road sat John Grosz's cowboys and vehicles, ready to retrieve their boss's cattle if the command was given and they could somehow shoot their way through the "Feds." On the valley floor, next to the gate of the WPA, sat a red Ford pickup that belonged to John Grosz. Joel and I rechecked our firearms, gave each other a look of *here we go*, and rode our mechanical yellow Ford "horse" into the "hoorah." When we reached the red pickup, I noticed only one man in the front seat, and it wasn't John. Getting out and flipping my parka hood over my head against the biting cold, I walked over to the Ford. As I did, I noticed a lone figure standing on a knoll about thirty-five yards away. Brother, what an idiot, I thought.

Recognizing the cowboy in John's pickup, I asked, "Where is John?"

Without saying a word, the cowboy pointed to the lone individual on the hill. Figures it had to be my uncle, I thought. No one else would be that tough and stupid all in the same breath! As I walked over to John, I noticed that all he was wearing were jeans and a wool shirt with a vest—no hat or gloves. Looking back, I could see Joel standing by the open door of the car where he could reach the AR-15 in an instant if need be. Good old Joel: not much of a body but a warrior through and through! Turning back to John, I could only feel admiration for the bastard. No matter how you cut it, he was one tough old man! Walking up to him, I said, "Well, John, do you want to redeem these cows or not?"

He looked at me through a blue face with snot frozen on the end of his nose and said, "Craazzzy gott-damned nephew ist going to blow my ass oft if I moof. I am vaiting for him here so he don't shoot my ass oft."

Realizing that he didn't know who he was talking to because of my parka, I removed the hood and repeated the question. He took one hard, cold look at me through squinted eyes that would have foretold trouble forty years ago in a faraway land and then said, "How much do I owe?"

I handed him the contract, which spelled out the amount the government had shelled out to get to this point: $2,190. He took a checkbook out of his pocket and, after two attempts to get the ink to work (at 40 below, ink won't hardly flow), wrote a check for the amount on the contract. That over and done with, I took out my citation book and, after getting my own pen to work, wrote him a citation with a mandatory appearance in federal court in Fargo for his cattle trespass violation. That pissed him off even more, and I explained, "You just redeemed your stock. You still have to pay the 'fiddler' for violating the cattle trespass law." I handed him the citation and was rewarded by being called a "pisskopf" as he turned and walked away.

Thus ended the cattle trespass standoff on a cold November morning in North Dakota. Joel let the cattle out of the fenced enclosure of the WPA, and John's cowboys gathered them up and headed for John's home ranch. All the folks on the government's side gathered up their gear and headed back after I paid them for their time and efforts with government purchase orders.

Several weeks later I met John in U.S. District Court in Fargo, North Dakota. The case went before Senior Judge Benson (an outstanding federal judge), and John was fined $500 (the maximum) for the violation and assessed an additional $170 for grazing costs on the two WPAs. The $170 went to procure native prairie grass seed so that the WPAs could be reseeded in part to offset the damage his cows had done.

Not one to harbor a grudge, I called it even and walked away from that chapter of my life ... or so I thought. I heard later, secondhand, that John, while driving home from federal court, stopped his pickup along a deserted prairie road and told the cowboy riding with him (the man with the aging disease) to think twice before he talked to me again. Then he made the cowboy get out and walk home. The cowboy almost didn't make it. He damn near froze to death about half a mile from his home, and if he hadn't been picked up by a neighbor as he lay alongside the road, he probably would have died.

As a sort of postscript, a member of my dad's family called me several weeks after the episode and said, "Terrrry, didt you take John's cows?"

I said, "Yes, I did."

He said, "But Terrrry, he's bloodt!"

I said, "John clearly broke the law and had to pay for that lapse in common sense."

He repeated, "But, Terry, he's bloodt!"

"That isn't supposed to make any difference here in America. I'm a federal law enforcement officer, and it's my job to treat everyone alike, kinfolk or not," I said gently.

There was silence for a moment, then a sharp click on the other end of the line. That was the last time he spoke to me, or I to him, before he died.

When John's brother, my grandfather, died, I was told that he left every surviving member of the family a considerable amount of cash, acres of land, and other valuables. There were two exceptions to the distribution of resources. One was a distant relative who had allegedly flown for the Luftwaffe in World War II, whom Grandpa never forgave for deserting his "new" country, the other one was me. Nonetheless, I called my aunt and offered to pay my share to bury my grandfather. She quietly answered, "No, thank you."

It appeared that Grandpa never forgave me for what I had done to his brother, even though the two of them were not close. I think "bloodt" had something to do with it. I did what I had to do, knowing the likely consequences. If I had it to do all over again, I would do it the same today. If what my biological dad said about the lost inheritance was true, I lost a lot personally—but professionally I still have the good "bloodt."

nine

The M-1 Abrams Tank

FROM FEBRUARY 1979 TO JUNE 1981, I was the assistant special agent in charge in Minneapolis, Minnesota. As such, I was the law enforcement operations supervisor (among other duties) in the headquarters office for the U.S. Fish and Wildlife Service, Great Lakes Region, or Region 3. What a unique region and learning experience those years provided me as a young senior manager! Those lessons followed me as I worked my way through the infrastructure of the Division of Law Enforcement.

My immediate supervisor was Bob Hodgins, the special agent in charge. One of the very best administrators and managers within the Division of Law Enforcement, Bob led his people by example, frequently assisting them as they experienced the difficult parts of the job from the field to the courtroom. He expected his subordinate supervisors to do the same, and woe unto the occasional lazy supervisor who wasn't in the front lines following Bob's lead. As Bob always said, you can't lead from behind.

The region was staffed by the youngest, least experienced officers in the land because our budget couldn't afford the more senior officers and their pricey pay scales. Young or not, our corps was an outlaw-catching bunch of agents, some of the best I ever had the pleasure to be associated with. Plain and simply, what they lacked in experience, they made up for in unlimited open-mindedness and youthful energy. They also had an uncanny way of collectively combining all their best talents until they were able to figure how to run to ground those poachers, smugglers, crooked animal dealers, and commercial-market hunters crossing over the line. Every man jack of them, including our one woman officer, Karen Halpin, always strove to catch every bad guy in sight. They wanted to please Bob—but I think they also enjoyed counting coup on their fellow man.

More than once Bob and I found ourselves letting junior-grade officers perform tasks or initiate covert operations that in other regions would only have been managed by the most experienced officers. We had no choice. We either tried to get the job done with our young, inexperienced gumshoes or had to sit on our last part over the fence, draw a paycheck, and let the outlaws have the run of Dodge. Unfortunately for the outlaw community, Bob and I loved a good challenge, and so did our young crew. So away we went into the wildlife wars. With Bob's leadership and our youngsters not bothering to look over their shoulders because "Hodge" was there to protect them from political threats, many a poacher fell to our baby-faced odd squad. In no time, the agents had the bit in their teeth when they saw that they could make a difference in the jungles of humanity hell-bent on the destruction of wildlife. It wasn't long before Bob's squad led the Service's twelve other law enforcement districts (since reduced to seven) in major investigations and prosecutions, even though we were so poorly funded that we often couldn't afford replacement patrol cars for our officers when theirs wore out.

It's pretty sad, when the Washington leadership criminally neglects funding a branch of an agency because of politics, ignorance, stupidity, animosity, jealousy, not knowing how to manage law enforcement, or all of the above. The Division of Law Enforcement historically and to this day, compared to the other branches of the agency, truly is the bastard cat. Yet the service officers perform far above the call of duty mandated by Congress and are an important tool of wildlife management. You can have all the laws you want on the books to protect the critters, but if you don't have the long arm of the law enforcing those laws, you have nothing more than fancy toilet paper with writing on it!

The region was unique in other ways than its officers and the leadership. It was populated in those days with about sixty-five million people and had wildlife resources to match. Anytime there are people and enough resources to tempt human ethics and morals, you will have illegal taking of wildlife, be it commercial or personal. The region and its people were no exception. In many enforcement arenas, such as the fur trade, warm-water game fish and the gamut of Great

Lakes fishery issues, big game, illegal wildlife harvest activities of every scope and degree on the numerous Indian reservations, killing and sale of waterfowl in the big cities, illegal goose hunting and baiting in the state of Illinois, and wildlife smuggling from Canada, the blood from the critters ran deep and red.

There was so much illegal activity that it was not uncommon to have four or five covert operations going on in the region at any one time. In my capacity as the region's operations officer, I spent many days running from state to state, assisting the young federal agents. It seemed as if every weekend somewhere in our eight-state region, every officer, me included, had to be mustered out to assist in a takedown of one sort or another. But by damn, did we ever catch a lot of people doing things they shouldn't. In short, times were fast and the catching was good, with as many as seventy-five to one hundred knotheads rounded up on any given time.

We put a lot of effort into the covert arena because plain and simply, the overt approach by the state Fish and Game agencies had not worked on serious wildlife crime. Covert work is patently more expensive in time, money, and emotional drain on the operatives, but bear in mind that our job was to put a stop to the carnage within legal bounds. We had an almost 100 percent rate of prosecution, even in the busy U.S. attorney's office in Chicago. That conviction rate was even more stunning when one looked at the nation's average conviction rate for all federal law enforcement agencies, which was around 85 percent in those days!

One particular undercover investigation within my several-year stint as Bob's second in command really sticks out in my memory. I remember going to work that morning with my mind for once at ease because I was almost caught up in my instant work and had plans for a very special event later that day. My four-year-old adopted Vietnamese daughter, Kimberlee, was going to become an American citizen. Suffice to say, I was looking forward to participating in that event as her father. I had planned my work day so I could take off early, meet my bride at the federal courthouse in Minneapolis, and attend this function of love with my family. What a wonderful feeling it is to take a child from near death, as she was when we received her in 1975, raise her in health, and start her down the long road toward the American dream. It doesn't get much better than that.

The ceremony was to take place at two in the afternoon, so once at work, I hurried to finish the case management disasters stacked up on my desk and settle any pissing contests between members of my office staff or field core of agents. Everything went like clockwork, and I found myself getting excited about the afternoon's events. About noon, as I scurried about my office finishing up the loose ends on the paperwork, my phone rang. For a fleeting moment I had that instant sinking feeling that comes from years of experience and the law enforcement intuition many of us possess. Trying to be optimistic, I dismissed that gut feeling and reached for the phone. My hand paused momentarily over the receiver as I tried to keep my instincts in check before I grabbed the angrily ringing phone and hefted it to my ear amidst my innate misgivings.

On the line was Don, one of our eager and aggressive officers, who was working on an illegal waterfowl commercialization investigation in the Bay City, Michigan, area. The tone of his voice confirmed my worst suspicions. Don had previously received information from an informant regarding an organized ring of commercial-market hunters operating under the guise of a legal commercial duck-hunting club. These folks were allegedly taking large numbers of ducks and moving them unlawfully in commerce. Don and his partner had covertly penetrated the group after months of hard work and were now fast on their way toward federal prosecution of the whole murderous lot for numerous felony violations of the Migratory Bird Treaty Act. All these officers needed was a couple more trips inside their ring of shooters to wrap up their evidence gathering, and then the whole rotten crew of outlaws was going before the courts.

Don's excited voice betrayed a concern and urgency I had heard many times from inexperienced officers during moments of extreme stress, when their investigation is headed for the toilet and they lack the experience to stand firm. Something had gone sour, and the officer, out of options, had turned to headquarters for assistance. It seemed that Don's partner, an agent named Peterson and the senior officer in the investigation, had been taken ill, and Don needed an immediate backup to continue a particularly sensitive stage of the investigation. Don was never very patient and was somewhat prone to stampede. That was especially true when he couldn't control the events facing him, a situation common in the field of law enforcement.

Calming him down, I let my mind race through my mental directory of officers in the region who might fill in for Don's partner. That first run-through told me there weren't any officers available of the caliber Don needed or who were talented enough to smoothly jump in. Running through my mental list again, I drew another blank when it came to the skill level needed to fill the bill. Then I thought over a list of officers from adjoining regions whom I might borrow to lend a temporary hand until Don's partner was back on his feet. But all those chaps came up as busy on their own projects or too expensive to "import" because of their distance from Michigan. Typical Fish and Wildlife Service law enforcement situation, I thought. Never enough officers to do the job the agency and Congress mandated. Damn, no matter how you cut it, I was the only one within grabbing distance with the experience required for the job! Not wanting to hear his answer, I asked Don when he wanted me there.

The relief in Don's voice at finding a heartbeat to assist him and provide another witness came through the phone loud and clear as he said, "Right now!"

I said, "Don, there is no way I can be in Bay City, Michigan, right now, seeing that I'm currently sitting in my office in Minneapolis!"

"I know," he replied impatiently, "but you can catch the next plane to Bay City and be here in time for tomorrow morning's hunt and waterfowl sales transactions in the evening. Without me there to make a buy at day's end, and without another federal witness, all our months of work could be down the drain. This is the first time they have trusted me enough to sell an entire day's kill, and I don't want to miss this opportunity to further the investigation. Besides, the assistant U.S. attorney wants at least two witnesses to every migratory bird sale or he won't file felony charges."

Damn, I thought, Don was really wound up, but I couldn't really blame him. He and his partner had worked hard to bring this investigation to fruition, and it looked as if it were going in the toilet if he didn't get some able-bodied assistance. Don and his partner had a good case going, in fact, the type of felony sale case dealing with migratory game birds that most agents never see during their entire careers. Calming Don down again, I assured him that I would be on my way as soon as the secretary could make travel arrangements.

"Great," he said. "I have to run to make some more preparations for the detail. When I finish that, I'll meet you at the baggage claim at the airport with your nonresident hunting license, shotgun, and ammunition for the detail."

Before I could say any more, he abruptly hung up. Looking at the telephone in my hand, I wondered whether Don ever looked past his nose and took the time to think about what I had to give up to provide a hand. Knowing Don the way I did, I doubted he even cared. Sitting there for a long moment, I just shook my head. Everything I had hoped for had turned to slop. It never seemed to fail. I would plan something special for my family, and this law enforcement thing would get in the way more often than not. Oh well, that is what the American people pay me for, I thought as I settled the phone back into its cradle and leaned back in my chair with supreme resignation.

Forgetting the earlier joy of anticipating my daughter's citizenship ceremony, I swung into action, calling Barb, Bob's secretary, into the office. I asked Barb to arrange for me to fly to Bay City, preferably late that evening. I figured that if I could do that, it would still be possible for me to share a little of my daughter's special day. Barb looked at me in utter disbelief, drew herself up to her full slender, six-foot-tall height, and said, "I will not! You have a date with the judge, Donna, and Kimberlee in the citizenship ceremony, and I will not assist you in any way in missing that event or the celebrations afterward."

For a moment, supervisor be damned, all I could see were her flashing dark eyes and the determined set of her face. Barb was a beautiful woman, even more so when she was riled up, and right now she could have won the Miss America contest. Finally, seeing tears well up in her eyes, I said softly, "Barb, I have to go. The Service has invested hundreds of hours and thousands of dollars in this investigation, and I can't walk away from it, especially in light of the request for assistance from the investigating officer. There is no one else I can send, so that leaves me. Hodge is out of town, and there isn't another experienced officer in the region, or at hand in another region, that fits the bill. Whether I like it or not, it has to be done, and the choice is not mine."

Barb's flashing brown eyes told me she would do as I requested, but it would be a cold day in hell before she would forgive me for going on a covert assignment instead of to my daughter's once-in-a-lifetime citizenship ceremony. She wasn't alone. I have yet to get over my personal sense of loss at not being able to attend that precious moment. Kimberlee has never said how she felt at not having her dad present on her special day, and I have never asked.

Throwing on a vest, I immediately left for home to pack the gear needed for this inopportune detail. When I returned an hour later, Barb informed me that the only flight available left at three that afternoon. *Damnit to hell anyway!* If I could have caught a flight around nine or ten in the evening, I could have enjoyed some of Kimberlee's ceremony and still arrived in time to assist Don. But as fate would have it, that airline schedule would give me only a few minutes at my daughter's citizenship ceremony before I would have to leave in order to have time to clear my weapons through airport security. Brother, what else is new? I thought, suppressing my feelings of disappointment so as not to rile Barb up again.

Finishing my office work, I hurried over to the federal building for my daughter's (and others') official entry into American life. The ceremony started late, and I was able to savor only about ten minutes before I had to leave. Running to my car, I sped to the airport, checked my war bag (a duffel bag holding everything I might possibly need for the detail) at the outside check-in, grabbed the rest of my gear, and sprinted through the airport. Without breaking stride, I dropped a dollar on a vendor's counter for a bag of corn nuts for my dinner and continued my run for the gate. I just made the plane, an old twin-engine, prop-driven Martin 404 Main Liner. After settling into my seat, I opened my "dinner," crunched down on the first corn nut, and promptly shattered a molar in my lower right jaw. That day, after starting out so beautifully, had turned into something dark, smelly, and viscous if my jaw, now throbbing in abject pain, was any indication.

Looking at the flight schedule to take my mind off the misery in my mouth, I noticed I was on a multiple-city "milk run" and would not arrive in Bay City until early the next morning! It was about a one-hour run to the work site, and we had to be ready to go at four A.M. So much for any sleep before going into a dangerous covert operation in which Don and I would be outnumbered at least seven to one. Welcome to the world of wildlife law enforcement, I thought as the plane vibrated off the runway, lifting noisily into the darkening winter night. I spent the next hour carefully digging the splinters, remaining filling, and roots of my shattered tooth out of my gum and spitting blood and fragments into the vomit bag until nothing was left but a large, sucking hole. Suffice to say, the corn nuts went unnoticed for the rest of the trip. ...

Arriving in Bay City late due to one hell of a storm, I met my harried officer, whose first words were not thanking me for coming but, "What is your cover?" Since I was more of an administrator than a field agent, I didn't have a standard deep-cover disguise, so I said I would have to think about an appropriate cover—one that was so far off the wall that no one would be able to question me about the details of who I was or what I did. Don's flashing black eyes had a questioning look, but he let the issue slide for the moment.

"Let's get my gear," I said. "That will give me time to think of a cover." I was trying to speak without opening my mouth too widely so the cold Michigan winter night air wouldn't hit the sensitive nerve endings in the hole once occupied by a tooth, sending me into painful orbit.

"What's the matter with your mouth?" Don asked as we headed for the baggage area.

"I just have a gum ache from what is left of a tooth, no big deal," I said.

"Oh, great," he said, exasperation running over his lips and spilling onto his shoes. "Now I suppose we have to find a dentist at this time of the morning to fix you up."

"Not really," I said. "Just some painkiller of sorts from my war bag, and I should be all right."

His look didn't convince me that he was settling down. For the record, the hole in my gum didn't feel too convincing of a good time to follow either! Especially when I remembered that I might have to experience the recoil of a 10-gauge shotgun later that day.

Grabbing my gear from the airport baggage carrousel, we trotted out to Don's undercover van, threw my gear in the back, and sped from the airport. I waited for the narcotic painkiller I had just taken to do its job and let my mind float back to the question Don had asked earlier about my cover. I thought about it for a few moments as we hurried down a rain-soaked Michigan highway, and an idea came to me like a revelation. Turning to Don with a partially closed mouth, I said, "I got it. I'll tell everyone I'm a casting engineer for the heavy-recoil system on the M-1 Abrams tank. That story will be so far off the wall that no one at the duck club will be able to ask me anything about my profession."

The Abrams tank was brand new at the time, and somewhat shrouded in mystery to keep the Russians "off their feed," so to speak. The lack of publicity about it would be one plus in using such a background story. A second plus was that I was a military history buff. With my newfound cover and military history background, along with the fact I had read everything I could find on the Abrams (which was scanty, to say the least), I was all set. Or so I thought. ...

Looking over at Don, expecting approval, I was greeted with a look of concern and utter disbelief at what he heard coming from the lips of the region's second in command. It was plain that his suspicions were being confirmed regarding the quality of officer one could expect if one was foolish enough to go to the regional office "pool" for assistance. Oh well, I didn't get as large as I was by being last in line, I thought as my double shot of codeine began to take effect. Dismissing Don's apprehension, I lay back deeper into the seat, trying to get some sleep as we scurried off into the dark and rainy Michigan night like a pair of fiddler crabs on the hunt.

About an hour later we arrived at some darkened buildings, which I assumed were the targets' duck camp. Staggering under our loads of equipment, we entered our assigned cabin, where I went to sleep in a bed that was far too short for my massive frame. Too soon the alarm went off, and we arose, dressed, and headed to the commercial duck-club kitchen for a typically heavy and greasy, not to mention large, waterfowler's breakfast.

As if from a distance, I kept hearing Don's worried voice giving me advice (after all, he didn't know that this was not my first time in a covert situation) on how to act as we plodded across the mud puddles in the parking lot in our chest-high waders. I thought, If Don doesn't settle down, he will have a hard time working effectively as an undercover officer, especially when the chips are *really* down. I had worked in similar situations many times before, both as a state and federal officer, and as a result of that experience found myself nowhere near as tense as my partner. After all, if the bad guys aren't looking for you, they won't see you. Another of Grosz's Rules. ...

The breakfast went somewhat as I expected in that everyone was polite to me after being introduced, but as a new face, it was obvious I wasn't going to be trusted. That trust would come only when I had proven myself to be "one of the boys" by committing some illegal act such as shooting an over-limit of ducks. That wouldn't be hard to do because I could wallow in the slop of a poacher as well as they could, if not better. That was especially true because I equated my "performance," if it were good, with saving a few critters for the future. Before day's end, I knew I would achieve the status of one of the boys, so I just grinned over the still distant but constant pain of the hole in my jaw and Don's many reminders to do thus and such.

While milling around the coffee pot in the large kitchen with the other chaps, I happened to notice another fellow about my size and sidled over to introduce myself (big fellows can usually get along with each other). It turned out he was *the* "Boss Hog" of the bunch of outlaws, and that he liked to eat (like me). As luck would have it, we got along famously right from the get-go. Occasionally, as the two of us were eating and visiting, I would look up at Don, who was seated at another table with some of the "boys," to see if he was resting any easier. Don, seeing the two of us getting along as we each plowed through our third plate of grits, appeared more relaxed but still very watchful of his regional office type "boat anchor."

After breakfast we were dropped off by boats at various stilt blinds in the marshes around Bay City to kill ducks like the rest of the duck-killing sons of bitches I had the luck of the German army to be hunting with. This killing went on all day, and I was pleased to know that my agents were working their way through the bowels of these bastards like a cancer, with a destination of the U.S. district court as a final resting place for this unsavory lot! Suffice to say, a lot of hearts were stilled that day in the world of wildlife.

Returning that evening, we discovered that as a result of my morning's successful interactions with "Boss Hog," Don and I had been invited to dinner in his home with all the other outlaw guides. Damn, what a lucky break for us and the investigation! I thought. This was the first time any such offer had been made to Don and his partner. So much for the low quality of the regional office officer corps, I chuckled after seeing Don's "how did you pull this off?" look. After

cleaning up, I took more codeine. We couldn't carry any "iron" because of our light dress, but I dismissed that concern as unfounded. A
short time later we were ushered into the private basement of "Boss
Hog's" home. Every chance Don got, he quietly cautioned me regarding how to act in this situation. His eyes told me he was uptight as a
full-fed wood tick over the questionable presence of his partner and
the sensitivity of the moment.

What a layout greeted my sleepless but still alert eyes. Taxidermic
ducks and geese of all species adorned the walls and hung from the
ceilings in natural-looking flying positions. Central to the large basement room was a long, solid oak dining table at least ten feet long and
four feet wide. All along the walls were hundreds of pictures of stacks
of ducks and geese taken by the outlaws gathered for the evening's fes-
tivities. Great little evidence photos, I thought. It was like the feeding
area for the "Knights of the Wrong Table," with "Boss Hog" sitting
at the end in a massive oak chair that was big even for a chap of his
and my dimensions!

What a surreal scene, I thought. I could just imagine what this did
for the egos of the guides surrounding us. Looking around, I could see
that they plain and simply represented the dregs of what *they* called the
sporting society. There probably wasn't a good job or education
among the lot of them, or much in the way of ethics or morals. That
didn't really matter, though. They could kill with the best of them, enjoyed it, and could keep their mouths shut. That was all that was required or mattered as far as "Boss Hog" was concerned. Later I would
realize that my arrogant sense of superiority showed how much edge
I had lost in my years as an administrative type. I had somehow forgotten Grosz's Rule: *Never underestimate your target or it will come
back to bite you in the ass!* I was soon to get my comeuppance. ...

The booze from a central bar was flowing, and the tongues were
wagging, as were the stories of the massive kills that had taken place
that day. Don and I circulated as newfound friends, pretending to
drink their booze but in reality not consuming much. Our job was to
keep a clear head, and instead of slopping down the booze, we were to
drink in the words and deeds of those present. We committed incriminating statements to our memory as they passed the guides' lips, to be
transferred to paper when we found ourselves alone for later use in federal court. It was a good and prosperous time for the "hunters." ...

The dinner bell rang, and as we seated ourselves around the enormous table, we were greeted with platters of roast duck in orange sauce; mounds of mashed potatoes with melted butter running down the sides in small rivers; slices of homemade bread, which by the smell was not long out of the oven; green salads of several types loaded with thick slices of red onion; several bowls of steaming hot vegetables, most notably pole beans with onion and bacon; fried yams; plates of deep-fried okra; and tankards of drink, all served by what appeared to be the wives of the "victorious" guides. No doubt about it, it was truly a meal fit for a "king" and his "knights."

For long moments after "Boss Hog" surprisingly said grace and then grunted, "Dig in" any talk around that table was punctuated by the sounds of men eating as if they hadn't eaten for days. Not to be outdone, Don and I joined right in as if we belonged. When the bowls or plates emptied, they were immediately filled by the ladies in waiting as the eating and drinking orgy noisily continued. As bellies filled and the whiskey consumed earlier on empty stomachs began to take effect, the serious killing and migratory bird sales talk returned, ramrodded by "Boss Hog." Don and I appeared to be concentrating on our food, all the while carefully recording in the annals of our minds the careless talk that would help us in convicting those with the loose lips. To make things easier, Don was to note the loose talk on his side of the table and I on mine. In the case of a particularly sensitive or major violation from one of the actors, both of us were to take mental note, that way meeting the U.S. attorney's request for two witnesses in felony situations. In so doing, we could cover more ground and wrap the noose tighter around the players' necks.

Suddenly a fellow sitting several chairs to my left leaned out over the table, turned his head toward me, and with a huge mouthful of food mumbled in a loud, whiskey-soaked voice, "Terry, what did you say you did for a living?" I took a quick look out of the corner of my eye at Don, who was showing more white around his eyes than I would have thought humanly possible—kind of like what a colt might show when confronted by a mountain lion. Damn, he has to learn to toughen up, I thought, or he will get us both killed. I slowly chewed my mouthful of food as I prepared my answer, all the while noticing the table talk had slightly abated as everyone waited for my response. Leaning over the table, I turned and fixed my eyes on the chap who had uttered the question and cheerfully said, "I'm a casting engineer for the heavy-recoil system on the M-1 Abrams main battle tank." Before that lad could say anything in response, "it" *really* hit the fan!

A portly fellow I hadn't noticed before, who was sitting several chairs farther to the left of my original questioner, said, "What did you say?"

Trying not to look surprised at the chap's rather pointed question, I looked him in the eye and repeated my answer.

There was a long pause before the fellow said rather heavily, "*Realllly,*" followed by an even longer pause. Then he said, "That's truly unique. I'm a design engineer for that same tank! In fact, we have one just a mile or so from here in our warehouse that has some problems we are troubleshooting as we speak."

I didn't respond to that revelation but continued to eat, all the while wishing I had more food so I would have reason to continue stalling. The chap continued in a questioning but not yet challenging voice, "That is *really* interesting. What company did you say you worked for?"

Finishing my mouthful of food, I again leaned over the table and told him in a tone devoid of any emotion, "Roberts Incorporated." Hoping that vagueness would put the matter to rest, I returned to my plate.

There was another long pause as the fellow digested my response. Then, in a pointed and challenging voice loud enough for all to hear, he said, "Roberts Incorporated ... Roberts Incorporated. I have been working on this tank project since its inception, and I don't remember any company by that name." Shoving his plate out of the way as if to make a point, he leaned further out over the table, turned his head, and asked rather sharply, this time in an accusatory tone, "Where did you say you were located?"

Turning to him as if I didn't like being continually interrupted during my meal, I said, "I didn't say. But," I slowly and forcefully uttered, "for your information, the company is located in Minneapolis." With that I continued to eat my now not-so-interesting duck dinner, trying to come up with a "Plan B" to get this fellow off my hind end before every chap there was on it. Looking slyly over at Don, I could see that he had the look of a freeze-dried human. I hoped no one else had noticed. If they did and put two and two together, it could get nasty in a hurry. As if I didn't have enough problems, my adversary continued to rag my ass.

"Minneapolis … Minneapolis … I sure as hell don't remember any firm by that name located in Minneapolis working on this tank project," he hissed through his teeth as he attempted to get to the bottom of the matter now strongly holding his interest.

"Been there in operation for over twenty years," I responded calmly, spooning more spuds onto my plate and liberally sprinkling them with salt and pepper like "Joe Cool." Snatching another quick look at my partner, I saw that he had backed his chair a bit away from the table in what appeared to be a defensive position to better run or fight when—not if but when—the discussion turned to a good old-fashioned, fist-swinging, head-breaking drunken brawl. By now the other conversations at the table had subsided and everyone was now listening with more than a general interest. *A whole lot more. …*

Knowing I was on deck and had to hit a homer, I again leaned over the table and, looking my big-mouthed tormenter coldly in the eye, said, "What kind of security clearance do you have?" I didn't even know where that thought came from, but the question sounded good to me at the moment, and over my lips it went. The man sat stunned for a moment as his buddies all looked at him and then, with an equally cold stare and a voice dripping with signs warning me not to go there, bellowed, "If you are who you say you are, you wouldn't have to ask me that question. You damn well should know what security clearance level I would have to have to work on this project!"

Now you could hear a pin drop, along with the thumping of my partner's rapidly beating heart. Even the ladies who had been so busy serving this multitude of noisy men moments earlier were now silent and unmoving in disbelief at the exchange taking place before their eyes. Out of the corner of my eye I could see that "Boss Hog" was also staring coldly in my direction, obviously thinking bad thoughts while waiting for my response, which his look said had better be a damn good one! With an air of confidence to gather some time, I spooned a large helping of fresh green beans with bacon and onions onto my plate. By the way, they were damned good! Whoever the cook was, she knew her stuff.

Knowing I had to deliver a killing shot to this sharp-tongued antagonist before he could do unto me, I gambled big time and attacked.

I turned to him and quietly said, "Since you insist on pursuing this matter, you need to be aware that I am in fact knowledgeable about the contents of your personnel file, *including your drinking habits*. I am also aware what your contribution to this project has been to date and know why you have the tank, not to mention what's wrong with it. I also possess a security clearance that is two levels above yours and am very much aware of the restrictions placed on you *personally*, and your coworkers, regarding loose talk involving this project. As you are well aware, *total* detail security about this tank is in the best interests of the government of the United States and you, my good fellow, are starting to cross over that line—*way* over!"

My eyes never left his, or his mine. Before I could come up with more bluff ammunition to follow that gamble and get that chap off my back, his expression changed to such a degree that I thought he was starting to choke on some food. For a few moments his face changed to every color under the sun while his eyes fairly bulged in their sockets. Careful, lad, I thought, you'll bust a gut if you keep going that way, and I'll be damned if I give you CPR.

Then he slowly said, "Damn, now I know … , goddamned stupid of me not to catch your drift earlier. The CIA! *Now I understand!* You're from the goddamned CIA!"

God, I thought, he couldn't have done a better job of bailing my hind end out if he had tried! With such a good "in," I just kept a stoic face, waited, and rode the crest that was to follow.

"Now I understand," he quietly said as he sat back heavily into his chair. "Now I know. *Wow!*" he said, his voice rising under the stress of the moment. "You are right! I have said too much already."

Calmly looking at him, knowing I now had the upper hand, I quietly said, "Buy me and my friend a drink, and what was said here tonight will die with the two hundred or so ducks lying on the floor in the picking facility that my partner and I hope to take home and put to good use." I continued my cold, all-knowing gaze into his eyes.

Jumping up from the table, he accidentally hit his plate of partially uneaten food, sailing it across the table and into the lap of the poacher across from him. Without apologizing, he said, "Let's go. That's a deal I can't refuse!"

I got up, slowly for effect, made sure I established casual eye contact with everyone around the table, and then walked around "Boss

Hog's" chair. Placing my hand on "Boss's" shoulder for the effect it would have on the group, I said to him, "Better hurry up and eat what's on your plate. I don't know how long the whiskey will last once I hit that bar, but it won't be long."

"Boss" just grinned a huge grin of relief at the turn the conversation had taken, pushed his chair away from the table, curled his upper lip in a challenge, and said, "Let's see just how much of a man you really are." With that moment of concern past, the four of us, including my partner with the white eye ring and brown stripes in his shorts, bellied up to the bar and drank double shots of whiskey—three of us out of relief and the fourth because he didn't know any better than to drink with a badge-carrying "casting engineer."

The air around the dining table was again filled with the day's talk of killing as the drama slowly receded from everyone's mind and the evening proceeded as hoped for, with the exception of my partner. Don's sphincter had sealed shut, and I think it was several days before it was operative again. He had never learned that to be young is to be immortal. ...

Months later, with this information and more that Don and his original partner had gathered over previous months, this whole bunch was rounded up and successfully prosecuted. As a result of that action, many lesser "Boss Hogs" got out of the commercial-market hunting business in the Bay City area, and the Service breathed a little easier, as did the critters. It was truly amazing to see the effect those trials had on the local illegal duck-killing populace. Bay City marshes, instead of sounding like a war zone on a daily basis, returned to the normal ebb and flow of hunting activity, and the critters once again had happy faces.

Don left the Service sometime later and took a job with the U.S. Customs Service. That move was probably for the best because it allowed him time to mature in the company of many fine officers in a far larger agency. With that comfort level and additional training, I am sure Don went on to develop into a fine officer serving the folks of this great land of ours.

As this story is being written, I am still in the Service but within months of retirement. I am trying to refrain from getting entangled in the webs we often weave in this business of putting those in the business of extinction out of business. But I know that if I ever get into a similar situation, I will always have my "best friend" in the form of wisdom gained over a thirty-two-year period in wildlife law enforcement and the commensurate "voice" to go into verbal battle. I guess I could also say I still have the CIA (a contradiction in terms) to get me and my critters safely past the "Palace Guard" and the "Knights of the Wrong Table." In essence, it's my own form of the "M-1 Abrams main battle tank."

ten

The Cornfields of Wisconsin

SPECIAL AGENT IN CHARGE Bob Hodgins stuck his head through the open doorway of my office saying, "What do you have on your schedule for the next week, starting today, 'Big-T'?" ("Big-T" was a nickname Bob used because of my size.)

Quickly looking through my calendar and finding nothing more pressing than a ton of office work, I answered, "Nothing terribly important, Chief. What's up?"

"Good," he said. "I need you to head over to Madison and team up with Senior Resident Agent Bob Thomas. He needs help working goose hunters in the Horicon Marsh area. Plan on hitting it so you can work this weekend through the next. That way, along with the rest of his people and a few refuge officers, you guys should be able to make a dent in the locals and out-of-state hunters taking too many birds."

"You got it, Chief," I said, looking forward to a stint in the field instead of my usual hectic days in the office. Satisfied, Bob ducked out of my office en route to another in a string of useless regional office meetings scheduled for all the division heads. Hurrying through my in box for items that needed to be addressed posthaste, I found none, so I prepared to get the hell out of Dodge before Bob changed his mind and went in my place.

The Horicon Marsh is located a few miles southwest of Fond du Lac, Wisconsin. It is a great natural marsh comprising the Horicon National Wildlife Refuge on the north and the Horicon Wildlife Marsh Area to the south. For as long as anyone can remember, this area has been a major migration and staging ground for thousands of subspecies of Canada geese, ducks, and shorebirds. Surrounding the marsh are thousands of acres of rich croplands. Principal among them, as far as the ducks and geese are concerned, are the freshly harvested cornfields, especially during the brutal Wisconsin winter weather, when geese and ducks by the thousands flock to those fields to fill up on the golden kernels of life-giving energy. As usual, humankind, seeing such a living bounty of fat, corn-fed critters waddling around the fields, soon had dreams of roast goose or duck, sage stuffing, mashed potatoes, gravy, hot biscuits, and a fresh green salad followed by a hot-out-of-the-oven blackberry cobbler. It didn't take long for the local farmers and the rest of the hunting public to venture forth with their trusty shotguns and a grin of better things to come. And it didn't take long, with such massive flocks of ducks and geese flying around, for some to "lose count" of the numbers of birds that could legally be taken. ...

As history shows, human nature can't leave idle or unharvested a good thing such as thousands of feeding waterfowl. Because of that nature, state and federal wildlife officers were regularly driven to distraction by this group of folks and their illegal antics in the cornfields of Wisconsin: shooting before legal shooting hours (one-half hour before sunrise); shooting after legal shooting hours (sunset); no federal duck stamp (required for hunters from age sixteen on when taking ducks, geese, swans, and brant); no hunting license in possession; possession of over-limits; double-tripping (going out two or more times in a day and taking a limit of birds each time, a strategy that makes it difficult to catch this type of shooter); shooting over a baited area; wanton waste (at the end of the shoot taking the biggest birds of ten to eighteen pounds and leaving the smaller subspecies of geese, the three- to four-pounders, to rot in the fields); and use of shotguns capable of shooting more than three times per event.

As if that were not enough, there were also problems with many of the local landowners. They hated what they considered interference from state and federal wildlife officers, especially when it came to checking paying hunters or their friends shooting on their lands. Many of the farmers were of German extraction and manifested a fierce spirit of ownership and total authority over their lands. No one, especially government representatives and run-of-the-mill trespassers, was welcome without the landowner's express blessing. To enter private land without it routinely courted a damn good ass chewing, often given just inches from the officer's face in several foreign languages. In rare circumstances, a damn good physical brawl resulted in cases dealing with the more hotheaded of the hardheaded.

Historically, many farmers augmented their incomes by inviting the hunting public onto their lands—for a hefty trespass fee, of course. In these cases, the landowners took on an additional self-imposed role of protector for those hunters. They wanted their paying customers to have the shoot of a life time, many times allowing them to freely break the conservation laws in the process. This shooting opportunity without fear of interference led to regular-paying, high-dollar customers. Illegal activity, when discovered during a warrantless inspection, led to many a serious discussion between the landowner and the officers regarding who could go where and when. Heated shouting matches took place on a daily basis during hunting season, many times more than once in the same day with the same landowner, when officers tried to enforce waterfowl regulations.

The bottom legal line under the Open Fields Doctrine (case law) was that any authorized conservation officer who believed migratory game birds were being taken had a legal right to check that activity without a warrant. Probable cause or a warrant was required if an officer was gathering information in and around lands considered curtilage (enclosed land surrounding a house or dwelling space holding a reasonable expectation of privacy). However, in the open fields or in plain view, the shooters were fair game. The purpose of this legal thinking was to provide for the conservation of a species without the undue hindrance of time-consuming administrative processes, yet still protect one's rights against violations of the Fourth Amendment to the Constitution, which guarantees against unreasonable search and seizure.

Another problem in enforcing wildlife laws was the deeds of a person we called a "Paul Revere." If you ran into the landowner before you got to your shooters, a heated discussion regarding the right of trespass would occur. In the ensuing "hoorah," the son or wife or other relative of the farmer would run ahead to warn the shooters of the law's presence. If that occurred, by the time you arrived all the evidence of the crime had long since disappeared. So what with the long hours, mud, weather, poor meals, cleverness of the illegally shooting public, birds not cooperating by not flying into the area you had staked out, and run-ins with the farmers, a good time was had by all. ...

Regardless of the hell-raising local farmers, I was happy to be free of my administrative duties as I headed for home to prepare for my trip to the fabled Horicon Marshes. Typically, I loaded up every kind of gear for weather from 60 degrees above zero to blizzard conditions, kissed my long-suffering bride and kids good-bye, and went out the door into another set of adventures. I always welcomed the opportunity to work in different areas of my district to better understand the people, the problems, and, most of all, the abilities of my officers. I had worked little in Wisconsin since my arrival in the region, and I looked forward to the learning that came from working in a new area for the first time. Especially an area with such a fabled history. For as long as I could remember, I had heard many tales involving thousands of geese being taken in this area, and I was finally going to get a firsthand look.

Meeting Senior Resident Agent Bob Thomas in Madison, we teamed up and convoyed in our unmarked patrol vehicles to Waupun, where we stayed in a small motel. Talk about exciting! For miles around the air was full of geese just arriving from the northern climes or flying around in hundreds of flocks looking for a place to land and fill up on the abundant waste corn. It was natural heritage in full bloom!

The next morning we arose early, to be greeted by a thick fog blanketing what appeared to be the entire marsh area. After a hearty breakfast in a local restaurant catering to the early-morning crazies of the goose-hunting fraternity, Bob and I headed off to the east side of the marsh near the small town of Knowles. Once there and with the commencement of shooting hours, we slowly patrolled up and down the county roads adjacent to the marsh and adjoining cornfields. Our technique was to stop and listen to the intensity of shooting in the fields, and if it was spotty or not heavy enough to arouse our suspicion, we would move on to look for "greener" pastures. Heavy shooting usually meant a good decoy set, great callers (those using legal goose calls or illegal electronic goose calls), lots of killing, or all of the above. We were most interested in the level of shooting where the birds were really getting hammered. A good officer always moves to the sound of the guns.

After forty minutes of roving, we finally heard a level of shooting that caught our attention. The fog was literally stacked up with calling, milling, confused, and lost geese over the shooting area. Their plaintive calls to buddies on the ground were so intense that it sounded as if at least a thousand geese were in the air around us! With numbers like that, the potential to exceed the legal bag limit could be irresistible. Off in the distance, I could hear someone working a Canada goose call, and *he was good!* He would no more than call and the air would be full of happy chaps requesting landing instructions! A killing was surely in the offing.

Stopping on the county highway to listen and get a better echo location on our hunters, I saw headlights of a vehicle slowly approaching from the north. Remembering what Bob Hodgins had told me about Wisconsin farmers and their likelihood of getting in our faces if we were on or near their lands, I bailed out of the car. I had Bob, who was driving, unlatch the hood, and I jerked it up just as a pickup drove up carrying what appeared to be a local farmer. Quickly leaning over, I jerked a spark-plug wire barely off the tip of the plug and then pretended to be looking over the motor for our "problem."

"Vott are you boys doing here?" came a gruff German-accented voice from the pickup.

Raising my head, I said, "We've been experiencing a miss in the engine, and I'm trying to find out what might be the trouble."

The farmer looked at me with a set of steely eyes as if he had heard that story before. Sensing his disbelief, I yelled at Bob to try it again. Bob turned over the engine, and the miss was very noticeable. I had Bob kill the engine as I went back under the hood like any good mechanic.

The farmer, still eyeballing us, said, "You boys hunters?" Since both Bob and I were dressed in hunting gear, I yelled from under the hood that we were but hadn't yet found a farm on which we could hunt. I noticed during the time we were playing games with the farmer that our hunters in the adjacent cornfield had gotten off two good volleys of at least ten shots each. Damn, I thought. I wished this dirt farmer would get the hell out of Dodge so I could haul my tail end over the fence and into that field to check the hunters. No such luck, however, as our farmer stayed put and watched me work under the hood.

"Try it again, Bob," I yelled. He did, and of course, the engine still ran rougher than a cob. "Must have water in the electrical system from this damn fog," I said loudly enough for the farmer to hear without raising my head out of the engine compartment. Reaching for the distributor cap, I unhooked it and, taking out my handkerchief, made a grand gesture of wiping off the points.

"Vell, votteber it is, I haff to patrol the edges uff my fields for trespassers ant dose damn game vordens," uttered the farmer. That was followed by a stream of tobacco juice that hit the road and partially splattered my boots. "If you boys are still here ven I return, I vill giff you a hand. Also, all da land around here ist private, so don't get any vild ideas on running oft into the cornfields for a little goose shoot, hear, now?"

"Yes, sir," Bob replied.

With that and another examining look, the farmer drove off into the fog. As soon as he was out of sight I grabbed my kit bag holding my binoculars, handcuffs, spare ammunition, citation book, and portable radio from the backseat. Running across the grassy right-of-way, I vaulted the fence, yelling over my shoulder at Bob to tighten down spark plug wire number eight. Sprinting into the fog of the harvested cornfield, I didn't slow down until I was at least one hundred yards inside the fence, where no one driving down the highway could see me because of my "aerial" cover.

Stopping to get my breath and bearings, I heard Bob slam the hood of the patrol car and drive off. Then, as if on cue, I heard another barrage of shots to the northwest. Trotting across the harvested cornfield, I would walk twenty-five steps and then run seventy-five like the old-time trappers when in a hurry. You can eat up a lot of ground that way and still have plenty of energy left if a dash of speed is necessary at the end. Finally getting close to my shooters, based on the caller's sounds, I slowed to a walk so as not to suddenly stumble on their blind in the dense fog.

The geese were milling overhead by the hundreds, and the caller with the damn good goose call would bring them in every time, slicker than cow slobbers. I could hear the heavy wet wings of the geese passing low overhead as they lumbered blindly toward the caller. In each instance, their approach would be followed seconds later by a barrage of shots. Stopping and listening carefully, I could hear the heavy goose bodies hitting the ground, never to migrate across this great land of ours again. I jotted down the number of shots fired, time fired, and the number of *whumps* I heard hitting the ground. I continued my stalk, swinging my binoculars from side to side, hoping to see dim figures in the fog. This is an old game warden trick enabling you to see your opponent before he sees you, thanks to the light-gathering and magnification properties of your optics.

About then I heard the sound of a vehicle engine slowly coming down a small, muddy farm road behind me. Running toward a pile of leftover cornstalks, leaves, and weeds piled on the ground where the harvester had made a turn, I dove headlong into the leavings. Cursing the lack of cover for a carcass my size as I burrowed into the mud, I saw a black pickup emerging from the fog. It was my German farmer from the road with the wad of tobacco between his cheek and gum. He drove by, slipping and sliding in the mud, out of sight into the fog to the east. He was so intent on keeping his vehicle on the narrow farm road and out of the soft winter mud of the field that he failed to see a grinning "pitcher's mound" partially hidden in a weed pile. Hearing him stop a few moments later and a door slam, I stayed put. He couldn't have been more than thirty-five yards away, but the fog prevented us from seeing each other. For the next few moments, all I heard was hundreds of confused geese milling overhead and then another barrage of shots with the now familiar resulting *whumps*. From the sound and number of shots, I figured I had five shooters. Looking at the *whumps* as kills, I figured the shooters had limits plus three over on geese, if my ears weren't playing tricks on me, *since I had started to count.* They had been shooting since long before my arrival, making my heart race with the realization that the chance for an overlimit of geese was in the offing.

I gave Bob a quiet update on the portable radio and asked him to respond with only a quick key of the mike if the transmission was acknowledged. *Click* came his quiet acknowledgment. Hearing talking between the farmer and his shooters, I got up, grabbed my armload of cornstalks and weeds, and ran toward where I figured he had parked his pickup. In a few steps, the truck hove darkly into view. Finding more weedy cover at the corner of the field near the vehicle, I again covered myself with the cornstalks and newfound roadside weeds. I had no more than covered up when my farmer emerged from the fog, carrying two large handfuls of geese! I couldn't get a good count, but he had to have at least four in each hand. Throwing them into the bed of his pickup, he backed out of the mud of the field onto the farm road and proceeded back from whence he came.

I choked down the urge to jump up and grab him as he went by with his over-limit. I knew he could be easily located, and I could personally account for at least eight geese in his possession, so I figured I would catch him later. Anytime anyone moves illegal birds away from the shooters, it makes it really tough on the officer unless he is right there to observe the deed. However, when he is, the "runner" of birds is involved under the law just as surely as if he had pulled the trigger, and rightfully so. Many times those birds have "disappeared" by the time the runner is apprehended, leading to a loud and prolonged denial yelling match. And when you get to court, testifying against someone for such an over-limit without the evidence in hand can be dicey, especially if the judge knows the individual standing accused before him. Basically, "law dogs" like to catch people with the goods, and many times, like this one, we are called upon to make tough decisions under hard circumstances. Grab everybody or let some go, taking your chances in order to get to the head of the snake?

Lying there trying to decide how to handle my shooters, I heard the farmer stop a short distance down the road and then silence. In a few moments, I heard him restart his pickup and proceed out of earshot toward the west and the highway bordering that side of his cornfield. That was strange, I thought. However, I quickly forgot about that moment because my lad was working the goose call again. In moments a flock of about sixty Canada geese flew over my hiding place, low enough for me to hit them with a cornstalk. They plowed out of sight into the swirling fog like ships of the line in the days of old, and into fourteen deadly shots. The characteristic *whumps* followed, and as near as I could tell totaled eight. Then there were the sounds of low voices as I assumed the men were picking up the spoils of their most recent shoot.

Soon the goose call started again, and I realized it wasn't a man doing the calling *but a machine!* Use of an electronic caller to take migratory game birds was illegal and had been since the 1930s! They were outlawed because they were so damn deadly and did not represent anything close to a fair chase. No wonder the birds were decoying into this death trap without a whimper. They were listening to their own on the airwaves, and what better way to lure game to the gun than to use their own kinfolk for the "talking"? (As I write this, electronic calling is now lawful for the taking of lesser snow geese because of their huge, out-of-balance population numbers. Wildlife agencies are using the management tool of hunting as a means of harvest to reduce the population to safe levels before the geese destroy the flora necessary for survival of the species on the arctic breeding grounds.)

Hot dog, was I excited! I had never made such a case, much less even heard an electronic caller in action, and boy, was I impressed! Once I concentrated on the difference between an electronic caller and handheld calls, the difference was easy to discern. Clear, crisp, concise notes of the same sequence emerged every time with the recorded calls. Irregular sounds and uneven spacing were the norm for handheld calls. Damn, I thought. Even though I had never worked such a case, I should have recognized the difference right away. Especially because every time the operator turned on the electronic caller, the birds came in as if they were on a string and there was no tomorrow. For many, there wasn't. ...

I decided right then and there through set jaws that I would let the fellows have one more shoot and then snap the trap shut. Canada geese being so common, I let the shooters hang themselves on a long rope, hoping it might make for a very good sentence to be hung around their necks in federal court. If so, perhaps the punishment would teach the gunners a lasting lesson, thereby saving a lot more birds over the long haul. I didn't have long to wait. On went the electronic call, and the birds boiled in on cue. This time there were not as many as before, but they were just as determined to find that "chap" on the ground calling to them.

The usual barrage of shots followed, along with the *whumps*. Getting up out of the weeds and making sure I still had my sidearm and that it was operable, mud and all, off I went toward the shooters at a ground-eating pace. I hadn't trotted twenty yards when I came upon a Dodge pickup full of hunting gear, shotgun shells, shotgun carrying cases, and the like. Quickly checking the bed of the truck for extra geese and finding none, I continued churning through the mud toward my shooters, recording their license plate number in my notebook in the process.

Soon I came upon about 150 full-body goose decoys, telling me I had moneyed shooters (giant full-body goose decoys were very expensive in those days), and within moments the cornstalk-covered lid over a sunken goose blind emerged from the fog. As I approached, the spring-loaded cover shot up and five men got to their feet. "Hey, we're having a goose shoot here," came my first greeting from one of the shooters.

I continuing my approach, watching for any signs of funny business.

"Who the hell are you?" came a pointed question from another man.

"Your friendly federal agent," I cheerfully responded.

With those words, one of the men quickly disappeared down out of sight into the bowels of the goose pit. I picked up the pace, figuring he was the person using the electronic caller and that he was trying to hide it to avoid discovery. I got there in time to see him hide a calling device in a military ammunition can.

Holding out my badge and credentials for all to see, I said, "Federal agent, gentlemen. I would like to check your shotguns for plugs, duck stamps, hunting licenses, numbers of geese, and *your electronic calling device* if I could, please."

The man messing with the lid to the ammo can froze when he heard me utter the words *electronic calling device*. "What are you talking about?" he said weakly as he watched me hovering over him.

"Just hand me that ammo can, and I'll show you," I retorted.

Up came the ammo can somewhat slowly, and I pulled out the tape recorder calling device. I turned it on, and out came the melodious tones of a bunch of "happy honkers." Soon the air around us was again filled with milling geese trying to locate their friend on the ground. About a dozen geese landed in the decoys not ten yards from me and just stood there looking at the six of us now standing around the blind in front of God and everybody. They stood stone still for a few moments before realizing something was amiss, and then off they went in a clatter of wings and panicked calls. I turned and stared hard at my shooters. I was met with nothing but five sets of downcast eyes of shame. Nothing like a testimonial as to the device's effectiveness, especially if one knows how cautious Canada geese are!

I called Bob to let him know what I had but couldn't direct him in to help me because I didn't know exactly where I was. I advised him to take the first farm road into the field above where we had been sitting on the highway before the farmer in the black pickup arrived. With that, I checked my now long-faced shooters' hunting licenses, duck stamps, and shotguns. All were in order. Then I walked through the decoys and with difficulty brought back to the blind seventeen large Canada honkers. Counting the birds in the bottom of their blind, the men had over-limits, not to mention being caught red-handed using an illegal calling device. Letting them know they were going to be cited for these violations, I seized the geese and electronic caller. As I gathered up their driver's licenses, I noticed that my shooters continued to be very quiet and subdued. Something isn't right, Terry, I told myself and began to look around for additional clues to wrongdoing. Finding none, I moved on with the administrative processing, but I still felt that something was wrong.

Moments later I discovered the reason for the tight jaws. When asked for their professions so I could fill in that portion of the citation, every one of them turned out to be an executive in the Herter's Manufacturing Company, a company that made a ton of items for the hunting and fishing public. Here they were supposed to know better, being in the sporting business, yet they had gotten greedy. I didn't say anything smart-assed, but I sure wanted to. Finishing up the citations, I asked if anyone had any questions. The only question was, "Is this going to get into the papers?"

I answered that the Service only filed the citations and let the chips fall where they may with the clerk of the courts. We were not in the business of providing information regarding someone's misery to the newspapers for their front pages. They were relieved, and several weeks later each of them forfeited bail of $950 in lieu of a courtroom appearance. ... But I am getting ahead of myself.

Then it dawned on me: What about the earlier pile of geese the farmer had removed from their shoot? He had driven just a short distance down the road and stopped, then started up his pickup a few moments later and left. That didn't give him much time to do anything out of the ordinary. I wondered if he might have hidden that mess of geese for his friends to pick up later. Holding on to my shooters' hunting and driver's licenses, I asked them about the load of geese the fellow in the black pickup had carried out. Everyone tried to play innocent, believing I didn't have any evidence in hand, so why say anything incriminating? Realizing I was going nowhere with that question, I advised them to gather their decoys because they were done for the day. I informed them that while they were doing that, I would backtrack the farmer and see whether I could find the missing geese.

Taking the point-and-shoot camera from my "possibles" bag, I took a picture of the over-limits of geese and the electronic calling device. Turning to my shooters, I said, "Now, if any of that disappears while I am gone, I will still have the evidence needed to convict you—plus, with those pictures, evidence to add the charges of destruction of government property. In short, gentlemen, all of you will be going to jail if the evidence is altered or disappears." I could tell from the looks in their eyes that they had had enough of me for the day and weren't going to do anything foolish.

Returning to their pickup, near which the farmer had parked, I memorized his tread design. Then I commenced following that track back down the road. Soon it led to several parked harvesters and a bank-out wagon (a self-powered wheeled device with high sloped walls that is pulled alongside a moving harvester to receive the harvest). The tread design I had been following backed up to the bank-out wagon and then moved off to the west. I crawled up onto the bank-out wagon and looked inside, and there lay ten still bleeding Canada geese!

As I crawled inside and began tossing them out, I heard a vehicle coming down the farm road toward me. That damn dirt farmer is on his way back! I thought. Bailing out of the bank-out wagon, I picked up my evidence geese before he and I got into a shouting match regarding whom the geese belonged to. I was relieved to see Bob coming (slipping and sliding would have been a better description) down the muddy farm road instead of the farmer. He was happy to see his boss, and a whole lot happier to hear what kind of case we had. Typical agent, I thought. To hell with the boss ... how did we do? With a grin, I tossed the geese into the trunk of his car and, getting on the front fender, rode the rest of the way in to our buddies still picking up their decoys.

Loading up the rest of the evidence, I informed the shooters of the additional geese I had recovered from the bank-out wagon. To a man, they knew where the geese came from and how they had gotten into the wagon. Yet none said anything regarding this new revelation. Handing them a card with my name and telephone number, I told them I would find the farmer (identified as Dan Krumpf by the Herter's folks) and cite him as well for aiding and abetting them in their violations. I also told them that when they got to the farmer, they should give him my card and let him know what my intentions were in case I hadn't found him yet. I figured I would beard the farmer in his own den since they had given me a general description as to where he lived, but if I was unsuccessful, he wouldn't be surprised by the arrival of a citation in the mail. Shaking hands all around, Bob and I slipped our way out of the area, eventually heading north on the adjacent state highway.

On the way we ran into a little house trailer alongside the road selling hot bratwurst, the Wisconsin-style breakfast of champions! Bailing out of the car, we ordered three each of the fresh pork sausages with buns. After covering them with onions and the like, we set off down the road, eating our bounty as we continued looking for someone doing something foolish.

A state highway crosses the refuge portion of Horicon Marsh, bisecting the closed hunting zone. Along both sides of that road were usually thousands of loafing geese. There were signs everywhere regarding the closed status of the area and the fact that shooting was prohibited. Driving down that road, Bob found a wide spot and pulled over. The two of us sat there wolfing down the bratwurst as if we hadn't eaten for months. Man, let me tell you, those folks in Wisconsin can sure make great homemade sausage! Bob was a slower eater than I, and as he finished his second sausage (I was already finished), I commented on the fact that it sure would be nice if someone drove past the resting geese on the refuge and blew them up. Bob just grunted at me in disbelief. He knew something like that, in front of two agents parked in front of God and everybody, would never happen. With that bit of disdain for what he considered an office orderly (Bob was crusty old school), he began eating his last sausage, hoping I would keep my future crazy thoughts to myself.

Always the dreamer, I got out my binoculars and began to watch every car that slowly drove by the thousands of resting geese alongside the highway. As expected, not hoped for, mind you, but expected, everyone just drove by looking at the winter spectacle of resting geese. Bob, grouchy as ever, kept grumbling out loud between bites on his bratwurst about having damn kids with screwy ideas for supervisors.

Then a carload of Japanese folks slowly drove by us toward the resting geese. As they got to the geese, their vehicle's taillights went on like those of everyone else before them as they slowed to observe nature in action. Then they stopped, and the geese, getting nervous, began to walk away from the parked car. The driver got out of the car and began taking pictures. Japanese tourists and their cameras, I thought as I lowered my binoculars, no longer interested. After taking a few pictures, the Japanese fellow walked to the rear of his car and lifted up the hatchback. I brought my binoculars back up and focused them on him once more. Into the back of the car went his camera, and *out came a rifle!*

"Bob," I yelled, "he has a gun!"

Bob just looked at me as if he thought I had gone crazy.

"Bob," I repeated, "that Japanese fellow has a rifle and is preparing to shoot at our geese!"

Bob, still unconvinced that anything serious was going on at the car parked sixty yards from us in the lifting fog, disdainfully lifted up his binoculars. Just then the man shot into the thousands of resting geese. *Roar* went the thousands of wings as the geese got the hell out of there for a quieter part of the refuge! Bob, suddenly convinced, started the car and headed down to our carload of tourists.

As we pulled up behind them, I was out the door in a flash and recovered the rifle from the still open hatchback of the car. Bob identified us as I checked the rifle. It didn't have any shells in the barrel, but the magazine was full, and there was a spent shell on the ground where we had seen the man stand and shoot. To make a long story short, the folks were from Japan, visiting the Japanese consul and out for a day in the country. They could hardly speak English, and we had one hell of a time explaining what the driver had done wrong. He was finally issued a citation (with a consulate address), and we seized the rifle as evidence (where in the hell they had gotten the gun was beyond me).

Even though they didn't have diplomatic immunity, Bob and I spent the next month explaining to our Washington-based leadership why those visitors had been cited for a refuge violation. We soon discovered that the Washington folks were under the gun because the Japanese Embassy was raising hell. The Refuge Administration Act makes it very clear that no individual, regardless of nationality, can break the laws pertaining to protection of wildlife or plants on a National Wildlife Refuge. It was some time before the Japanese shooter finally paid off his $100 in the form of bail forfeiture, but what a political "hoorah" in the meantime. And, to be sure, what an unlikely event to occur in front of two special agents feeding their faces with bratwurst. ... Also, so much for the idiot ideas from the region's second in command. Bob was still grumbling about being saddled with such a chap—but not quite as loudly as before!

Finished with our Japanese shooter, Bob and I moved over to the east side of the Horicon Marsh, and this time it was Bob's turn to move through the fields on foot while I stayed in the car as a backup. The cover of fog was getting heavier again, as did the surrounding shooting. The air, even over the road on which I was sitting, was alive with low-flying birds. In the heavy fog, they were lost as they looked for a place to set down, rest, and get some grits. It was a real display of nature in all its glory, and I got out of the patrol car and just stood there reveling in the sounds and occasional glimpses of the birds as they tried avoiding crashing into each other. That, and a good cigar I was now puffing, really made for a day to remember.

Somewhat later Bob "scratched" three guys with an over-limit of mallard ducks, and while he tended to that, I gathered the full wrath of the farmer's wife as she recognized our car and its occupant as the one responsible for pinching the Herter's folks on her land to the south. Then her husband, Dan Krumpf, drove up and bailed out of his pickup like a man on a mission! Figuring it was going to be "fist city" before his burrs got knocked off, I squared my stance in preparation for what he was bringing to the party. Running up to me, he began screaming at his wife to go get the sheriff because this fat-assed bastard, meaning yours truly, was going to jail for trespassing. I quietly identified myself and informed Dan that as agents of the federal government, we had a legal right to be on private lands checking hunters. Looking at me as if I were a lying SOB, he notched his abusive behavior one level higher and dared me to try and drive off before the sheriff got there. He made it very clear that to do so would get me killed on the spot. Suffice to say, he was pissed and a tad out of control! Seeing that I was going nowhere talking to this lad, I just sat on the fender of our car, smoked another cigar, and waited for the local sheriff.

Soon I could see a blinking red light coming through the fog, and moments later the deputy sheriff drove up. Getting out of his car, he walked over to Krumpf and got his side of the story as I calmly sat on the fender. Then he came over to me, with the farmer angrily breathing down his neck, to hear my side. I identified myself and explained what had transpired in the field that morning. I also explained that the federal laws I enforced superseded state laws, and he agreed. Turning to Dan, the deputy told him that as a federal officer, I had every right to be on private property, and there was nothing the county could do.

Hearing that, Dan blew up and began threatening the deputy. He told the officer in no uncertain terms that if he didn't arrest me for trespassing, Dan would do it as a civilian, and then the deputy could transport me to jail. Sliding off the fender, I walked up to Dan and said, "Now, wait a minute. You, whether you care to believe it or not, have been told by two officers of the law that I have every legal right to be here. If you persist in this foolishness of arrest as a citizen, it will be a false arrest. If you do that, I will go to jail peacefully, but when I get out and the court sets you straight, I will sue you for false arrest, and your farm will be my farm. Do you understand?"

I think the "your farm will be my farm" statement finally got through that damn German stubbornness and rang his bell. He was so mad and frustrated by now that all he could do was spit. Turning to the deputy, I requested that he remain for the next few minutes because I was going to write Dan a citation for his involvement in the over-limits of geese belonging to the Herter's folks. Damn, you talk about turning several different shades of purple when those words were spoken! One on the wild side from Dan, and one of a trapped rat from the deputy. To his credit, the deputy stayed, and after a few more minutes of calming discussion, Dan more or less settled down and received a citation for his part in running the birds from the hunt site that morning.

I had just finished with him and thanked the deputy for his assistance when Bob called me on the portable radio. He needed an assist, and this time I knew where he was. Within moments I was able to slip and slide up to him and his group of hunters. As I drove up, I could see that he had a large farmer stuck in his face. This time the farmer had a couple of big, strapping sons my size, which didn't bode well. Stepping out of the car, I walked up behind Bob and just stood there as he introduced me as another federal agent. I could see both sons sizing me up in case Dad told them to take me. No matter how Bob and I cut it, this was not a winning situation. After a few moments, I could see that Bob was getting nowhere with the landowner as to the government's right in checking hunters, so I interceded. Normally I would not have done that; I would have let my officer carry the mail, so to speak. However, Bob looked like he could use some assistance in trying another approach. So before this got into a good old-fashioned wrestling match in the mud of the cornfield with nine hundred pounds of farmers, I felt it best to save what was left of our hides.

"Good morning, gentlemen," I said in a strong voice, sliding around Bob and quickly sticking out my hand to shake theirs before they could get their feet under them and refuse. Keep in mind that most men, mad or not, when offered another man's hand in friendship will usually shake it without thinking. I was banking on that reflex, and it worked. Seeing the flash of surprise at this move, I kept advancing. "Bob, the deputy is at the end of the farm road [he wasn't; he had gone back], and if you want I can radio him and have him come in as well."

That statement caught the farm folks by surprise, and then the dad did something I didn't expect before Bob could respond. "The hell you say," he said. "If that's the case, what's his name?"

"Dale Treatmann," I quickly responded, having introduced myself to the deputy earlier. The farmer's face just flushed beet red when he heard that I had the correct name, knowing the deputy would complicate matters if he or his sons started anything. Trying to stay on my roll and not get into a boar's nest with these three beefy (Durham bull variety) fellows, I said, "I am this man's supervisor, and aside from the trespass issue, has he done anything unprofessional here today?"

"Well, no," came the farmer's limp reply, "but the son of a bitch sure as hell doesn't belong on my land harassing my hunters."

"Wait a minute," I said. "Bob says your hunters shot over the limit on ducks. Is that true?"

"Well, yeah, but only a few, and they claim it was a mistake," he lamely responded.

"How many over are they, Bob?" I asked.

"Nine over," Bob replied.

"Gentlemen, I don't really see an issue here," I said flatly. "It is pretty hard to miscount to the tune of nine over the limit, and I don't care what school you went to."

I could see my farmers were kind of rocked back on their heels, so I kept coming. "If my officer had been out of line, I would have fired him on the spot [I lied—it would take a lot more than that to fire any-one, but any port in a storm], but you say that isn't the issue. If not, we need to let him finish up with these men who shot the over-limits so we can get off your lands and let you folks get back to your lives." Bob was a good officer and had treated all concerned professionally and they knew it! As such, I had them cold.

The burly farmer stood for a long moment looking at me, and I at him, and then said, "Let's go, boys. I can see we're not going to get anywhere with this damn bureaucrat." With that, they loaded up in their pickup (how they all got into the front seat is a tribute to the Ford Motor Company), and left with a "Meet us at the farm when this is over" to the long-faced hunters. Before they drove off, in order to keep my little charade going, I told the farmer that I was going to re-lease Dale so he could assist some other farmers with real trespass cases. Before he could say anything, I walked over to my radio mike and, without pressing the key, talked as if I were speaking to Dale. I wanted Dale to be "gone" when the farmers got to the gate at the state highway so my story would appear to be true, rendering a subsequent wrestling match unnecessary. Damn, I thought, this having a go-around with a farmer every time we catch someone on their land is getting old.

Our fog started to lift after that, and it seemed as if the hunters had settled down now that their cover and confidence to violate was gone. Also, the birds flew higher and were a lot more careful in their choice of fields. For the rest of the day Bob and I made routine checks of hunters, managing to scratch out only a few with minor violations. Many of the hunting fraternity are pretty honest folks. It is just at cer-tain times that a number of them drop off the edge and do something foolish, requiring a closer look by the likes of us.

We had fog and rain off and on for the rest of the week, with fewer hunters in the field than on the weekends. However, we still managed to catch about a dozen people with over-limits of geese and ducks. However, I knew I would be ready to go home by the end of the de-tail. I was tired and wet all the time. The food eaten at every greasy spoon was getting old, and it seemed that just about every third farmer I ran across had something nasty to say about my lineage. Some farmers would come out to see who we were, and others would send their wives or kids ahead to warn their hunters while they kept us tied up in verbal exchanges. Ethically and financially, it made no sense. It was pretty sad that they were all charging the hunters big bucks to hunt on their lands. In so doing, they could make many thousands of dollars (most of it unreported and tax free, I would bet) to augment their incomes as farmers. However, if all the geese were shot, some by legal and others by illegal means, then the farmer's hunting revenues would diminish or vanish. I found it hard to swallow their policy of warning the hunters in light of the farmers' financial plight and need for extra revenue. You would have thought they would have fiercely protected their golden Canada goose so that would be an annual form of income during future southward migrations. It was also pretty sad that many of those farmers were passing this "run and cheat" ethic on to their children.

The last weekend in Horicon came quickly. When one is working from before daylight to after dark every day catching those in need of catching, time moves right along. I was going to work my last two days alone because Bob had been taken sick. However, that was no big deal because I had learned the area well and was looking forward to having a go at it alone. After all, it wasn't as if I hadn't done this kind of enforcement work before, having cut my waterfowl enforcement teeth in the Sacramento Valley of California, another horn of plenty.

Rising early on Saturday, I stepped out into another heavy winter fog. Good, I thought, that will make it easier for those so inclined to violate and easier for guys like me to catch them. Realizing this might be a long day, I ordered three hamburgers and fries for breakfast. That drew a lot of funny looks around the room from folks helping themselves to the usual pancakes, bacon, and eggs. This was typical game warden fare: high in fat, representing about nine thousand calories, and enough to sustain you all day if necessary if no other food was forthcoming. I'm sure that's part of the reason why many of us representing "the thin green line" have heart or bypass surgery before we make sixty!

Walking into the welcoming fog with a full gut, I headed for an area where I had heard a lot of late shooting the night before. I hadn't been able to get there in time to put a cramp in my illegal shooters' styles, so I had held back, figuring there would be another day. Today was the day! I had discovered over years of wildlife enforcement that if someone violates the law big time and is not caught, they will often return to the same area to do it again. Hence my planning to bring Christmas early to such folks if they showed.

Parking my unmarked patrol car on the state highway, I lifted up the hood as if the car were disabled. Grabbing my gear, I quickly headed out into the cornfields before I met another mad farmer wanting to discuss my lineage. The area was a patchwork of harvested and unharvested cornfields. As near as I could remember, the late shooting had occurred in a five-hundred-acre harvested cornfield surrounded on all four sides by unharvested corn. That would be good, I thought, because I could hide at the edge of the unharvested corn and set up my surveillance from the cover it offered.

Moving through the damp standing corn in the dark of the morning, I soon came out at the edge of the harvested area I wanted to work. Realizing I still had at least an hour until legal shooting time, and because it was so foggy (the fog would create an extra twenty minutes or so of darkness), I headed out into the field to look over the shooters' setup. Within minutes I located a huge decoy spread of about three hundred giant Canada goose shell decoys. Walking through the decoy area to check for any signs of bait, I could see numerous footprints around a dozen or so of the decoy shells through the diffused light of my two-cell flashlight. That meant only one thing. The folks using this area, to avoid apprehension, were shooting over-limits of ducks and geese and hiding the overages under the shells of the decoys. Turning over nine shells with lots of footprints around them, I could make out splotches of blood and many feathers lying on the ground, a typical sign of experienced violators hiding their over-limits. I grimly thought, now I just need these same boys in the decoy set that morning hiding the birds in such a manner, and I will be in business. Walking out of the decoys past their pit blind, I took a long way around to avoid the possibility of discovery through my size fifteen footprints, returning to my hiding place in the standing corn. I made sure I could observe the shooters from behind their goose pit and yet, with a little luck, be able to run and cut them off before they could escape to their vehicles. Then I settled in for a damp wait.

Legal shooting time came and went. The only thing I saw was the fog swirling in and out of the decoys. The air was jug-full of confused ducks and geese, all looking for a place to get some breakfast. It was amazing. The calls of the birds were of such number and intensity that in watching and listening to them, I almost failed to see five hunters quietly approaching the blind on foot through the dense fog. Without a word, they climbed down into their pit blind, and after arranging their equipment, two of them started blowing goose calls. They hadn't blown but a few notes when *whoosh,* in came about fifty mallards low over the decoys, looking for a place to land. Swooping just as quickly back up into the fog, they disappeared before the men in the blind could shoot. A couple of quick "highball" calls from a mallard call, and back the ducks came, announced by their clattering wings. This time they were even lower than before. The men were ready, and with a barrage of shots, eleven low-flying ducks dropped stone-cold dead into the decoys. The remaining ducks rocketed back into the fog, and the fellow on the duck call gave the "high-ball" call again and then stood silently. His doing so and understanding how confusing the fog was for the fliers told me I had an experienced killer on the end of that call. The clattering sounds of wet duck wings hitting other wings in the flock came through loud and clear as the ducks confusedly circled overhead. Then they mistakenly returned to the field where they had gotten a hot lead reception moments before. A couple of quick calls and then the chuckling sound of feeding ducks were the ticket to bring them back. This time they came right over the shooters in the goose pit, and before all was said and done, another dozen were scattered on the ground. Damn! I thought. These guys are some sort of shooters! As near as I could tell, the five of them had shot a total of thirty times and had twenty-three ducks on the ground! I grimly decided I would stay with these lads until they stopped at their limits or strayed over into mine.

So my morning went from my hiding place, until another twenty-six ducks and thirty-two geese lay on the ground. With that the shooters got up and began picking up their dead and crippled birds during a break in the flights. Three of them picked up large handfuls of birds, looked all around to make sure the coast was clear, and then shoved them under several of the shell goose decoys. They brought in only ten Canada geese and ten ducks to lay or stand around their pit blind with cornstalks stuck under their necks, making them look like additional feeding birds. Then they went back into their blind for more of the same "fun."

Figuring it was time to move from my hiding place to where I could do a better job in cutting off the lads when they went to their vehicles,

I took off. My fellows were way over the limit on ducks and geese. I figured I would give them one more time in the "barrel" and then slide in and ruin their day. Hustling through the corn, I damn near ran into a farmer servicing his farming equipment. Quickly dropping to the ground at the edge of the cornfield, I crawled backward into the standing corn. Once I figured I was far enough out of his eyesight, I changed course a little and continued to run through the unharvested cornrows toward my cutoff point. Running flat out, I could hear the shooters calling again on their goose call, and then another barrage of shots. Since I was breathing hard and making a hell of a racket hammering through the standing corn, I could not hear or count any *whumps* from birds hitting the ground. But they were already in trouble with their over-limits, and what they had just killed would be frosting on the cake, I thought.

Then my luck turned sour! Running between cornrows over the top of a slight hill, I looked back to see the farmer standing on the platform of his corn harvester, *looking right at me!* Damn, I thought as I dove to the ground to hide, still some one hundred or so yards from my cutoff point. About that time, my guys cut loose again, and the surviving geese roared right over my head to escape the danger behind them. Running another forty yards in a crouched position, I carefully stood up with my binoculars to see what the farmer was doing. *He was looking right at me with his own set of binoculars!* Dang it, he had the high ground, and I couldn't get out of his sight even in the tall rows of corn. That meant I had a "pissin'" contest in the making!

I took off in a beeline for my shooters before the farmer could get there to warn them or haul off their extra birds. To hell with the cut-off plan! In the background, over the sounds of myself moving through the corn, I could hear his harvester start up. Hoping against hope he would think I was one of his shooters looking for a cripple, I figured he would get on with his farming. Well, get on with his farming he did. After cranking up his corn harvester, he started cutting a path in the standing corn directly toward me! Realizing the jig was up, and since he had the angle on me, I accelerated into a dead run for my goose shooters. Hearing the hell-raising going on, my shooters were standing up in their pit blind trying to figure out what the dickens the farmer was doing. Yep, he was cutting across one of his cornfields in his harvester directly toward them! I broke out of the standing corn just below their blind, and when they saw me, they got the message. Walking as fast as I could (in case I had some runners at the end of my walk and needed the energy to chase them), I cut across the harvested cornfield and into their huge decoy spread. There was a method to my madness. The farmer and his harvester were now not far from my hind end, and I was not sure what he had in mind. Moving into the decoy spread would stop him from chasing me unless he wanted to destroy many hundreds of dollars' worth of decoys. If he chose to do that, I knew that what he had in store for me was not good. ... In that case, my options were rather limited: to be run over with a corn harvester or stand and fight. The latter left the farmer with only one choice—sitting up in the front of that harvester with only the glass of the cab between him and a lot of other ethereal cornfields, that "trip" being sped along with the aid of a 230-grain bullet from a Colt .45 ACP!

Slamming to a stop at the edge of the decoys, he stepped out on the platform of his harvester and began yelling at me. "What the hell do you think you are doing? This is private property, and you are trespassing. If you don't stop, I will have you arrested and thrown into jail."

I turned, showed him my badge, and resumed my fast walk through the decoys to my shooters before they could get organized.

"I don't care who the hell you say you are, you are trespassing!" he yelled. He got back into his harvester and headed my way again, going around the edge of the decoys.

I arrived at the pit blind, identified myself to the five shooters, and requested their hunting licenses, duck stamps, shotguns, and birds. Without a word, they all reached for their wallets and their licenses. By now the farmer had arrived and managed to drive the front end of his corn picker right next to my left leg. In fact, he moved so close to the pit blind that two of the fellows jumped out to get out of his way if he kept coming! I turned to look at the farmer, who was now out on the cab's platform with a fuming look on his face, and pleasantly said, "Good morning." Then I turned back to the men at the goose blind as if there weren't the front end of a corn picker just inches from my hind end and commenced to check their licenses and shotguns. The farmer didn't move from his perch on the platform but stood glowering at my back. All my men's licenses and shotguns were in order, so I moved to the front of the blind and began counting their ducks and geese. I asked one of the shooters to gather up all the birds scattered around the blind to be used as decoys and to bring them to me as well. When that was done, my shooters were just three birds shy of full limits of ducks and geese. Asking them to sit down, I walked out into the decoys and picked up an additional twelve ducks and eleven geese scattered where they had recently fallen. Walking back to my shooters, who by now had a bad case of the big eye, I laid the extra birds at their feet. "This lot of birds puts you fellows a pile over the limit," I said.

No one said anything! They just continued looking at me as if they were holding their breath. Looking up at the farmer, I thought I could see a change in his demeanor. I turned back to the shooters and said, "Is this all you fellows have?"

They kind of looked at each other and then more or less in unison said there were no more birds. The farmer, realizing the men had a gross over-limit in their possession, said, "Damn, you guys know better than that."

I didn't look at the farmer, but I could tell from the tone of his voice that he was a little embarrassed at going to bat for his hunters and pissed for looking like an idiot in having done so. Kneeling at the edge of the pit and looking at my shooters all sitting there in the field, I asked, "What about those extra birds under the decoys?"

For a moment, all you could hear was the wind rustling through the cornstalks and the milling birds in the fog overhead calling to their kind on the ground. Then the farmer jumped down off his harvester and walked over to me. "What the hell do you mean extra birds under the decoys? These guys are from the local chapter of Ducks Unlimited, and not one of them would violate the law unless it was a mistake. If I thought for a minute they were violators, I would personally kick their hind ends off my land until time stood still."

Holding all the men's hunting licenses, I told them to remain seated, turned to the farmer, and asked if he would like to accompany me into the decoy set. He nodded, and we both walked in among the decoys. After a few false turnovers of the decoy shells because I had forgotten the exact ones under which the birds had been hidden, I found an additional thirty-nine ducks and twenty-two geese. I picked up all I could carry and asked the farmer if he would help. He looked long and hard at the sorry pile of broken and wet duck and goose bodies on the ground, then said something I didn't hear, picked up two hand-fuls of birds, and followed me to the blind. A second trip by both of us collected the remainder.

"Well, gentlemen, does anyone know who shot what?"

There was a lot of mumbling and the realization among all that in shooting so fast and furiously, no one really knew who had shot what. With that understanding, I wrote each shooter for an over-limit pos-session of ducks and geese with the total overage of birds from the field that day on each man's citation. I figured I would let the judge sort it out in a court of law. One of the men asked if they had to ap-pear in court when I said that was one of their legal choices.

"No," I said, "but if you don't and choose to forfeit bail, the bail will be higher than a kite because each of you is charged with the en-tire overage since none of you know who shot what."

Looking around at his soulmates, the man turned and said, "That will be all right. We just want to get this settled in the simplest way possible and without any publicity."

Looking at the men for a moment, I asked, "Is that the way you other fellows want it? The bail in an offense such as this will run each of you a thousand dollars [$500 for the duck and $500 for the goose over-limit] and loss of all the birds."

They all nodded acceptance, and that was the way I wrote it up.

The farmer had remained silent after we removed the extra birds from under the decoy shells, but now he said, "That's it! You meat-heads get your decoys picked up, and never ask again to shoot on my property. By God, I can't believe I have a bunch of violating bas-tards from Ducks Unlimited spoiling my hunting for me and my family. I suggest all of you get cracking before I change my mind and personally whip the hell out of every one of you for what you did here today!"

The shooters got up and started collecting their gear and stacking the decoys. One turned to the farmer, who was named Larry, and asked if they could bring their four-wheel-drives to the area to haul the decoys out of the field.

Larry said, "Hell, no! You damn knotheads can just pack them out one bunch at a time as far as I am concerned!" The men went back to work without comment, and I started gathering evidence birds for the long trek to my vehicle. "Need a lift, Officer?" Larry asked.

"That would be damn nice," I said. "Otherwise I will be hauling out evidence birds the rest of the day." That was the first time in my career I hauled out evidence birds on a corn harvester. The thought that it sure would have made damn good cover for the rest of my weekend's work ran through my mind as we bounced across the fields. By the time I finished gutting the birds and logging my evidence, the fog was starting to burn off. Soon the shooting, enhanced by the fog, did so as well. For the rest of the day I walked the various cornfields around the marsh checking duck and goose hunters without much success. That was all right, though. I liked seeing members of the hunting fraternity observing the laws, and most of them were.

Getting back late to my motel and not being hungry (three hamburgers with three orders of fries for breakfast will do that for you), I just sat in front of my room in a chair smoking a cigar so I could watch the antics of the hunters staying there as they returned from their fields of dreams. When a mass of hunters returns to a central point all at once, you have barking dogs, dog fights, loads of ducks and geese being brought into the rooms to be drawn and hung in the showers, ice chests filled with fresh ice for the next day's hunt, and more dog fights. Just part of the "spice" of hunting.

There was one room two doors to the right that caught my eye that evening. Occupying it were two neatly bearded fellows, and it now dawned on me that they had been there for the last three days. The only reason I remembered them was that when they came in, all their birds were beautifully picked and cleaned, not in the whole carcass, feathers, hide, guts, and all, that the other hunters usually dragged in. The two men would first unload all their hunting gear and then bring in their day's limits of birds.

Damn, Terry, I thought, if my memory serves me correctly, they have hunted for the last three days, and two of those three days, I saw them bringing in what appeared to be limits of birds from their truck to their room. If they did that for the third day, today, that would put them over the normally allowed double possession limit! Standing as if I were stretching and taking a few steps to the right, where it didn't appear too obvious, I peered into their room. They or the maid had opened the curtain partway, so I could look in from my vantage point. Between the first bed and the outer wall was a huge white ice chest like the kind used on deep-sea fishing boats—in other words, one that could hold a lot. About then both men lifted what appeared to be limits of Canada geese and mallard ducks on their duck straps from under their camper shell and walked briskly to their room. No birds were placed in the cooler that I could see, and shortly thereafter, I saw one man placing both shotguns in the corner of the room by the cooler.

With nothing to go on but the duck straps of birds just hauled into the room (they could have donated or shipped the previous day's birds off to others, thereby ridding themselves of possession over-limit issues), I headed the final few feet to the door of their room. Walking by the partially open window, I could see my chaps pouring themselves drinks from several liquor bottles. Not seeing the duck straps of birds anywhere in my quick glance, I faced the door to their room and knocked. Seconds later it was opened by Robert Bowen (as I later learned), who said, "Yes, may I help you?"

Going on nothing more than a gut hunch and the birds they had just brought into the room, I held out my badge and credentials and said, "Gentlemen, my name is Terry Grosz, and I am a special agent for the Fish and Wildlife Service. Over the last few days I have observed the two of you bringing into this room what appeared to be limits of mallards and Canada geese. If all those birds were kept on site, that would place the two of you over the possession limit and in violation of state and federal wildlife laws. I would like to start with checking the two stringers of birds you just brought into the room."

Bob just looked at me as if to say, "Just who the hell do you think you are, barging in here like this?" His partner, at last galvanized into action, said, "I will get them for you," and hustled off to the bathroom. I just stood there in the doorway, ignoring Bob's menacing looks. Within seconds the other man returned with two duck straps loaded with birds and laid the still dripping and bloody carcasses on the rug. Brother, I thought, I'm glad I am not in the motel business in a hunting town, especially if the rest of the hunters are as careless as these.

Bob stepped aside with a glower still on his puss as I walked into the room to examine the birds lying on the floor. There were exact limits of ducks and geese, nothing more. Damn, Terry, I thought, now what? Standing back up, I said, "I would like to take a look in the bathroom where these came from, if you don't mind?"

Dick Ball (as I was soon to learn), said, "Be my guest," and before he could change his mind on the consent search, I walked into their bathroom. It was a mess, to say the least. There was blood dripped across the floor from the freshly drawn birds, looking like something from the Bates Motel of Alfred Hitchcock fame. It was apparent that the lads had washed out the birds in their shower and then hung the duck straps from the shower head to drain. Seeing nothing else of interest, I came out of the bathroom and walked over to their huge cooler. Reaching this point of my search, I looked over to Dick (since he had given me the go-ahead to search the bathroom so quickly) and asked, "May I look in this cooler as well?"

Dick flashed a worried look over to his partner and then looked at me. "Well, I guess so, but it has nothing inside but our food and some beer."

"No, I don't want you snooping in our cooler," erupted Bob. "What is in there is our business, and you keep your damned self out of there!"

Knowing the only way I could legally search the cooler was with their consent or a warrant, I swung Plan B into action (every good officer always has a Plan B). "Gentlemen," I said, "why don't the two of you sit down because what I have to say may take some time." Both men sat heavily on the ends of their beds and looked up at me. "I am going to be very frank with you. Counting today, I have observed the two of you entering this room three times with what appeared to be daily limits of picked and cleaned ducks and geese [I fibbed a little]. During that period of time, I have not observed you leaving with any of those birds like you were going to divest yourselves of possession or ownership. So I think the birds are still in this room, and in fact in that cooler. If that is the case, then both of you are now in a possession situation of over-limits of ducks and geese. Since you will not give me permission to look in that cooler, and since I do not have a warrant, I am precluded from doing so. However, the rules involving search are less constricting once possible contraband is loaded into a motor vehicle. That is because the courts realize there is a very real possibility that the evidence of a crime may disappear because of the vehicle's mobility. Since that is a possibility, you need to be aware of what I am going to do when you decide to leave. First I am going to contact the innkeeper and get a key to your room. Then I will radio for some extra help, and we will sit on you and your room until you finally leave. Once that ice chest is loaded into your vehicle and you leave your motel room, I will use my key to enter and search the room since it will no longer be under your legal control. If the extra birds are not there, I will call my fellow officers, who will be tailing you at that point, and notify them that you did not leave the extra birds in the room. With the possible contraband now moving down the highway and the probable cause I have developed to date, I will have my partners stop and search your vehicle. This they can legally do because of the mobility issue and possibility of the loss of contraband via that motor vehicle. If they find those extra birds, which I suspect are in that cooler, you will be issued a citation for the violation and have to settle up with the judge on this matter. In the process, I will have your vehicle seized because it is being used to further the crime. In the interim, I will try to obtain a warrant with the probable cause I have developed, which, if successful, will shortly settle the 'what's in the cooler' issue. Now, that is what I am prepared to do. Does any of what I said change your minds about opening that cooler? You don't have to, and you have every right under the Constitution to deny me access, but I am asking you to reconsider your earlier denial. If the extra birds are there, we need to face this issue like the men we are and settle it."

Bob looked over at Dick for a long moment and then asked if I would leave them alone for a few minutes. Nodding, I walked out of their room and closed the door behind me. I kept an eye through the front window on the two shotguns stacked in the corner of the room, just in case conversation alone was not what they had on their minds. The occurrence of a deadly event was not likely, but the first rule in law enforcement is to come home safely every night. I did not intend to break that rule.

In a few minutes Dick walked over and lifted the lid to the cooler. From where I stood, I couldn't see the contents because the back of the lid was facing me and blocking the view of the chest's contents. Then Bob came to the door and asked me in. Walking in, Dick said, "You were right. We have all our birds in the cooler except those we got today. There are three possession limits in the cooler, plus the one we have in the shower [hunters were allowed two daily bag limits *after the second day of hunting*—more than that would put the person over the possession limit]. Officer, we are both assistant county attorneys from Minnesota, and if this gets out we could lose our jobs."

I felt like saying, You should have thought of that before you got carried away, but I wisely held my tongue. "I have no plans to post the error of your ways publicly, so the issue is what you make it. However, I need to see some hunting licenses, duck stamps, and driver's licenses, if you please." With that, I commenced to count out the birds in the cooler and confirmed that they did indeed have three limits of ducks and geese in their possession. Just for the hell of it, I checked both of their shotguns. They were unplugged! However, since I had not seen the men using them to take those birds in their possession, there was nothing I could do other than give them a hard look ... which was not returned.

I wrote citations for exceeding their possession limits of ducks and geese and seized their cooler so I might have something large enough to carry and preserve the birds. Both men were subdued, and upon completion of the business, Bob asked, "Would you have done it?"

"Done what?" I asked.

"Staked us out until we left and then searched our vehicle for the birds."

"Yes, I would. That was why I leveled with you so you would know what you were getting yourselves into. That plus the fact that by being so frank, there wouldn't be a Fourth Amendment issue on illegal search and seizure if this matter went to court. I was hoping my honesty would get you to reason out the consequences of your acts and, instead of making it harder on yourselves, give it up and get it over with. And to your credit, you did."

"Well, we knew you probably had us on the search issue with the mobility of the vehicle, and we weren't prepared to stay in our room for two weeks to eat all the evidence, so we gave up," said Bob with a weak grin.

Finished and *now* hungry, I started to leave with the evidence. "Terry," said Bob, "anytime you are in my county and need to prosecute anyone for a Fish and Game violation, give me a holler. I will be there for you regardless of this dimwit act of ours these last few days."

I thanked him, and Dick basically reiterated the same thing. Thanking both of them again, I left their room, loaded the ice chest with difficulty into the backseat of my sedan, and headed for the café. I hope they still have some prime rib I thought, because *now* I am ready to eat! As it worked out, Bob and Dick followed me shortly into the same café, and the three of us ended up having a great prime rib dinner together like old friends. I even picked up the dinner tab for my newfound but highly embarrassed attorney friends.

Opening the motel-room door the following morning, I was greeted with the promise of a beautiful fall day in Wisconsin. It was clear as a bell if the zillions of stars were any indicator of the day to come. A breeze of about ten to fifteen miles per hour was blowing steadily out of the north. A portent of a storm in a day or two, I thought as I loaded my gear into the patrol car. I still had a ton of prime rib resting in my gut to get rid of before I would be hungry again, so I swung out onto the highway, heading for a spot on the southwest side of the marsh. Come daylight, I was proven correct in my predictions for the day. It was bluebird weather with a breeze, and what a day it was. Birds by the tens of thousands traded back and forth across the azure skies from the great marsh, all looking for a safe breakfast in the cornfields. Sporadic shooting came from all points of the compass, but nowhere was it as heavy as it had been during the previous foggy days.

I checked about a dozen hunters and found all well and legal. However, off to the north I heard a lot of shooting in one area, so I started working that way. I always did enjoy working my way to the sound of the guns, and many times it led to a pot of gold, if you get my drift. I found a lot of interesting hunters needing a look-over between me and the shooting to the north, so my progress was slowed. Finally I got to where I figured it was occurring. The first swing of the binoculars showed that I was too late. The hunters in question were finished. Setting up an intersect point, I watched the hunters through my binoculars, three adults and a boy, leaving the fields with what appeared to be full limits of ducks in their duck straps.

The party approached the edge of a weedy cornfield where I was kneeling, and when they were close, I stood up. There was the usual surprise at being confronted by a stranger, but once I had introduced myself they all settled down except the boy, who was about twelve. I could tell he was uneasy with me and found out later that this was the first time he had been checked by a game warden since he had passed the hunter safety program. He just didn't know quite what to expect and was a little nervous — or so it seemed. In the ensuing inspection, all the party checked out with their limits of ducks, licenses, and duck stamps. The boy, a son of one of the hunters, continued to show signs of stress and I figured maybe he was cowed by my size, not to mention authority. Realizing that this was an excellent opportunity to educate the young man as well as make this contact memorable, I turned to the boy. Kneeling down in front of him so I wouldn't be so imposing a figure, I took out my badge and credentials, handing them to him for examination. "Son, I am a special agent for the Fish and Wildlife Service. Do you know what I do for a living?"

"Well, check hunters to see if they have broken the law," he replied.

"That is one of the things we do, but we do a whole lot more. We talk to schoolkids about conservation, we band ducks and geese sometimes when our people on the national wildlife refuges need help, we work with sportsmen's groups on wildlife projects, and in general we try to help the wildlife. Why do we help the wildlife?" I asked.

"I don't know ... so it won't go extinct," came his pretty good reply.

"One of the main reasons we protect wildlife is so young boys like you, and someday hopefully your sons and daughters, can go hunting and have quality time together like you and your dad did this day. In fact, you are the only young man I have checked in the eight days I have been working the hunters in this area. To me it's pretty sad that more dads aren't taking their kids out hunting and for a morning of being together. I didn't have a dad to raise me when I was young, and all the hunting and fishing I did was by myself. I am here to tell you, it was fun but not as much fun as if I had had a dad to go with me. You are very lucky that your dad loves you so much that he takes the time to take you with him on special occasions like this."

Looking out of the corner of my eye at the three adults, I could see them shifting uneasily from foot to foot as I talked with the youngster. Damn, that was strange behavior. Nothing I had said should have outraged or made anyone uncomfortable. Well, the small boy was still intently listening to me, so I continued. "Son, I have a suggestion. The next time you make some money mowing lawns or helping your neighbors, you might want to take your dad out for a Coke and a hamburger as a way of thanking him for being such a great guy and father to you."

The boy looked back at his dad with an odd expression, whereupon his dad growled, "*All right, enough is enough!*" Digging down into the tops of both hipboots, he dug out two plastic bread bags partially filled with duck breasts and tossed them at my feet!

Talk about surprised! I no more than the man in the moon had suspected this person of doing anything illegal. The members of the hunting party had been perfect gentlemen the whole time, giving me nothing in the way of body language or discussion to suspect foul play. Yet here at my feet lay two plastic bags, which when counted out represented the breast meat portions of eight more large ducks! Picking up the two bags of duck breasts, I stood up, switching gears from educator to officer, and requested his hunting license and driver's license for the second time.

"Are these duck breasts yours?" I asked.

"They are all mine," he responded quietly. Man, you could have cut the air with a knife. I could tell the other men in the party knew exactly what had happened. The looks of disgust on their faces said it all. However, they hadn't stopped the man's illegal actions, just stood by and let him have at the resource. No one seems to want to get involved these days, I thought with a grimace. Now they stood in the glaring light of day, embarrassed at what their partner had done and embarrassed for the boy, not to mention themselves for condoning such an act.

With little discussion, I issued the citation and seized his ducks in the duck strap plus the ones in the plastic sacks. Realizing my educational responsibility was just starting, I knelt back down so I could look the boy in the eye and said, "You know, son, sometimes people make mistakes and have to pay for them. What your dad did here today was a foolish mistake. Kind of like when you don't tell the truth or don't do your homework after saying you did. Nevertheless, you should be very proud of your dad because he was honest enough to admit his mistake and take his medicine. If I were you, I would still take him out for a Coke and a hamburger for being such a great dad."

The boy beamed and looked back at his dad with the look I had hoped to achieve from him in the first place. Standing up, I walked over to the dad and shook his hand, in the process thanking him for being honest and for taking the time to take his son out on a duck hunt. The look in his eyes said it all. He was ashamed for what he had done for a few extra duck breasts but thankful I didn't rub his nose in it in front of his friends and son. Thanking all the others for their patience, I gathered up the evidence and strode away so the situation would have time to work itself out, especially between the boy and his dad. I hope the boy did take his dad out for that Coke and a hamburger. I know if I still had a dad, I would do so gladly. ...

Realizing it would be nice if my three children had a dad for a few hours that week, I hung it up and headed for home. Traveling east on state Highway 49, I chanced to see a ragtag flock of about fifty green-winged teal flying over an unharvested cornfield at cornstalk height. Suddenly they swooped down out of sight into the cornfield and then, all at once, shot straight up into the air as only a flock of speedy little green-wings can when surprised. Four of the flock suddenly folded dead in the air, dropping into the cornfield, while the rest headed for safer climes.

Stopping the car, I bailed out and glassed the field. It was about a thousand acres in size, and all I could see was unharvested corn. That was strange, I thought. Green-wings won't land in standing corn. They are small seed eaters who like shallow watered areas, and I sure as hell didn't see any of that in the standing corn. Then, from the middle of the field, I heard the unmistakable sound of a poor imitation of a mallard call. What the hell? I thought. Looking around, I spotted a pair of mallards heading for the middle of the field. After a couple of passes, they set their wings and disappeared into the tall corn. *Boom-boom* went the quick shots of two shotguns, and no mallards flew out of the area.

So that was it! There was a pond or small shallow pan of water in the middle of that cornfield! What a great place to hunt. Food all around and total seclusion in the standing corn. And, with the right kind of people and mind-set, a great place to violate. ... The shooting area was so well hidden that if I hadn't seen the flock of teal decoy into the area, I would never have discovered it. I hurriedly got back into my car, the thought of spending time with my kids lost for the moment. Driving down the highway to the closest angle that would allow me access to the shooting area, I parked off the roadway. Ever mindful of the possibility of interference from the landowner, I raised the hood as if I had experienced a breakdown. Hurriedly looking around, I saw I had at least three hundred yards to go to get to my shooters, so I grabbed my gear, went over the fence, and trotted into the field of corn.

Soon lost in the tall cornstalks, I plowed along in the general direction of where I suspected the hunters were located. After plowing through about one hundred yards of corn, I stopped to listen and gather my breath. Nothing happened for about twenty minutes; then I heard five quick shots about 250 yards away. Heading in that direction, I moved through the field for about another hundred yards before stopping again. I had no sooner stopped to gather my breath and wipe the sweat off my face than I heard two more shots directly before me, still about a hundred yards away. Getting my bearings on the area by using a distant large barn, I continued working my way toward the shooters.

I always liked sneaking up on folks to see how close I could get before being seen. This noisy, dried-out cornfield would be a good sneaking challenge, I thought. I had on a canvas hunting coat, which was unduly noisy going through cornstalks. However, that would make it even more of a challenge, I thought, and now, I was into the game big time! I took a quick assessment and saw that I had several advantages. One was the element of surprise, and another was a covering soft cornstalk-rustling breeze that would provide cover if I were careful. With that, I began to sneak and slowly edge my way through the cornstalks toward my shooters. They shot several more times as I slowly approached between row after row of cornstalks until I was about thirty-five yards away. Then I really started sneaking, moving only when the breeze rustled the cornstalks. Whenever that happened, I would traverse several rows of corn and then stop, waiting for the next breeze to ripple across the field. Soon I could hear my shooters talking but still could not see them. A couple more sets of breezes and I was within fifteen yards of my quarry. Then a dozen wigeon came barreling into the decoys, and I saw two shooters stand up in a previously hidden pit blind at the edge of a small watered area and blaze away. I heard two ducks plop into the water as the rest winged away.

Both shooters ducked back down into the blind without making any effort to pick up their dead birds. Once again I could hear excited talking, only this time I was close enough to make out what they were saying. There was lots of talk about how good the shooting was. Then along came a breeze, and I was able to make six cornrows before stopping. Several more gusts came in the next minutes, and I managed to quietly sideslip across cornrows between plants until I was no more than eight feet away. A pair of pintail dropped in over the heads of my shooters, taking them by surprise. Jumping up, they managed to only kill one bird with five shots. During that shooting distraction, I managed to move across two more cornrows. Standing there like Bigfoot, I listened in on a conversation meant only for their ears.

"What does that make?"

"I don't know, but I bet we have at least twenty on the water, and except for the teal and wigeon, most are big ducks," replied the other voice.

"When the next bunch comes in, we need to go out and pick up what we have and hide some," came the first voice. With that, he commenced to blow his poorly blown duck call at six ducks working the edge of the cornfield. Soon they headed toward the pond for a look. Overhead they came, just out of shooting range. Liking what they saw, they began circling the pond. Finally convinced that the decoys in the pond were some of their own, in they dropped with a vengeance as the air *swooshed* out of their wings. Four of the six never pulled out of their glide as my two gunners dropped them with some clean shooting. Both men stood up in their blind to look over their secluded pond, still unmindful of the chap standing just a few feet behind them!

Finally one of the shooters said, "I am going out to pick up that bunch of ducks that fell near the far side of the pond before we lose them." He got out of the blind and walked across the shallow pan of water, picking up dead ducks and wringing the necks of those still living among the decoys. Working his way to the other side, he picked up several more ducks at the edge of the pond. Working the far edge of the pond, he eventually disappeared out of sight to my left. With another fresh breeze, I continued moving forward through the cornrows until I was now separated from my remaining fellow in the pit blind by *just two rows of corn!* I could almost reach out and touch the man and couldn't help but grin from ear to ear at what it would be like when I made myself known. It dawned on me that I might scare the shooters so badly that they might react out of fear by whirling and shooting!

As that thought spun through my mind, the other shooter returned from his duck retrieval trip. Holding out two handfuls of ducks, he said, "How is that for some damn fine shooting? *Holy Jesus Christ, who are you?*" he added, suddenly seeing me looming directly behind his partner. His partner whirled and damn near jumped clear out of his skin when he saw a human of such proportions standing at arm's length.

"*Who the hell are you?*" he bellowed.

"Federal game warden, gentlemen," I quietly replied. "How is the hunting?"

Neither man could say much of anything. They just stood there looking at the "thing" that had managed to sneak up on them, now identified, with the potential to ruin their afternoon.

Walking through the last two rows of corn, I identified myself with the badge and credentials. They were still speechless from the scare. Finally the one with the ducks said, "Mister, where the hell did you come from?"

"From this cornfield," I calmly replied. "May I check some hunting licenses, duck stamps, shotguns for plugs, and in light of the number of ducks you have over the limit, some driver's licenses as well?"

Without a word, one man dropped the ducks and the other laid down his shotgun as they began digging in their pockets for the requested items. While they did that, I looked the area over. It was one sweet setup. They had a small, shallow pan of water in the middle of a huge cornfield and seclusion like I had never seen. It was a great hideaway for a duck shoot, and the ducks lying on the ground by the blind and still in the center of the pond spoke to that cold fact. I had the men gather up the rest of the ducks in the pond while I checked their licenses and gear. Damn if one of them didn't have the last name of Krumpf! I wondered if he was the farmer Krumpf's son or perhaps a more distant relative. The other man, with a last name of Routon, was still so upset by the turn of events that he was shaking like a dog passing razor blades.

"Relax, son," I told him. But being surprised at so close a range in an area where they felt secure had really unnerved him. All their paperwork was in order, but when it came time to count the ducks, the men, both twenty years old, were twenty-four over the limit. I issued the appropriate citations and seized the ducks.

Both men had little to say until I finished. Finally Krumpf asked, "You aren't going to tell my dad, are you?"

"First of all, I am not sure who your dad is, and second of all, that will be up to you. Just remember, things like this usually have a way of eventually coming out of the woodwork. If it does, and it's a surprise to your dad, I'm sure he will be hurt."

The other kid, Phil Routon, recovered some of his "sand" and volunteered, "I don't have a pa, so it won't make no difference to me."

I looked at the young man for a moment and then said, "Someday you will be a dad, and then think back on this moment. What would you do if your son strayed across the line and didn't have the heart to tell you?" With that, I gathered up all the birds, binding them together with a short piece of nylon rope from my game bag. After a quick handshake all around, I started the long trek through the corn to my vehicle.

I hadn't walked ten feet when Routon said, "Hey, mister. I'm not trying to be a smartass or anything, but how can a guy as big as you sneak through a dry cornfield without us hearing you?"

"No offense taken, son. When my dad was alive, he taught me how to move like an Indian. Today I just put into play what he taught me when I was a young man about your age." I continued on toward the car, walking between cornrows and stalks as quietly as I could for effect until I was out of sight and hearing of the men. Once out of sight, I just grinned my famous "Robert Redford" grin at the joke I had played on my two unsuspecting shooters. What a hell of a lesson they got today, I thought.

When I came out of the cornfield, who did I see but Dan Krumpf in his black pickup sitting by my patrol car. Seeing me emerge with two loads of ducks, he got out of his truck and walked over to my car. "I figured dis car might belong to a fed vith da Minnesota plate on it, and it being a Plymouth and all. It seems all you feds drife Plymouths. Picking on some other poor son of da bitch, huh?"

"No, sir," I responded, "just doing the job you and others pay me to do."

I could tell the thought of having to pay my salary in some manner really pissed Dan off. "Dis ist mine cornfield as vell, and no vone hunts it but mine kid and his friends," he said. Then it dawned on him that I had a huge load of ducks and had just come from the field where his kid hunted. "You bastard," he said, "I suppose you haff now caught my son too?"

I started to respond when, looking over his shoulder, I noticed black smoke billowing out from under the hood of his truck. "I think you have a problem," I said, pointing to his pickup. He turned and said, "Now vott da hell," as he raced for his truck. Unlatching his hood latch and flinging it up, he created a backdraft. A massive fire-ball completely engulfed him for several seconds in what had to be the surprise of a lifetime! Stumbling back from the explosion, Dan fell to the ground with a smoking torso, head, and face, yelling as he rolled around in pain and fear! Dropping my load of ducks, I sprinted for the fire extinguisher under the front seat of my car and raced back to the burning truck, giving Dan a squirt of white powder on the head and shoulders as I went by. I applied the retardant to the entire engine compartment and quickly put out a gasoline fire that had been caused by a split gasoline line. The two of us got the gas line crimped off and put out the remaining fire in the grass under the engine, thereby saving his new pickup.

"Think you'll be needing a lift," I said. He was a mess. Half his mustache was gone, and his face was turning beet red. He had no eyebrows, and his thick black hair was mostly gone from the front third of his head. Not to mention that after a short bout with my extinguisher, he looked like Al Jolson in reverse. I couldn't help it; I just started to laugh, and once he got a look at himself in his truck's side-view mirror, he started laughing as well.

"Vell, tank you for saffing mine truck," he said.

"No sweat," I said. "I'd do the same for anyone."

Making sure the fire was out, we got into the patrol car, and I took him to his farmhouse. Upon arriving, whom did we see in the front yard but the Krumpf I had just pinched in the cornfield. Uh-oh, I thought. I didn't want the kid to think I had gone right to his old man and spilled the beans. But the kid took one look at his old man and started to laugh, and pretty soon we were all in stitches. When we stopped laughing, Dan told the kid to go in and see what "Ma" had for lunch and if there was enough for one more. Turning, Dan said, "Giff me a hand, Terrry." Walking over to a machine shed a short distance away, Dan produced a can of Bag Balm, and I gave him a hand covering all the burned areas with the greasy concoction. Then we walked to the house to wash up. "Don't say a gottdamned thing, voman," Dan said when his wife first saw him. "I vill tell you later." With a second look of disbelief, she hustled off to the kitchen.

I had a great lunch, especially after Dan cooled his wife down once she saw who her luncheon guest was. To set things straight, Dan let her know in no uncertain terms that I was now a friend. If it hadn't been for me, he would have lost his pickup and probably his life to the fire. With that explanation, she softened, and I was her friend too as she applied more Bag Balm a little more lovingly to Dan's beet-red head and arms than I had.

Her homemade strawberry pie was great, but not as good as my bride's rhubarb pie when I finally got home later that night. That evening, sitting in my big leather chair with all three of my kids happily sleeping in my arms or at my feet, I had a chance to think back on my trip to the Horicon Marsh and the cornfields of Wisconsin. It had been a great several days, and my memories of those times, the cases, and the vast hordes of geese will last until I step over the Great Divide. True, I had run the gamut of nasty, hardheaded farmers, but I had survived and learned. I had also caught a few really bad chaps who needed catching. No telling how long they had been breaking the law to the degree they had, but for the moment they had their wings clipped, and the birds were getting a little relief. Last but not least, I had made several friends. One had been a hotheaded farmer who, although it took a squirt from my fire extinguisher to "cool" him off, became a friend nonetheless. Another, well, I hope he bought his dad that hamburger and Coke and ... twenty-one years later, as I write this story, I hope his kids are doing the same for him.

About the Author

TERRY GROSZ earned his bachelor's degree in 1964 and his master's in wildlife management in 1966 from Humboldt State College in California. He was a California State Fish and Game Warden, based first in Eureka and then Colusa, from 1966 to 1970. He then joined the U.S. Fish & Wildlife Service, and served in California as a U.S. Game Management Agent and Special Agent until 1974. After that, he was promoted to Senior Resident Agent and placed in charge of North and South Dakota for two years, followed by three years as Senior Special Agent in Washington, D.C., with the Endangered Species Program, Division of Law Enforcement. While in Washington, he also served as a foreign liaison officer. In 1979 he became Assistant Special Agent in Charge in Minneapolis, and then was promoted to Special Agent in Charge, and transferred to Denver in 1981, where he remained until retirement in June 1998 (although his title changed to Assistant Regional Director for Law Enforcement).

He has earned many awards and honors during his career, including, from the U.S. Fish & Wildlife Service, the Meritorious Service Award in 1996, and Top Ten Award in 1987 as one of the top ten employees (in an agency of some 9,000). The Fish & Wildlife Foundation presented him with the Guy Bradley Award in 1989, and in 1995 he received the Conservation Achievement Award for Law Enforcement from the National Wildlife Federation. Unity College in Maine awarded him an honorary doctorate in environmental stewardship in 2002. His first book, *Wildlife Wars*, was published in 1999 and won the National Outdoor Book Award for nature and the environment. He has had three books published since then: *For Love of Wildness*, *Defending Our Wildlife Heritage*, and *A Sword for Mother Nature*. In 2003 filming began on a reality-based television series that features the stories in Terry Grosz's books. He lives in Colorado.

B

GROSZ

Grosz, Terry.

No safe refuge.

3-04

$20.00